THE SCIENTIFIC ORIGINS OF NATIONAL SOCIALISM

Social Darwinism in Ernst Haeckel
and the German Monist League

History of Science Library

Editor: MICHAEL A. HOSKIN
Lecturer in the History of Science, Cambridge University

THE ENGLISH PARACELSIANS
Allen G. Debus
Professor of the History of Science, University of Chicago

WILLIAM HERSCHEL AND THE CONSTRUCTION OF THE HEAVENS
M. A. Hoskin
Lecturer in the History of Science, Cambridge University

A HISTORY OF THE THEORIES OF RAIN
W. E. Knowles Middleton

THE ORIGINS OF CHEMISTRY
R. P. Multhauf
Director of the Museum of History and Technology at the Smithsonian Institution

THEORIES OF LIGHT FROM DESCARTES TO NEWTON
A. I. Sabra
Reader in the History of the Classical Tradition, The Warburg Institute

MEDICINE IN MEDIEVAL ENGLAND
C. H. Talbot
Research Fellow at the Wellcome Institute of the History of Medicine, London

THE EARTH IN DECAY
A HISTORY OF BRITISH GEOMORPHOLOGY, 1578-1878
G. L. Davies
Lecturer in the Department of Geography, Trinity College, University of Dublin

THE CONFLICT BETWEEN ATOMISM AND CONSERVATION THEORY 1644-1860
W. L. Scott
Professorial Lecturer, School of Business Administration and Department of Mathematics and Science, American University

THE ROAD TO MEDICAL ENLIGHTENMENT 1650-1695
L. S. King
Professorial Lecturer in the History of Medicine, University of Chicago

WILLIAM HARVEY
AND THE CIRCULATION OF THE BLOOD
Gweneth Whitteridge
Lecturer in the History of Medicine, University of Edinburgh

History of Science Library: Primary Sources

VEGETABLE STATICKS
Stephen Hales
Foreword by M. A. Hoskin
Lecturer in the History of Science, Cambridge University

SCIENCE AND EDUCATION IN THE SEVENTEENTH CENTURY
THE WEBSTER-WARD DEBATE
Allen G. Debus
Professor of the History of Science, University of Chicago

FUNDAMENTA MEDICINAE
Friedrich Hoffmann
Translated and introduced by L. S. King
Professorial Lecturer in the History of Medicine, University of Chicago

THE PNEUMATICS OF HERO OF ALEXANDRIA
Introduced by Marie Boas Hall
Reader in History of Science and Technology, Imperial College

Ernst Haeckel at Eighty: The Volkish Prophet.

THE SCIENTIFIC ORIGINS OF NATIONAL SOCIALISM

Social Darwinism in Ernst Haeckel and the German Monist League

DANIEL GASMAN
*Assistant Professor of History, John Jay College,
The City University of New York*

MACDONALD : LONDON
AND
AMERICAN ELSEVIER INC : NEW YORK

To my Parents

© Daniel Gasman 1971
First published 1971
Sole distributors for the United States and Dependencies
American Elsevier Publishing Company, Inc.
52 Vanderbilt Avenue
New York, N.Y. 10017

Sole distributors for the British Isles and Commonwealth
Macdonald & Co. (Publishers) Ltd
49-50 Poland Street
London W1A 2LG

All remaining areas
Elsevier Publishing Company
P.O. Box 211
Jan van Galenstraat 335
Amsterdam
The Netherlands

Library of Congress Catalog Card Number 77-132637
Standard Book Numbers
British SBN 356 03411 9
American SBN 444 19664 1

All Rights Reserved. No part of this publication may be reproduced, stored in a retrieval system, or transmitted in any form or by any means, electronic, mechanical, photocopying, recording or otherwise, without the prior permission of the publishers.

Printed in Great Britain by W. & G. Baird Ltd., Belfast

Contents

	Preface	ix
	Introduction	xi
	Ernst Haeckel and the Volkish Tradition	xi
I	Ernst Haeckel and the German Monist League	1
II	The Political Assumptions of Monism	31
III	Monism and Christianity	55
IV	Monism, The Corporative State and Eugenics	82
V	Monism and Marxism	106
VI	Monism, Imperialism, and the First World War	126
VII	Monism and National Socialism	147
	Selected Bibliography	183
	Index	203

List of Plates

Frontispiece

    ERNST HAECKEL AT EIGHTY: THE VOLKISH PROPHET.
    Reproduced from the journal of the Monist League, *Das monistische Jahrhundert*.

Appearing between pages 8 and 9

I.   A POSTER ANNOUNCING A LECTURE ON EVOLUTION TO BE DELIVERED IN BERLIN BY HAECKEL.
    Reproduced from Peter Klemm, *Der Ketzer von Jena*, Leipzig: Urania, 1968.

II.   A GNARLED EVOLUTIONARY TREE DRAWN BY HAECKEL.
    Reproduced from Peter Klemm, *Der Ketzer von Jena*, Leipzig: Urania, 1968.

III. ILLUSTRATION OF BIZARRE BOTANICAL SPECIMENS.
    Reproduced from Haeckel's *Kunstformen der Natur*, Leipzig: Verlag des Bibliographischen Instituts, 1899-1904.

IV. (a) A DETAIL FROM GUSTAVE MOREAU'S *Galatea*.
    Reproduced from *Odilon Redon, Gustave Moreau, Rodolphe Bresdin*, New York: The Museum of Modern Art, 1961. *Galatea* is held in the collection of Mr & Mrs Harold Weinstein of Chicago, to whom acknowledgement is made.

    (b) A SYMBOLIST WORK BY HAECKEL DRAWN IN CEYLON.

Reproduced by permission of Johannes Hembleben from his book, *Ernst Haeckel in Selbstzeugnissen und Bilddokumenten*, Hamburg: Rowohlt, 1967.

Preface

ALTHOUGH much attention has been paid by scholars during the last few years to the ideological content of National Socialism, the role of science, and especially of biology in the origin and evolution of German fascism has been relatively neglected, partially perhaps because fascism, stemming as it does largely from a conservative reaction on the part of certain social classes and individuals to the modern industrial world, has seemed to be rooted also in opposition to modern culture and science. Yet science—distorted and crudely popularized as it was by the Nazis—did play an important part in their thinking and in the official ideology of the National Socialist state. This study, a somewhat revised version of a dissertation submitted to the graduate faculty of the University of Chicago for the doctorate in history, seeks to trace certain key features of National Socialism back to the conception of science and to the social Darwinism of Ernst Haeckel, Germany's most famous nineteenth-century biologist.

The original idea for a work on Haeckel and social Darwinism in Germany emerged from discussions which were held with Professor S. William Halperin of the University of Chicago. Since beginning graduate studies he has aided me not only in the research for this project but has given freely of his encouragement, assistance, and counsel in all that I have undertaken at the University. It has been a rare experience to have been his student and I owe much to his profoundly sensitive understanding of European History. For their genuine interest and helpfulness in the preparation of this work I should like also to thank Professors William H. McNeill and Allen Debus of the History

Department at Chicago, Dr. Michael A. Hoskin, the editor of the History of Science Library, Professor Lawrence Kaplan of the City College of New York, and Earl Fendelman, a discerning critic and friend. Professor Bernard Semmel of the State University of New York at Stony Brook has given not only the benefit of his criticism but has been a true friend in so many ways that I could not even begin to acknowledge my debt to him. Were it not for the understanding and patience of my wife, Lydia Csató Gasman, this book certainly could never have been written.

I should like also to mention the unforgettable friendship of the late Professor Solomon F. Bloom of the History Department of Brooklyn College. His sad loss, now almost a decade ago, is still deeply felt.

Poughkeepsie
New York
January, 1970

Introduction

Ernst Haeckel and the Volkish Tradition

THE *annus mirabilis* of the intellectual history of Europe in the nineteenth century was 1859. Among the impressive and important works to appear during that year were John Stuart Mill's influential essay, 'On Liberty,' and at least two other books by different authors which were of overwhelming significance: Karl Marx's *Critique of Political Economy*, and Charles Darwin's *The Origin of Species*. It is, of course, a truism to say that both Marx and Darwin were prophets of the age of realism and materialism that largely dominated European civilization during the last decades of the nineteenth century. In retrospect, and on its brighter side, the period after 1859, until the outbreak of war in 1914, was one of developing technology, of industrial and scientific progress, of a growing sense of tolerance and civilization, and of overriding confidence in human ability to solve the 'riddles' of the universe. And despite the existence of some isolated voices of pessimism and despair, the last decades of the century represented an era of optimism in the power of science and faith in humanity to realize the older eighteenth-century vision of Condorcet, the potentially infinite progress of the human mind.

On its darker side, however, the same period appears as one of crass materialism, self-assurance to excess, and smugness. In addition, as we now rather painfully know, it harbored latent within itself the basis of twentieth-century totalitarianism. A number of years ago, Professor Carlton Hayes correctly indicated the complex and dual character of this age. In the Introduction to his popular book, *A Generation of Materialism* (1941), he gave evidence of his own feelings about the period. He wrote that as a student he had viewed the last decades of the nineteenth century as a 'stage, indeed a glorious stage, in the progress of Europe and our Western Civilization toward ever greater liberty, democracy, social betterment, and scientific control of nature.' However, some thirty years later these decades also appeared to him as a 'fertile seedtime' for the 'quite different harvest of personal dictatorship, social degradation, and mechanized destruction' which appeared in the twentieth century. And it was, he felt, the 'dual character of the age— at once climax of Enlightenment and source of disillusionment' which gave it its 'peculiar interest and significance.' [1]

In addition to this Janus-like character of the 'Generation of Materialism,' it is important to recognize that the writings of such representative authors of the age as Marx and Darwin, contain along with their realistic, secular, and mechanistic appraisals of life and society, also a strain of romanticism—a strain perceptible not only in their own writings but also in the underlying consciousness of the age itself. Repelled by the harshness of reality, be it in the natural world or in the factory town, many Marxists and Darwinists were captured by visions of better things to come, and of course, by utopianism, conceived frequently in dream-like and mythologically styled fantasies. Marx allowed himself just such a fantasy when he envisioned in all seriousness his communist utopia which he said must emerge from the struggle of the classes, and which would, for the first time in history, transform, in a fundamental way, the nature of all human existence. Even Lenin, the archrealist, and seemingly 'orthodox' Marxist, did not see fit to base his revolutionary theories on the inevitable and spontaneous laws of Historical Materialism. Rather, he accepted, somewhat unconsciously, to be sure, the romanticised revolutionary theory of the *Narodniks*. These Russian populists had taught that the outcome of a revolutionary struggle was determined by the decisive action and influence of the critically thinking individual who refused to submit to the fortuitous flow of history. Thus, in his famous struggle with the *Mensheviks* at the turn of the century, Lenin opted for consciousness and action and opposed a reliance upon the inevitable, mechanical, progressive, and 'spontaneous' laws of history for the Russian Social Democratic Party. And for Darwin, despite his painful vision of nature, 'red in tooth and claw,' and fraught with competition and death, there did seem to be an optimistic conclusion inherent in the nature of things. It is to be observed that he closed *The Origin of Species* with a utopian and prophetic vision of the inevitability of progress and perfection.[2]

In response, thus, to the bleaker effects of industrialism, technology, urbanism, and shallow materialism, the second half of the nineteenth century witnessed also a search for a spiritual essence within society. The neo-romanticism of the *fin de siècle* was an ideology framed to meet the dilemma of man's existence in the modern industrial world. It reflected above all else a lack of spiritual values in the face of the predominance of the material and therefore sought for the 'true' and the 'genuine.'[3] It represented a search for roots and belonging within the shadows created by the harsh reality of the Industrial Revolution and mass urbanization. Many Marxists and Darwinists seemed to believe that by penetrating the secrets of society or nature, they would find their own identities, either historical, class, or racial. In a sense, as one historian has pointed out, this search for deeper reality would 'lead to totalitarianism because it was always the search for some sort of authority with which one could identify and which would liquidate the present situation of man.'[4] Neo-romanticism, in other words, sought an absolute sanction for its ideas in either history or nature. And even though Marx and Darwin themselves were highly suspicious of the pursuit of unity and final authority in either history or nature, nonetheless, as frequently occurs, many of their followers and epigones were not careful enough to draw a line and to heed, as it were, the Kantian exclusion of ultimate knowledge, of the quest after 'Things in Themselves.' Certainly, among the disciples of Darwin, none pursued the ultimate secrets of nature and society more avidly than Ernst Haeckel, the self-appointed spokesman of Darwin and Darwinism in Germany.

It may be said that in no other country of Europe, or for that matter even in the United States, did the ideas of Darwinism develop as seriously as a total explanation of the world as in Germany. But Darwinism in Germany was a system of thought that was often transformed almost beyond recognition. *Darwinismus* was far from the biological ideas or underlying moral and philosophical views of Darwin himself. Professing a mystical belief in the forces of nature, insisting on the literal transfer of the laws of biology to the social realm, and calling for a religious reformation in German life, Haeckel and his immediate followers held to ideas which were remote from the familiar naturalism of Spencer, Darwin, and Huxley.

A close investigation of the major ideas of Haeckel and his followers reveals a romantic rather than a materialistic approach to biology and a striking affinity not with liberalism or socialism but with the ideology of National Socialism. It will be the principal purpose of this study to demonstrate that the content of the writings of Haeckel and the ideas of his followers—their general political, philosophical, scientific, and social orientation—were proto-Nazi in character, and that the Darwinist movement which he created, one of the most powerful forces in nineteenth- and twentieth-century German intellectual history, may be fully understood as a prelude to the doctrine of National Socialism.

There appears to be substantial reason and evidence to view Haeckel in this light, to call most previous generalizations about him into question and to subject them to renewed examination. In virtually all studies of the history of ideas in the nineteenth century, Haeckel is seldom, if ever, separated from the general progressive, scientific, and modernistic tradition of European culture and his name is found to be synonymous with materialism, naturalism, mechanism, and of course, Darwinism.[5] He has traditionally been thought to embody optimism, progress, liberalism, socialism, and tireless opposition to arbitrary state power.[6] He is invariably accepted as the intellectual embodiment within Germany of the feeling of optimism and security, engendered by science and industrialism, which suffused bourgeois civilization before the cataclysm of 1914.

Our analysis, however, of the social Darwinist ideas of Haeckel and the German Monist League which he founded will question the traditional view of Haeckel as a progressive liberal or socialist. It will reveal Haeckel's prophetic synthesis of romantically inclined Volkism with evolution and science—which provided an ideological basis for National Socialism. It will maintain that proto-Nazi Volkism did not invariably originate in opposition to science and modernism,[7] but will seek rather to show that one of the earliest, if not the earliest comprehensive program embodying National Socialist principles in Germany arose in the context of a movement which prided itself on its scientific ideology and modern view of the world. And finally, the underlying purpose of our investigation is that these insights into the nature of Haeckelian thought must alter our conception somewhat of the historical origins of National Socialism in Germany.

Ernst Haeckel was born on February 16, 1834, in Potsdam.[8] Shortly after his birth the family moved to Merseburg, a town in Saxony, where his father was a government lawyer. Haeckel remained with his family in Merseburg until 1852, and it was there that he received his basic education. At home the influence of Goethe, Schiller, Schleiermacher, and Humboldt helped to shape his early mind. As a child Haeckel had wanted to become a botanist and had even kept a herbarium of his own, where he noticed that not all of the varieties of plants could be classified according to the rigid definitions of the textbooks which assumed that nature was immutable. He was to remark many years later that he had noticed that there were 'good and bad species,' and therefore made two collections. 'One, arranged on official lines, offered to the sympathetic observer all the species in "typical" specimens, as radically distinct forms, each decked with its pretty label; the other was a private collection, only shown to one trusted friend, and contained only the rejected kinds that Goethe so happily called "the characterless or disorderly races, which we hardly dare ascribe to a species, as they lose themselves in infinite varieties," ... In this a large number of specimens arranged in a long series, illustrated the direct transition from one good species to another. They were the officially forbidden fruit of knowledge in which I took a secret boyish delight in my leisure hours.'[9]

Haeckel's parents, however, wanted him to become a physician and adhering to their wishes he studied medicine at Würzburg, Vienna, and Berlin between 1852 and 1858. He received his medical license in 1858. However, the life of a general practitioner did not appeal to the young Haeckel and after a brief medical practice he returned to the pursuit of pure science. Moving on to the University of Jena he undertook to do a dissertation in zoology under the direction of the well-known anatomist, Carl Gegenbaur. Thus Haeckel became a zoologist and never returned to the practice of medicine. Gegenbaur prevailed upon him to accept a position at the University of Jena and it was there that Haeckel remained for the rest of his life.[10]

Haeckel's adult life (he died in August, 1919), spans the years from the time of the accession of Bismarck to power in the early 1860's to the demise of the German Empire at Versailles in 1919. In 1866, Bismarck engineered his war against Austria and established his own state, the North German Confederation. In that same year, Haeckel, as a young man of thirty-two, published his first and what proved to be his most elaborate theoretical statement, his two-volume *Generelle Morphologie*, in which he attempted to subsume all of science under Darwinian principles and guidelines. Thus, the publication of his scientific manifesto coincides with the Bismarckian achievement of German unification. The future evolution of his political and scientific thinking was intimately allied with the history of the Second Reich.

As a young member of the faculty of the University of Jena, Haeckel entered the decade of the sixties as a free-thinker and a liberal, but with strong nationalistic sentiments. Despite an oft-flaunted commitment to political and social freedom, Haeckel, like most German liberals, looked to a strong state for help in the task of nation-building. One should bear in mind in discussing the history of liberalism in the nineteenth century that a relatively powerful middle class came into political prominence in such western countries as England and France where a strong state structure and a sense of national and historical identity were already in existence. Jealous of its own political prerogatives, liberalism in western Europe proclaimed a belief that that government is best which governs least and professed an attachment to the natural and inalienable rights of man. In Germany, on the other hand, the middle class was comparatively weak and a stable state structure was non-existent. As a consequence, and particularly after 1848, and even more so after Bismarckian unification in the 1860's, liberalism in Germany, aware of its own weaknesses, looked increasingly to the advantages which a strong state could offer for the realization of its own program. For the German liberals, the organization of the national state appeared to be much more important than the abstract and somewhat alien western liberal conception of the freedom of all men, and revealingly enough they called themselves National Liberals. Abandoning in practice many of the political principles to which they were abstractly committed, they were able to throw virtually unqualified support to the authoritarian Bismarckian state.[11]

In his political and intellectual evolution Haeckel may be cited as an illustration of the tendency of German liberalism to seek authoritarian solutions to Germany's problems. Haeckel was early a fervent supporter of Bismarck,[12] and as liberalism after the foundation of the Second Empire in 1871 moved more and more to the political right and increasingly retreated from the cosmopolitanism inherent in the older liberal ideology of the French Revolution, so too did Haeckel in his own development advance along the same path. In the decade of the seventies, Bismarck, with liberal support, was engaged in the *Kulturkampf*. During the same decade Haeckel began to fight his own *Kulturkampf* against all Christianity and on behalf of his own vision of modern culture and science which he opposed to traditional ethics and religion. Of course, Haeckel viewed Bismarck's battle against the Catholics as of the utmost importance and deeply regretted its cessation. During the 1880's, Bismarck fought what he considered to be the new menace to Germany, the socialists and the Marxists. Paralleling the efforts of Bismarck, Haeckel, along with his social Darwinist followers, set about to demonstrate the 'aristocratic' and non-democratic character of the laws of nature. And finally after the dismissal of Bismarck by William II in 1890, an act which Haeckel condemned in the strongest language, he proceeded to ally himself with the most active imperialist and chauvinistic trends in German life. Until the end of the First World War, and up to his death in 1919, Haeckel contributed to that special variety of German thought which served as the seed-bed for National Socialism. He became one of Germany's major ideologists for racism, nationalism, and imperialism.

Haeckel's politics, his vision of science and the world, in short his personal brand of social Darwinism, was in reality an uneven composite of three streams of thought: German philosophical romantic idealism, scientific positivism and materialism, and Darwinism. Let us, therefore, briefly examine the nature of each of these aspects of European thought and indicate in an introductory way how they were absorbed and changed both consciously and unconsciously by Haeckel.

Haeckel was first of all influenced by and heir to the powerful forces of German romanticism.[13] Though a European-wide phenomenon, romanticism had been particularly strong in Germany, where it had become an all-embracing *Weltanschauung* capable of merging with many different social and political ideas. For one thing, German nationalism had been able to achieve a means of expression in romanticism, so that once science came to challenge the romantic vision of nature it also became willy-nilly a threat to German nationalism, national expression, and national self-consciousness. More than a literary movement, romanticism, in the writings of Schleiermacher, Fichte, Novalis, Goethe, and the Schlegels, was really an expression of German life and feeling. Historically, romanticism arose as a reaction to the ideas of the Enlightenment and the French Revolution, which had been brought to Germany by the invading armies of France during the revolutionary and Napoleonic periods. German patriotic opposition to the invader became in the realm of ideas opposition to the way of thinking of the Enlightenment.

The French *philosophes* had taught that reason was superior to authority, tradition, and human intuition. The romantics, on the other hand, believed that certain truths were outside of the province of reason, and they appealed to man's need for faith and deeper emotional feeling. As a form of conservative nationalism, romanticism held that the abstract concept 'Man' was a fiction and substituted in its place the notion of the uniqueness of national and cultural identity. Thus, whereas for the French *philosophes* nationalism was subordinate to the universal human community, for the German intellectuals it was the other way around.

Despite its call for faith, romanticism, as it developed for the most part in Germany, lacked a religious sense of God, and substituted in place of a deity the worship of nature and the religion and philosophy of pantheism. On this basis it proceeded in the realm of science to probe the secrets of nature by intuitive comprehension. Intent on finding unity in the world, romanticism and *Naturphilosophie* sought for the all-embracing laws of the universe. A search was undertaken for cosmic principles, and it was in the midst of this quest after the unattainable that romanticism and its derivative science, *Naturphilosophie*, deteriorated into charlatanism and quackery and assumed a mystical and falsely speculative character.[14]

However, romantic *Naturphilosophie* had one idea which was to be of monumental importance later on in the century—the idea of evolution and development. For the romantics, nature was in a continual process of becoming. This was expressed at times in the form of a belief in the existence of a Chain of Being in nature.[15] From inanimate matter all the way up to man and God, there was a unity and interconnectedness. In the course of its development, nature realized itself in all of its manifold forms.[16]

It was not only in science, however, but also in history that the romantics looked for development. In their philosophy they opposed the eighteenth-century notion of abstract and universal man who supposedly organised his society after an abstract social contract. Culture and not abstract ideas was the key, they said, to a nation's history. All aspects of culture were organically related to the same universal process. Religion, art, mythology, and science were therefore intimately bound up with the political and social structure of any given age. Taken together they expressed the spirit or *Geist* of a society. In this unity both the internal world of man and the external world of nature were one. Mind, by intuition, could grasp the essential reality of the whole, of which it was both part and reflection. The appeal of this kind of thinking is obvious. The individual who believed in this form of secularised pantheism ostensibly found himself able to know the Absolute, the true spirit of the world, and to have communion with all of nature and history. By intuition, which the romantics regarded as a form of reason, the individual, as it were, created the world after his own mental image.[17]

In addition, German romantic idealism saw an organic link between one age and another. All nations and all ages were, they believed, united in one historical process of development and becoming, from lower to higher cultural forms. Fichte, for example, developed his cultural romanticism into a form of nationalism. For him, the Germans had certain distinctive qualities which gave them the potential to develop into the highest form of nation—a nation in which full human freedom would finally be realised.

If romanticism was the first influence on the mind of Haeckel, then the second was the materialism of mid-nineteenth-century German philosophy. It may be said that the materialistic break with idealism and romanticism came from two directions. Firstly, the students of

Hegel—Strauss, Feuerbach, Bruno Bauer, and then Marx—derived materialism from his idealist philosophy and began to pay more attention to the actual workings of history rather than to the vague movements of the world-spirit. They looked to the 'true' nature of man and history. Among the left-Hegelians it was discovered that Christianity stood in the way of the full development of mankind. In 1835, David Strauss published his famous book, *The Life of Jesus*, and in 1841, Feuerbach's *Essence of Christianity* appeared. Recognize, they all taught, the mythological nature of religion and mankind will then be free.

Secondly, idealism was seriously threatened by developments within science itself. Influenced by positivism, science sought only that which could be empirically verified. In Germany, Emil DuBois-Reymond, Johannes Müller, Helmholtz, and Rudolf Virchow, all disdaining idle philosophical reflection and abandoning *Naturphilosophie* which they correctly considered to be sterile,[18] retired to the laboratory to get on with the practical work of discovery and verification. In their hands science took on an experimental and empirical character and made progress which was both tangible and observable. But the very success of science also brought with it cultural tensions. By its success laboratory science threatened the mystical unity of man and nature which had been the basic creed of the idealists. Science, it was felt, had the capacity to destroy the deeper sense of things. The same criticism which had been levelled by the romantics at the Enlightenment, the neo-romantics advanced against modern industrial society.[19] In this situation some intellectuals retreated from an acceptance of the modern world. Such was the case, for example, with the two 'Germanic critics' Paul de Lagarde and Julius Langbehn.[20] There was, however, a second alternative, a new unity between science and idealism. In 1859, Darwin's *Origin of Species* appeared, and Haeckel, about to enter upon his career, sensed its possibilities. Here was the opportunity to bring the old *Naturphilosophie* into harmony with modern science. It was for this reason that he wrote conspicuously in his first major work, the *Generelle Morphologie*, that 'all true science is *Naturphilosophie*.'[21]

The third major constituent of Haeckel's thought, therefore, was Darwinism. It may be said that if Darwinism in England was an extension of *laissez faire* individualism projected from the social world to the natural world, so too was Haeckel's biological work in Germany a projection of German romanticism and philosophical idealism. Like Darwin, Haeckel moved from the social world of ideas to the natural world. In both cases, interestingly enough, it was not science which shaped their conceptions of nature and man, but rather national, historical, and philosophical consciousness.

Broadly speaking, English Darwinism signified two things. Firstly, it meant of course, the theory of natural selection, or the fortuitous[22] and mechanical choice of favored individuals and species in the struggle for life. Secondly, it may mean social Darwinism, or the application of the theory of natural selection and evolution to explain human society. Evolution, which is often equated with Darwinism, is only, in Darwin's theory, a consequence of natural selection. It is not the other way around. Thus, from the purely biological and scientific point of view, Darwinism has this rather restricted meaning and is of definite significance for science, for the philosophy of science, and for scientific method.

Darwin's significance for philosophy and scientific method resided in his eliminating the need for explanations of final causes from the organic world and in the success which he had in providing a mechanical basis for the explanation of organic change. Even though the actual mechanism of heredity was unknown to Darwin, the theory of natural selection heralded a break with teleological, anthropomorphic, and religious explanations in the organic sciences. By his theory Darwin accomplished for the organic world what Newton succeeded in doing for the inorganic world in the seventeenth century. However, Darwin's theory was even more thoroughgoing in its destructiveness of cosmic purpose than Newton's conception of a universal law of gravity. There were no universal forces in Darwinism, and even the term evolution was not to be found in the early editions of *The Origin of Species*. Once Darwinism was accepted, nature could no longer be conceived as a creative whole, nor as giving evidence of possessing directional character. Rather, according to the implications of Darwin's theory, nature changed and sometimes 'progressed' by accidental and wholly unprepared random variations—which, of course, implied that there is neither finality nor purpose in nature.[23]

However, apart from being a biological theory, Darwinism has seemed to some to have major implications for traditional religion, philosophy, and social science.²⁴ This was especially true for Haeckel and his followers. Haeckel combined in his own person the natural scientist and the social theorist and political activist. Although he did not have an active political career, as did his contemporary and ideological opponent, Rudolf Virchow, the famous pathologist and leader of the *Fortschrittspartei*,²⁵ Haeckel was able, nonetheless, to carry great weight and authority in matters outside the realm of science. Indeed it is safe to say that few men in modern times have had more of a general cultural influence than Haeckel.²⁶ As the recognized spokesman of Darwinism in Germany he was taken as the virtually incontestable and exacting voice of science, both among many of the scientists and certainly among the general public.

In Haeckel's thinking and writing the traditional elements of social Darwinism were present in bountiful supply. It is apparent that he advocated an ethic of competition and struggle as the foundation of the laws of human society. And his ethic of the inherent struggle to be found in the world did play an overwhelmingly important role in stimulating the growth of National Socialism. But there were other very important reasons why Haeckel's social Darwinism became one of the most important formative causes for the rise of the Nazi movement. At the basis of National Socialist ideology in Germany lay not only the idea of struggle and the notion of racial conflict between the 'higher' and 'lower' races of men (for example, Hitler's formulation of the differences between the human races was taken directly from Haeckel)²⁷ but also the equally important religion of nature which implied among other things a contempt for rationalism and history. The Nazis, like Haeckel, sought to bring man back within the purview of nature. By stressing in their ideology the importance of rootedness, of *Blut und Boden*, the Nazis wished to deify the primitive forces of nature. History and civilization, they felt, had separated man from his true character and destiny. This ideology, in the form in which the Nazis used it, had its immediate source to a surprising extent, in the social Darwinism of Haeckel and in the Monist League which he founded and directed. Biology in Germany, which might have been expected to stand in the way of the mystically false ideas of the Nazis, came rather to their support and much of the basis of that support is directly traceable to the influence of Haeckel himself.

ERNST HAECKEL AND THE VOLKISH TRADITION

In the decades around the turn of the century racially inspired social Darwinism in Germany, which was almost completely indebted to Haeckel for its creation, and which on the whole had little, if anything at all, to do with Charles Darwin, played a very important and decisive role in the intellectual history of the period. Haeckel's ideas on social Darwinism were brought to fruition in a milieu that was particularly German. His ideas served to unite into a full-bodied ideology the trends of racism, imperialism, romanticism, anti-Semitism, and nationalism which were floating around among various dissatisfied and frustrated groups in German society, especially among the lower middle classes. Finding themselves in danger of being forced down into the working class, the lower middle classes expressed their anxiety through the medium of certain ideas which were mystically nationalistic and anti-Semitic, and which grasped for roots in German life and history. The form which social Darwinism took in Germany was a pseudo-scientific religion of nature worship and nature-mysticism combined with notions of racism. It was based on both the social Darwinian ideas of Haeckel and the ideology of Volkism which was related to and largely inspired by his writings.

In *Mein Kampf*, Hitler, despite his criticism of the political ineptitude and naivete of the Volkists, made use of the broad concept of the Volk and of the Volkish state to describe his vision of a racially powerful and united Germany. These terms and their ideological content are to be found throughout the literature of National Socialism, and indeed Volkism was the 'chief source of inspiration for most leaders of Naziism, ... and it undoubtedly helped greatly to pave the way for the victory of Hitler's party.'[28] Many of the important theoretical leaders of the Volkist movement were in one way or another connected either ideologically or personally with Haeckel. However, it should be pointed out also that not all of the Volkist writers or intellectuals were necessarily potential Nazis or harbored exclusively National Socialist ideas. It may even be said that many of their social criticisms of German society were often correct in a general way. On the other hand, they did help to provide a proper cultural environment which led to the development of Hitler's movement. And in retrospect many of their ideas and sentiments appear ominous indeed.

But what do the terms 'Volk' and 'Volkish' really signify? Perhaps these terms are best explained in a recent study on the origins of National Socialism.

> 'Volk' is one of those perplexing German terms which connoted far more than its specific meaning. 'Volk' is a much more comprehensive term than 'people'; for the German thinkers ever since the birth of German romanticism in the later eighteenth century 'Volk' signified the union of a group of people with a transcendental 'essence.' This 'essence' might be called 'nature' or 'cosmos' or 'mythos,' but in each instance it was fused to man's innermost nature, and represented the source of his creativity, his depth of feeling, his individuality, and his unity with other members of the Volk.[29]

The Volkists thus represented a strain in German thinking which diverged sharply from traditional Western nationalism and traditional Western religion. Largely an ideology which appealed, as we have already noted, to the socially and economically threatened lower middle classes, it attempted a fusion of nationalism with neo-romanticism. It tended to worship nature, and frequently gave rise to crackpot occult and faddist movements. In place of the *Rechtsstaat*, that is, the legally constituted state, it stressed the importance of 'blood' and the supposed basic racial differences between people. In the Volkist conception of the Chain of Being, the Volk, or race, stood in between the individual who was himself isolated and alienated by the forces of modern society and the universe or cosmos at the opposite end of the scale. The Volk, or race, which partook of the universal allowed the individual to belong to something greater than himself. It gave to him a sense of identity with a cosmic significance. In this mystical union of the people with the life forces of the cosmos the Volkists dreamed of binding the individual German to his natural and topographical surroundings, in short, to his regional landscape. Nature and individual, they felt, must be tied together in an indissoluble bond.[30] These were also the essential ideas of Haeckel's pantheistic religion of evolutionary Monism. In this way he and his followers, brought science to the defense of Volkism, and attached themselves to the pseudo-scientific myth of the racial unity of the Aryans.

It may be said that Haeckel gave to the idea of race a modern and scientific guise by the addition of a social Darwinist ingredient. In 1853, the Alsatian Frenchman, Count Arthur de Gobineau, published his famous book, *The Inequality of the Human Races*. In it he developed the idea that the Aryan race was the superior one among the world races and of course also among the Europeans. In actuality his book was an attempt at universal history with race and its significance as the key. He felt that the Aryans were destined to lose their strength because of racial mixture. This, he believed pessimistically, was the fate of every race.

At the time when this book was published Gobineau's ideas were not given much of a reception in either France or Germany.[31] But in Germany later on in the century his ideas were revived in a new guise. By invoking the social Darwinist idea of the inevitability of racial struggle in human life, it was proposed that the Aryans or really the Germans need not succumb to a fate of deterioration as Gobineau had predicted. The Germans, it was felt, could fight and win against the double threat of racial contamination and deterioration from within and racial threats from without. Haeckel, who accepted the Aryan myths of Gobineau, supported the idea of the need for maintaining the racial purity of the Germans. He warned repeatedly against the mixing of races and campaigned throughout his life for the most radical use of racial eugenics.

The fact that Haeckel was a reputable scientist helped Volkism to gain a respectable and appealing character. Because of this respectability and the apparent scientific character of many of its leading ideas, a good number of teachers and academicians were attracted to the Volkist movement and became participants in it in one way or another. Its ideas were disseminated in the classroom or in the many books and articles that were written in support of its major premises. It was Haeckel who brought the full weight of science down hard on the side of what were Volkism's essentially irrational and mystical ideas. In contrast with the ideas of those who had sought to escape from the harshness of industrial reality into the idyllic communities and idealized spirit of the Middle Ages, the Volkism that was being urged by Haeckel and by his followers was essentially modern.[32] No need, they felt, to deny industrialism or the scientific revolution. On the contrary, once allied with a new pantheistic religion based on evolution and led by a biological elite forming the nucleus of strong state power, German life would be reconstituted. The German people would then be 'in harmony' with the laws of nature and with the animated and sentient forces of the universe. The liberation of Germany for Haeckel and his followers resided not in history but in freedom from history. The Germans, they felt, must return to the laws of nature.

This study, therefore, will attempt to analyze the ideological content of Haeckelian social Darwinism. It will be concerned both with the social Darwinian ideas of Haeckel and with those of his closest followers, generally in the context of the organization which Haeckel founded and led, the German Monist League. Monism in general, of course, was not only a German, but was also an international movement and ideology.[33] Its program could be equated with the rebellion against revealed religion and metaphysical ways of thinking which had been sparked by nineteenth-century positivistic and materialistic science. Indeed, prominent scientists like Ernst Mach, Svante Arrhenius, Jacques Loeb, and Eli Metchnikoff openly and forcefully identified themselves with Monism and the attempt to bring science and its methodology into the domain of all areas of human thought and endeavor. In Germany, Haeckel's Monist League could be identified with this larger international movement based upon science. For many, if there existed one organization which truly expressed the modern temper, it was the German Monist League of Haeckel with its radically scientific and positivistic spirit and program. And, as such, its significance and fame loomed large in Germany, a country which had witnessed the large scale application of science and technology to the national economy and to the larger national purpose. However, it was the positivistic content of the ideology of the German Monist League combined with Volkish nationalism which gave to it its peculiar significance and importance for the history of the development of National Socialism. In its program science and nationalism were indissolubly combined and, as such, the German Monist League of Haeckel assumed a character quite different from that of scientific Monism in other countries.

To be sure, not all Monists were necessarily proto-Nazi. There were many who abhorred racism, Germanic nationalism, and Volkish mysticism. There were Monists who were simply positivists, pacifists, freethinkers, and Marxists of varying persuasions who viewed Monism as an up-to-date ideology dedicated to the destruction of theistic metaphysics and religious obscurantism. The membership roster of the League included the sociologist, Ferdinand Toennies, the Art Nouveau painter, Henry van de Velde, the pacifist, Alfred Fried, and political writers and intellectuals like Carl von Ossietsky, Otto Lehmann-Rüssbildt, Helene Stöcker, and Magnus Hirschfeld. The latter four were active contributors to the left-wing, strongly anti-fascist journal, *Die Weltbühne*.[34] But these individuals were not representative of the main ideology or prevalent mood of the Monist League in the years before the First World War. Under the leadership of Haeckel, and then of Wilhelm Ostwald, it was the proto-Nazi and Volkish character of the Monist League which was predominant.[35]

This study, therefore, confines its attention to the predominant ideology of Haeckel and the Monist League up through the period of the First World War. It seeks to analyze the ideas and programs of those individuals who were typically representative of Monist thought up until that time, and concentrates on the writings and statements of those who were the elected leaders of the League, who edited its journals and wrote books on its behalf, and who enjoyed the confidence of Haeckel and Ostwald.

The chronological limit of our study is 1919, the year of Haeckel's death. Under the Weimar Republic the character and content of the ideology of the Monist League underwent a significant shift away from racism and Volkism in the direction of radical liberalism and sympathy for the social experiment of the Russian Revolution.[36] It was only after the rise to power of the Nazis in 1933 that the older character of the Monist League reasserted itself and especially those who had been closest to Haeckel quickly and forcefully expressed their deep loyalty to and affinity with National Socialism.[37]

NOTES

1. Carlton Hayes, *A Generation of Materialism* (New York: Harper, 1941), p. xi.
2. Charles Darwin, *The Origin of Species* (Variorum text; Philadelphia: University of Pennsylvania Press, 1959), p. 759.
3. George L. Mosse, *The Culture of Western Europe* ([New York]: Rand McNally, 1961), p. 7.
4. *Ibid.*

5. For Haeckel as a 'mechanistic' and 'materialistic' philosopher and scientist, see Hayes, *A Generation of Materialism*, p. 115 and *passim*. The Marxists of East Germany have also recently 'rediscovered' Haeckel's materialism. See Peter Klemm, *Der Ketzer von Jena* (Leipzig: Urania, 1966), *passim*.
6. For a typical, but incorrect, view of Haeckel as a socialist, see Donald H. Fleming, 'Introduction,' Jacques Loeb, *The Mechanistic Conception of Life* (Cambridge, Mass.: Belknap Press, 1964), pp. xi, xvii, and for a typical, but incorrect, statement of the nature of Haeckel's liberalism, see Eric Nordenskiold, *The History of Biology* (New York: Tudor, 1928), pp. 505–507, 525. Two recent and significant articles, however, briefly allude to Haeckel's influence on the development of National Socialism: See Fritz Bolle, 'Darwinismus und Zeitgeist,' *Zeitschrift für Religion und Geistesgeschichte*, XIV (1962), 143–178, and Hans-Günter Zmarzlik, 'Der Sozialdarwinismus in Deutschland als geschichtliches Problem,' *Vierteljahreshefte für Zeitgeschichte*, XI (1963), 246–273.
7. An assumption frequently made in studies of the origins of National Socialism is that the Volkish and proto-Nazi movement arose largely as a reaction to the mechanistic and materialistic science of nineteenth-century Germany. And almost invariably the ideas of Haeckel and the German Monist League are brought up as the example, *par excellence*, of the kind of mechanistic materialism and superficial modernism which excited the rebellion of the Volkish authors and launched them on the ideological road towards National Socialism. This thesis, for example, constitutes one of the themes of Fritz Stern's influential study of the 'Germanic critics,' Lagarde, Langbehn, and Moeller van den Bruck, *The Politics of Cultural Despair*. Stern singles out Haeckel and the Monist League as one of the most important sources of their discontent with German culture and describes Haeckelianism as typical of the tendency of German life against which they devoted all of their energies. However, their opposition to Haeckel and Monism is overstated. As we shall see there were in fact important ties both ideologically and personally between the 'Germanic critics' and the Monists. For Stern's comments on Haeckel and the Monist League, see *The Politics of Cultural Despair* (Berkeley and Los Angeles: The University of California Press, 1961), pp. 123, 282.
8. There are a number of standard biographies of Haeckel, all written more than fifty years ago by his followers. See, for example, Wilhelm Boelsche, *Haeckel, His Life and Work* (Philadelphia: Jacobs, 1906) and Walther May, *Ernst Haeckel, Versuch einer Chronik seines Lebens und Wirkens* (Leipzig: Barth, 1909).
9. Quoted in Boelsche, *Haeckel, His Life and Work*, pp. 38–39.
10. *Ibid., passim*.
11. For a general analysis of German liberalism, see Guido de Ruggiero, *The History of European Liberalism* (Boston: Beacon, 1961), pp. 211–274; and Leonard Krieger, *The German Idea of Freedom* (Boston: Beacon, 1957), *passim*.
12. How little this appears to be known may be seen in Nordenskiold's *History of Biology*, p. 507, where Haeckel is described as a firm opponent of Bismarck and as a person who took little or no interest in politics. In fact, as we shall see in more detail, the very opposite is true.

13. For an account of the influence of romanticism and *Naturphilosophie* on Haeckel, see Nordenskiold, *History of Biology*, pp. 511–515, and for a general discussion of the significance of romanticism in European and German thought, see Mosse, *The Culture of Western Europe*, Chapter I. On romanticism and science in Germany, see Alexander Gottfried Gode-von Aesch, *Natural Science in German Romanticism* (New York: Columbia University Press, 1941).
14. For an account of *Naturphilosophie*, see Nordenskiold, *History of Biology*, pp. 286–298. Nordenskiold credits *Naturphilosophie* with a 'deep influence on the development of biology,' but at the same time comments that 'its extravagances cannot . . . be regarded as other than features tending to retard the sound progress of science.'
15. Arthur O. Lovejoy, *The Great Chain of Being* (Cambridge, Mass.: Harvard University Press, 1957), Chapter X.
16. The idea of evolution which the romantics entertained was, of course, similar to the idea of evolution proposed by Darwin later on, but it was at the same time very different from it. For Darwin, each event in the evolutionary process was a new event. On the other hand, for the romantic nature-philosophers the evolutionary process in a sense, went no place. For them the idea of nature in its fulness existed before the event. It was for this reason that Goethe (whom Haeckel admired as much as Darwin) in his biological work, for example, was constantly looking for archetypal forms in nature.

    For the differences between Darwin and earlier romantic evolutionary theory, see John Dewey, *The Influence of Darwin on Philosophy* (New York: Holt, 1910). On Goethe as a biologist and nature-philosopher, see Rudolf Magnus, *Goethe as a Scientist* (New York: Schuman, 1949). On the connection between Haeckel and Goethe, see Nordenskiold, *History of Biology*, p. 512, and Haeckel, 'Die Naturanschauung von Darwin, Goethe und Lamarck,' in *Gemeinverständliche Vorträge und Abhandlungen aus dem Gebiete der Entwicklungslehre* (Bonn: Strauss, 1902), I, 217–280.
17. For an analysis of the philosophical presuppositions of early nineteenth-century German romanticism, see Martin Malia, *Alexander Herzen and the Birth of Russian Socialism, 1812–1855* (Cambridge, Mass.: Harvard University Press, 1961), pp. 69–98, 218–256.
18. Oswei Temkin, 'The Idea of Descent in Post-Romantic German Biology: 1848–1858,' in Bentley Glass (ed.), *Forerunners of Darwin* (Baltimore: Johns Hopkins University Press, 1959). On the influence generally of positivism on the development of nineteenth-century science and biology, see Nordenskiold, *History of Biology*, Part III, Chapter IX.
19. Mosse, *The Culture of Western Europe*, pp. 19–20. Professor Mosse has written: 'By mid-century, the unity between man and nature was being challenged. As nature seemed more and more to become the domain of scientific investigation, the essential romantic unity was in danger of being rent asunder and the stimulus which it had offered to the poetry of life seemed threatened. As this point melancholy set in among many intellectuals . . . . Nature was no longer animate and sentient but mechanical and necessary.'

20. For a comprehensive account of Paul de Lagarde and Julius Langbehn and their reaction to modern industrial culture, see Fritz Stern, *The Politics of Cultural Despair*.
21. Ernst Haeckel, *Generelle Morphologie der Organismen* (Berlin: Reimer, 1866), II, 447.
22. On the fortuitous character of Darwinism, see Charles Coulton Gillispie, 'Lamarck and Darwin in the History of Science,' in Glass, *Forerunners of Darwin*, p. 287. Professor Gillispie has written: 'Instead of explaining variation, [Darwin] begins with it as a fundamental fact of nature. Variations are assumed to occur at random, requiring no further explanation and pre-supposing no causative agent for science to seek out. This is what opened the breach through which biology might follow physics into objectivity, because it introduced the distinction, which Darwin was the first to make, between the origin of variations and their preservation. Variations arise by change. But they are preserved according as they work more or less effectively in objective circumstances.'
23. Dewey, *The Influence of Darwin on Philosophy*.
24. For a general introduction to social Darwinism, see George E. Simpson, 'Darwin and "Social Darwinism,"' *Antioch Review*, XIX (1959), 33-45.
25. Erwin Ackerknecht, *Rudolf Virchow* (Madison, Wis.: University of Wisconsin Press, 1951), *passim*.
26. Nordenskiold, *History of Biology*, pp. 505-506: 'There are not many personalities who have so powerfully influenced the development of human culture—and that, too, in many different spheres—as Haeckel.' And as Rudolf Steiner, the noted Theosophist, wrote in 1907: 'Despite all German philosophy, despite all other German culture, Haeckel's phylogenetic thought is now the most significant achievement of German intellectual life in the second half of the nineteenth century.' Quoted in Johannes Hemleben, *Rudolf Steiner und Ernst Haeckel* (Stuttgart: Freies Geistesleben, 1965), p. 165.
27. See Chapter VII.
28. Walter Z. Laqueur, Review of George L. Mosse's *The Crisis of German Ideology*, in *The New York Review of Books*, January 14, 1965.
29. George L. Mosse, *The Crisis of German Ideology* (New York: Grosset and Dunlap, 1964), p. 4.
30. *Ibid., passim*.
31. *Ibid.*, pp. 91-92.
32. Peter Viereck has noted the essentially modern character of German neo-romanticism: *Metapolitics* (New York: Knopf, 1941), p. 147. Viereck writes:
'Where the romantic revolution differs from the first is in political method. Here the romantic "will to power" no longer *rejects* the "uninspired" world of materialism—efficiency-industrialism but *swallows* it, swallows and thereby assimilates it. Thus, in the person of Wagner, the romantic "spirit of music" combines with a tough, practical, and politically shrewd Naziism. Thus, in the whole movement of Naziism itself, the fantastic goals of romanticism are sought in 1941 not with the inefficient "blue-flower" of the earlier, ivory tower romantics

but with the most rational and scientific means of modern technics, modern propaganda, modern war. This swallowing and assimilation of its direct opposite, of rational technics, which alone explains the victories of Hitler Germany, is what makes the second romantic revolution the most important "event" of the last hundred years.'

33. For an account of Monism as an international movement, see Paul Carus, *The Monist, A Review of its Work and a Sketch of its Philosophy* (Chicago: Open Court, 1891–1892).

34. But even these 'left-wing' Monists frequently expressed ideas which were not typically Marxist or liberal. Their concern with society reflected rather a general radicalism based upon naturalistic premises and it is this which helps to account for their membership in the Monist League. For example, Helene Stöcker, who was the first woman to earn a Ph.D. in philosophy in Germany, and who was also a leading pacifist, was at the same time a strong advocate of eugenics and a close follower of Wilhelm Schallmayer, who, as we shall see, influenced the rise of Nazi eugenics. In the *Bund für Mutterschutz*, which she founded in 1905, and led in close conjunction with the Monist League, she campaigned for the 'biological' emancipation of women, Her position was that women could not be expected to maintain the same role in society as that of men, but had rather certain feminine rights and obligations. The *Bund für Mutterschutz*, therefore, fought for the support of women during pregnancy, care for illegal children and unwed mothers, and legislation to prevent the unfit from marrying. Insofar as the *Bund* emphasized the biological differences between men and women, its program was ideologically closer to that of the National Socialists on the woman question, than it was to that, say, of the suffragettes, who minimized the differences between the sexes. In any event, the leaders of the Monist League assumed a position on the woman question, which was, in fact, identical with that of the Nazis later on. And although Helene Stöcker was, of course, a bitter opponent of the Nazis, and ended her life in New York as a refugee from Nazi Germany, it is still of interest that in 1914, she thought it important enough to record the influence of Alexander Tille's book, *Von Darwin bis Nietzsche*, on her intellectual development. As we shall see, Tille was an important proto-Nazi writer. See Helene Stöcker's untitled article in Heinrich Schmidt, ed., *Was wir Ernst Haeckel verdanken. Ein Buch der Verehrung und Dankbarkeit* (Leipzig: Unesma, 1914), II, 324.

Otto Lehmann-Rüssbildt was also a pacifist. His attachment to the Monist League stemmed mainly, it would appear, from his fanatical opposition to Christianity. As a Monist he organized mass meetings which urged departure from the traditional religious faiths. And Magnus Hirschfeld was a noted physician who founded an Institute of Sexology and was a member of the left-wing of the SPD. He was famous for advocating advanced views on sexual problems and campaigned against the inclusion of homosexuality and abortion within the criminal code. Hirschfeld apparently found a congenial milieu in the Monist League because of its concern with man as a 'natural' creature.

Alfred Fried was also an important pacifist who, in fact, won the Nobel Peace Prize in 1911. He joined the Monist League a year or two before the World War and attempted to bring pacifist doctrines into harmony with Monism. His articles in the Monist journals are a curious mixture of Monism and pacifism. In defining his 'pacifist' position Fried insisted that struggle is the basis of all culture, that pacifism had nothing at all in common with internationalism or total disarmament, and that the advanced countries had to retain some arms to protect themselves from those nations who were 'less cultured.' Thus some of his 'pacifist' statements are worth noting: 'Conflict should not be done away with, but only its crudest, its physical form.' 'Only conflict is the father of all things.' 'International in the modern sense does not mean antinational, but highly national (*höchstnational*).' 'Justice means regulated power.' Thus, when an 'Apache kills a wanderer, he is acting anarchically, but when a gendarme kills an Apache, this is regulated power.' 'One sees, that the fable of "eternal peace" is not part of the pacifist program.' See Alfred Fried, 'Friedensbewegung,' *Das monistische Jahrhundert*, II (1913-14), 71-76.

For more details on these left-wing Monists, see Istvan Deak, *Weimar Germany's Left-Wing Intellectuals* (Berkeley and Los Angeles: University of California Press, 1968), *passim*.

5. For a typical, but incorrect view of the leadership of the Monist League as left-liberal, see Hajo Holborn, *A History of Modern Germany, 1840-1945* (New York: Knopf, 1968), p. 396.
36. For an expression of opposition to the new liberal tendencies of the Monist League after the First World War and complaint that the policies and ideas of Haeckel were being abandoned, see *Monistische Monatshefte*, VI (1921), 321-324.
37. For an expression of Monist thought under the Nazis, see *Natur und Geist*, (1933-1938), a journal edited by Haeckel's close friend and collaborator, Heinrich Schmidt.

Chapter One

Ernst Haeckel and the German Monist League

ERNST Haeckel grew to maturity in the decade and a half following the abortive German Revolution of 1848. The failure of the Revolution to achieve for Germany a united and modern state structure caused political passions to smolder from frustration and bewilderment, and the era left an indelible impression on the youthful mind and outlook of Haeckel. Because of the failure of the Revolution, the political, social, and intellectual problems which had plagued the fragmented states and provinces of Germany before 1848 not only persisted but became more intense in the years that were to follow. Prussia did not succeed in resolving its old enmity with Austria, nor did it very quickly succeed in reconciling the differences within the Confederation between itself and the lesser states. After the agreement of Olmütz with Austria (1850), Germany, and especially Prussia, 'entered into several years of a deep sleep of repression.'[1]

Throughout the decade of the 1850's many kept alive the hope for a change in the political fortunes of Germany and nourished ideas of unification and national revival. It is true that there was a great confusion about the form the new Germany should take once change came about. There were those who argued for a Germany under the leadership of Prussia and separated from Austria, and there were others who looked towards an overthrow of the Hapsburgs in Austria, and the creation of a large Germanic *Mitteleuropa*. And there were still others who assumed positions in respect to unification which were variants of *klein-* and *grossdeutsch* solutions to Germany's political dilemmas. But the general concern with the question of union is clear.

Towards the end of the decade two significant changes, one internal, the other external, offered the supporters of unification new hope. In 1858, William I took over the leadership of Prussia from his ailing brother, Friedrich William, and in 1861 he succeeded to the throne. Though a pious and somewhat conservative man, William I took an active and positive interest in the unification question and offered the possibility of hope to aspiring nationalists. Secondly, and very significantly, the nationalist movement in Germany was stimulated by events in Italy. In 1859, under the leadership of Cavour, Mazzini, and Garibaldi, Italy threw off the Austrian occupation in all her provinces save one, and largely succeeded in unifying herself. This success on the part of the Italian nationalists could not but suggest to the Germans that their political destiny was very similar. Both countries were involved in an intimate way with Austria and both were beset by the need for national self-realization.[2]

It was in this atmosphere of impending change, of national tension and awareness, that Haeckel completed his scientific and professional training, and began taking a passionate interest in the political condition and future of Germany. Even as a young student he had shown marked and strong nationalistic sentiments,[3] and given a family tradition in which service to Germany and the state was venerated, this was not unusual. Reaching back more than a century into Prussian and Rhenish history, Haeckel's family, on both sides, included prominent members of the upper governmental bureaucracy. His maternal grandfather served as a lawyer with the Prussian judicial administration and during the Napoleonic wars voiced noticeable German patriotic sentiments. The French considered him to be one of the more important government administrators in the Rhine district and for a time removed him to Paris as a hostage where he continued to verbally defy French authority.[4] As we have already noted, Haeckel's father was also a lawyer, and he ended his career as a friend of Gneisenau, and as state councilor for the Prussian government in Berlin.[5] So now, in the heat of the struggle for unification, Haeckel became intensely involved, albeit only in a very personal way, in the political tempest which was brewing. In 1859, he was in Italy, preparing and gathering material for his doctoral dissertation in zoology. The letters which he sent home to his fiancée, Anna Sethe, and the letters to his friends, especially to the writer and poet, Hermann Allmers, who was then also in Italy, were full of the drama of Italian unification and revealed his intense German nationalism and the profound hope that Germany would follow in Italy's footsteps. Haeckel recognized that it was in Italy that he had finally become aware of how deeply he felt about Germany. Writing from Messina on October 16, 1859, he explained how the time spent in Italy had 'stirred up and cultivated' more than anything else a 'heightened inner love for our incomparable German fatherland.' He wrote that wherever he went in Italy, no matter how magnificent the scenery and how beautiful the countryside, his love of Germany had to be expressed. 'It had to be heard over all of Italy and Sicily, in the majestic environment of Naples, as well as on the glorious plains of Palermo, among the quarries of Syracuse, as well as on the peak of Aetna: *Deutschland, Deutschland über alles, über alles in der Welt!—Ich bin ein Deutscher, will ein Deutscher sein*!' And it was in Italy that he became acutely aware of the racial ties which bound all the German people together. In Sorrento he and his friend Allmers had come upon a Norwegian traveller. 'The common bond,' Haeckel wrote, 'of our German racial nature quickly allowed us to become acquainted with him and we were overjoyed to hear so well expressed . . . the noble and great ideas of the free German spirit.' He met other Germans and described them as 'sons of the north' and 'relatives' of the 'same great national race.' On New Year's Day, 1860, Haeckel discovered a German ship in the harbor of Messina and boarded it. He drank to the new year with the crew and later wrote: 'This experience strengthened anew in me my belief that there exists in our common German nation a healthy embryo which is capable of evolution and it is only because of this that one may hope for a healthy surge in our social relations.'[6]

By the spring of 1860, when Italy had already won her independence, Haeckel was back in Germany, and the letters which he continued to write revealed the depth of the impression which Italy had also left upon him in political matters. 'I have no doubt,' he wrote, 'that this wonderful example of the union of a free people is also of the greatest significance for Germany.' If the 'degenerate' Italians could unify, then so too could the Germans, who stood far above them in 'moral development,' in the 'complexity of their deep spiritual life,' and in their 'highly developed sense of justice.' The real impediment to unification was the particularism of the feudal aristocracy, the 'thirty-six parasitic robber princes, who, together with their lackeys' deny freedom to the rest of Germany. But the 'noble disposition' which 'slumbers' in the German people will ultimately allow them to realize their 'fate.'[7]

Haeckel's youthful vision of a united Germany was, even more than might be expected, strongly chauvinistic and expansionist. The Germans, he believed, were superior to all other people and had thus to be allowed to dominate all of central Europe. This attitude was clearly expressed in 1860, when shortly after his return from Italy he attended a *Turnfest* at Coburg and noted the profound impression which it had left upon him. He observed with joy the 'fraternization of young and old from all classes and estates, from all the cities and provinces of Germany from the Eider to Lake Constance, and from the Vistula to the Rhine.' He saw the athletically oriented *Turnfest* as symbolizing a 'single people of brothers,' who, by 'developing their bodies' contributed to the 'defense and strengthening of the entire people.'[8]

In addition, Haeckel looked to the creation of a strong government which would be able to bind Germany solidly together. Upon his return to Germany in the spring of 1860 he recorded having passed through Paris on his way home and apart from the 'unbelievable' opulence of the Napoleonic capital he noted that France possessed a 'centralisation for which one must have deep respect' and thus found that the 'military despotism' of Napoleon III was quite 'bearable.'[9] It was clear that his brief experience with France had served to accentuate for him the pitifulness of German particularism and political fragmentation. He believed, of course, that the Germans could imitate the French because they were superior to them. He had written earlier from Paris: 'We will not only reach the [level] of the French in other things but will also surpass them, since we still possess an inner essence which is lacking among the French: an earnest deep morality, a full inner soul, a happy pure family life, and a forceful striving for the essence and essentials of a thing.'[10]

Then in the 1860's unification finally came to Germany, but the longed-for consolidation was instigated by Bismarck, rather than by the liberal middle class. By uniting Germany under Prussia's leadership and by excluding Austria from the new state, Bismarck attempted to maintain the historical existence of the Junkers while fusing their interests with those of the middle class under a cloak of nationalism.[11] At first Haeckel opposed Bismarck and wrote to Rudolf Virchow in May, 1860, that Germany should not be united by a policy of '"Blood and Iron."' However, six years later, once Bismarck's[12] Austrian war was over, Haeckel and his friends, despite their underlying *grossdeutsch* point of view, enthusiastically welcomed the new Germany and seemed to express no further regrets that political unification was bought at the price of true political liberty and real parliamentary government. At the time of the outbreak of the Austrian War, Allmers wrote to Haeckel that he was excitedly 'following Prussia with true and happy exaltation on its energetic path to victory,'[13] and he noted that a 'unified Germany with Prussia at its head would be able to defy half of Europe.'[14] Within a few weeks, when this short war had already ended, Haeckel wrote back to Allmers that he hoped that the diplomats would not destroy the newly arisen state and would grant to Germany her just demands.[15]

Four years later Haeckel and his friends greeted the Bismarckian War with France even more ecstatically than they had greeted the events of 1866. In November, 1870, Allmers wrote to Haeckel: 'What a time this is! What exaltation, what victory!'[16] In the future, Germany would become so powerful that 'every people around her from near and from far will bow to the majesty of the German people.'[17] A short time later, Haeckel assured Allmers that he agreed with his appraisal of the events of the Franco-Prussian War. 'Naturally,' he wrote, 'I have followed all the victories of the newly blossoming fatherland with enthusiasm and like yourself hope for a promising future.'[18]

While Germany was thus in political ferment and was embarking upon its modern path of unification, Haeckel was also busy launching his own scientific career. In 1861, he received his doctorate in zoology and during the same year was appointed *Privatdozent* at Jena, having been recommended for the position by his former instructor in comparative anatomy, Carl Gegenbaur.[19] During these first years of teaching, Haeckel, along with the rest of the German scientific community, began making the acquaintance of Darwin's book, *The Origin of Species*. It had been translated into German in 1860, and the scientific and intellectual community was, on the whole, prepared to accept evolutionary ideas in biology. At the same time many looked upon evolutionary theory with suspicion, knowing that, in the past, evolutionary ideas had been a refuge for philosophical idealism and teleological interpretations of the workings of nature. The German intellectual community remembered that the older *Naturphilosophie* of the opening decades of the nineteenth century had also espoused an evolutionary view of nature and had developed a number of theories of organic descent. It was well remembered that *Naturphilosophie* had been, because of its boundless and undiscriminating taste for vague and valueless theorizing, a 'destructive influence on German science.'[20] Nevertheless there can be no doubt that by 1859, the year that Darwin's book appeared, many German biologists and naturalists held to some belief in the transmutation of species.[21]

Haeckel himself read *The Origin of Species* for the first time during the summer of 1860, and studied it with increasing care over the next two or three years. In November, 1861, he wrote to his fiancée, Anna Sethe, that he was *'vertieft'*[22] in Darwin's book. Then over the next year or two Darwin's ideas seemed completely to pervade his thinking and he began to make Darwinism the focal point of his entire scientific and professional life. His conversion to Darwinism did not, by any means, take the form of a painstaking intellectual process of discovery, nor of a conviction slowly arrived at. Rather, Haeckel's belief in the truth of evolution was realized in a virtual flash of immediate revelation and inspiration. He was later to remark that when he first read Darwin the 'scales fell from my eyes.'[23] He related that he 'found in Darwin's great unified conception of nature and in his overwhelming foundation for the doctrine of evolution the solution of all the doubts which had bothered me since the beginning of my biological studies.'[24] Thus, from the very start his attachment to Darwinism was more than the acceptance of an interesting and possibly fruitful scientific theory. He immediately raised evolution and Darwinism to the status of a complete and final rendering of the nature of the cosmos. Through evolution he studied the world and everything in it including man and society as part of an organized and consistent whole. He therefore called his new evolutionary philosophy 'Monism,' and contrasted it with all of traditional thought, which he rather disdainfully labelled 'Dualism,' condeming the latter for making distinctions between matter and spirit, and for invidiously separating man from nature.[25]

How are we to explain the ready and enthusiastic acceptance of Darwinism by Haeckel? Perhaps part of the answer is contained in a letter which he wrote to Allmers in December, 1863. In this letter Haeckel repeated a theme which had already occupied him very much in the past, the question of the political emancipation of Germany. However, he also implied that it was not enough to free Germany politically, confiding to Allmers that he was dismayed by the shallow intellectual and spiritual level of the ordinary German. He wished to recreate the Germans, to make them into brave new men who would be at home in the natural landscape of the fatherland. Every German, he wrote to Allmers, should be urged to rise from 'impotence' to 'full independence.'[26] To accomplish this required a philosophy which could not only explain the world but would also at the same time provide a key to the spiritual and intellectual as well as the political emancipation of Germany. In 1863, when Haeckel wrote these words to Allmers, he had already found in Darwinism a solution to his problems, and he set about elaborating what he considered to be the full scientific and social implications of Darwin's theory.

In 1862, Haeckel became Professor of Zoology and Comparative Anatomy at Jena, and during that same year was also married. With his academic position now secure, Haeckel began lecturing at Jena on Darwin and concentrated heavily on expositions of Darwin's theory. He presented Darwin as the most important and significant thinker of the nineteenth century, and he reported that his talks were warmly greeted by his students and by the audiences at his public lectures. To his parents Haeckel wrote during this period that what he had to say about Darwin was being received with overwhelming enthusiasm.[27] In September, 1863, he undertook to defend the idea of biological descent and evolution before the thirty-eighth Congress of German Naturalists at Stettin. In his address, *'Ueber die Entwicklungs—Theorie*

Darwins,' which became a kind of semi-official manifesto of the Darwinian movement in Germany, Haeckel proposed that evolutionary theory be accepted as the most important generalization of the nineteenth century, providing not only the basis for the science of biology, but for a whole new cosmic philosophy. Darwinism, Haeckel declared, was of fundamental significance for science and for the study of man's social institutions. Going beyond Darwin, who had not yet committed himself in public on the question of the origin of man, Haeckel explained that mankind had unquestionably evolved from the animal kingdom and that man's social existence was governed by the laws of evolution and biology. Furthermore, he said, evolution teaches that change is the outstanding characteristic of history, and he took advantage of the occasion to point out that evolutionary theory provided a justification for the overthrow of 'tyrants' and 'priests,'—those, in other words, who stood in the way of German emancipation and freedom.[28]

In February, 1864, just a few months after the Congress at Stettin, Haeckel's wife suddenly and unexpectedly fell ill and died on the fourteenth, Haeckel's thirtieth birthday. The shortlived marriage had been a very happy one and Haeckel often described their brief time together as the best and most satisfying period of his life.[29] Now, to mitigate his own suffering, which was intense,[30] Haeckel threw himself into his scientific labors. In 1866, as we have already noted, he published his first lengthy and important book on Darwinism and evolutionary philosophy, the *Generelle Morphologie*. In an earlier work on single-celled sea organisms, *Die Radiolarien* (1862),[31] Haeckel had briefly mentioned the need to understand and evaluate the problems of organic classification in terms of Darwin's theory. However, it was only in the *Generelle Morphologie* that Haeckel actually presented an entire view of the organic and inorganic worlds from the standpoint of evolution. The *Generelle Morphologie*, however, did not become a popular book and Haeckel himself admitted that its style was overly abstruse and ponderous. But it was followed by two popularizations of his evolutionary ideas, *Natürliche Schöpfungsgeschichte* (1868), and *Anthropogenie* (1874), which immediately became best-sellers and quickly transformed Haeckel into one of the most renowned scientists and writers in Germany. In all three of these works, the *Generelle*

I. *A poster announcing a lecture on evolution to be delivered in Berlin by Haeckel. The charts and skeletons provide a sinister environment for a Darwinian Passion Play.*

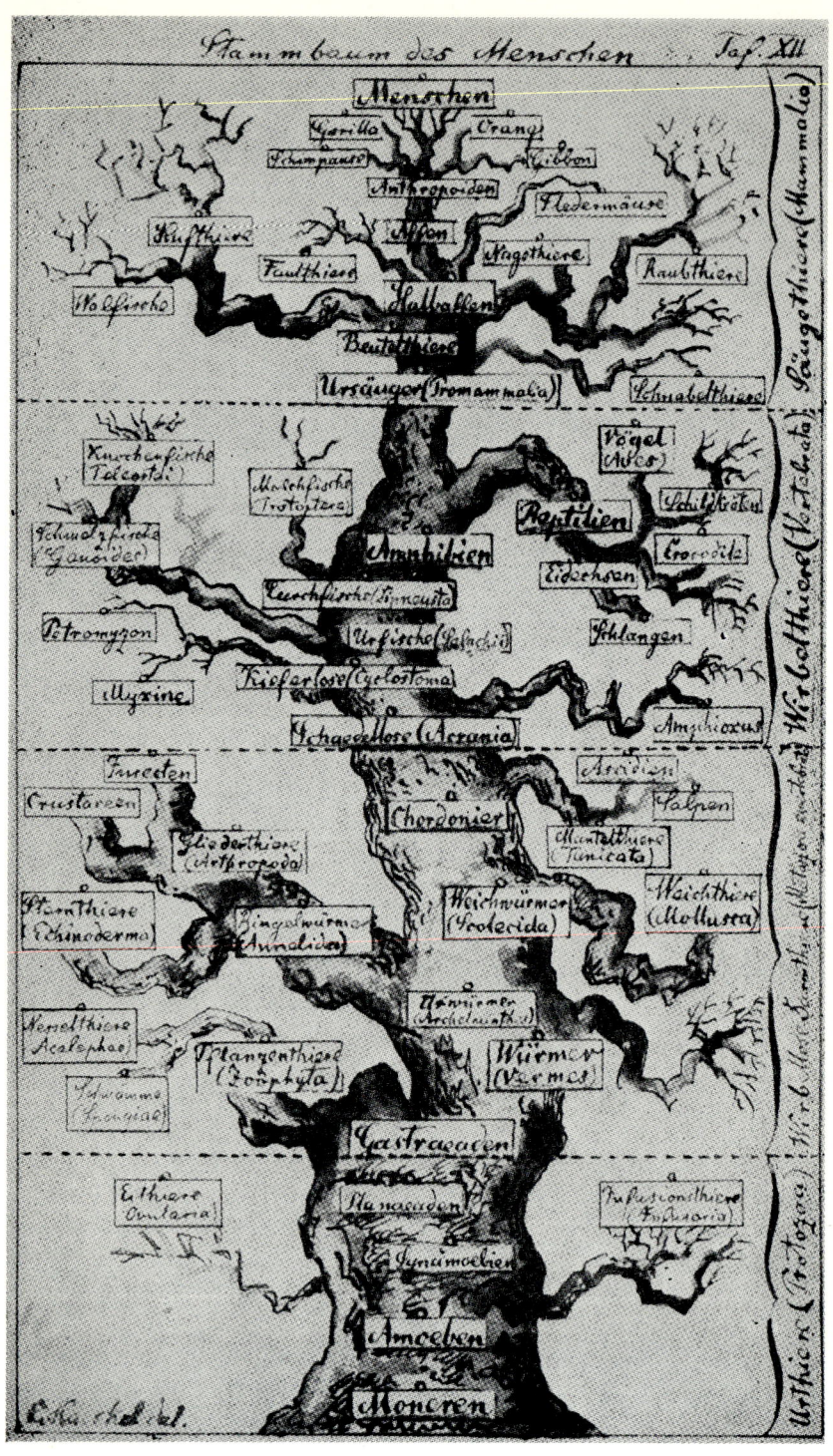

II. *A gnarled evolutionary tree drawn by Haeckel.*

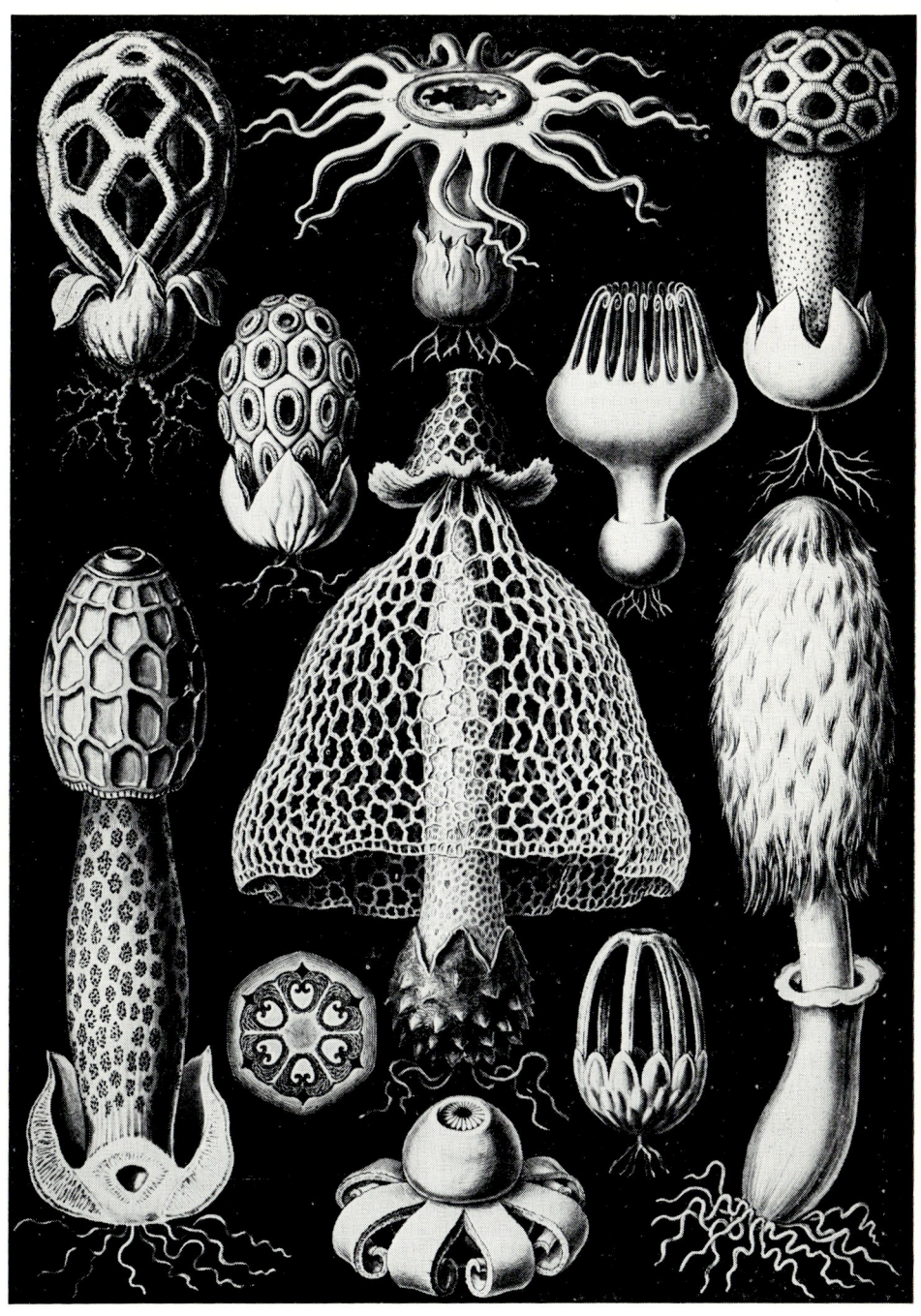

III. *In this illustration appearing in Haeckel's* Kunstformen der Natur, *objectivity is forsaken in favor of bizarre beauty.*

IV. (Right) A detail from Gustave Moreau's Galatea.

(Below) A symbolist work by Haeckel drawn in Ceylon.

A dream-like exoticism is common to both Haeckel, the self-appointed prophet of 'materialism', and to Moreau, the symbolist fin de siècle believer in the 'unseen'.

Morphologie, the *Natürliche Schöpfungsgeschichte*, and the *Anthropogenie*, Haeckel discussed in great detail almost every area of biology known to nineteenth-century science and made it a point to stress that evolution was much more than a theory of natural selection. Darwin's theory, he contended, repeating the thesis of his address at Stettin in 1863, was 'only a small fragment of a far more comprehensive doctrine—a part of the universal theory of development which embraces in its vast range the whole domain of human knowledge.'[32] And it was the 'whole domain of human knowledge' that Haeckel was actually seeking to encompass, including the laws governing the behavior of mankind and history.

In 1867, Haeckel was married again, this time to Agnes Huschke, the twenty-four-year old daughter of an anatomy professor at Jena.[33] With his family life stable and relatively happy (Haeckel did not seem to feel the same deep affection for his second wife that he had felt for Anna Sethe) he was able to dedicate himself fully to his biological and scientific work. In the three decades following the appearance of the *Generelle Morphologie* he published an extraordinary number of impressive, highly detailed, and important studies of various aspects of biology related primarily to problems of organic classification and evolution. Thus, Haeckel was to achieve fame not only as a popularizer of the ideas of Darwin and of nineteenth-century evolutionary biology, but also as a famous zoologist in his own right. He was an indefatigable researcher in zoology and some of his work is of enduring value.[34] For example, in *Die Radiolarien*, Haeckel described about one hundred and fifty new species of one-celled sea organisms and provided expert illustrations of them.[35] In addition, and for its time, *Die Radiolarien* contained important descriptive material on assimilation in single celled organisms and contributed to the contemporary discussion of the nature of protoplasm. Haeckel even came close to the discovery of phagocytes, a number of years before their actual description by Metchnikoff later in the century.[36] In the 1880's Haeckel added another two volumes of research to *Die Radiolarien* by describing, illustrating, and classifying a few hundred new species of primitive organisms. Apart from the Radiolaria, he also did pioneer work in the investigation of the properties of the sponges and the medusae. In *Die Kalkschwämme* (1872), and in *Das System der Medusen* (1879), he described many new species of these types of organisms, and his classifications have in a number of instances been retained in modern biology.[37] In the 1890's Haeckel completed an enormous three volume work, *Systematische Phylogenie*, which contained much material on the classification of both the vertebrates and the invertebrates. This work was warmly received. For example, the noted Swiss anatomist, Arnold Lang, lauded this work for its 'intellectual achievement' and recorded his 'amazement' at the 'enormous amount of knowledge which perhaps will never again be combined within one mind.'[38]

Beyond his work in direct zoological research, Haeckel also advanced a number of highly speculative biological theories which he considered to be not only indispensable corollaries of the theory of evolution but fundamental tenets of his evolutionary religion as well. Throughout his life Haeckel held tenaciously to the present existence of spontaneous generation, to pan-psychism or the belief in a world soul, to the Gastraea Theory or the supposition of a common ancestral form for all of the metazoa, and to the Biogenetic Law. For Haeckel these biological hypotheses were proven realities and he believed them to be more crucial supports for evolution than the theory of natural selection itself. No amount of evidence that these ideas were at best premature hypotheses could shake his conviction as to their reality. For him they provided solid evidence of the unity, sentiency, and constructive logic of the cosmos.[39] The most famous of these theories was, of course, the Biogenetic Law, that ontogeny recapitulates phylogeny; the idea that the biological history of an individual must in abbreviated form repeat the biological development of its ancestors. Although this theory is now, at least, partially defunct, along with Haeckel's other evolutionary hypotheses, it was of enormous influence in the nineteenth century and for fifty years biological literature was under its influence.[40] Scores of biologists came under its sway and it was not until the second or third decade of the twentieth century that biology began to free itself decisively from its allurements.[41]

For all his fame as a zoologist, however, and as a scientific worker, the Darwinism which Haeckel urged was more akin to religion than to science. Although he considered himself to be a close follower of Darwin and, as we have seen, invoked Darwin's name in support of his own ideas and theories, there was, in fact, little similarity between them.⁴² Haeckel himself openly thought of evolution and science as the domain of religion and his work therefore assumed a character which was wholly foreign to the spirit of Darwin. Darwin's empiricism, his caution in the face of speculative theories, his general mechanical conception of the workings of nature, were all in striking contrast to Haeckel's biology. For Haeckel, evolution did not only mean the process of change from one species to the next. Evolution for him was a cosmic force, a manifestation of the creative energy of nature. In his science-religion, therefore, he sought constantly for meaning, beauty, and regularity as inherent characteristics of nature and as signs of its divinity. For him poetry and science were one. His books and articles were interlaced with quotations from Goethe and as he himself conceded, his pan-psychism was in large measure derived from Goethe. And since evolution was not theory, but religion, his works exuded a mystical fascination with the processes of life and regeneration. Haeckel saw nature through the eyes of an artist. He devoted his zoological study primarily to the primitive organisms of the sea because in his mind's eye they were at the beginning of the upward spiral of the evolutionary tree, and he was certain that spontaneous generation was perpetually in progress in the depths of the ocean. He therefore studied the lower sea organisms, he painted them, and in the end he began to worship them. Haeckel also campaigned vigorously for the acceptance of the animal origin of man. Of course, ultimately, so too did Darwin. But the emphasis was different. For Haeckel knowledge of the animal origin of man did not deepen one's knowledge of man *qua* man, as much as it showed how man was rooted in nature and how meagre his distinctively human characteristics were. He emphasized not how far man has travelled from his animal past, but how close he really was to his animal forebears. And thus, if Haeckel was the major source of Darwin's ideas in Germany, then he ultimately helped to deny to Germany a true Darwinian revolution—the rendering of the processes of nature in terms of mechanism and empiricism.⁴³

It was this desire on Haeckel's part to make of evolutionary theory a religion which was so bitterly condemned by his erstwhile teacher and friend, Rudolf Virchow.⁴⁴ Contrary to Haeckel's assertions, Virchow was not unalterably opposed to Darwin or to the theory of natural selection, but he did take serious exception to Haeckel's attempt to make of evolution a cosmology. He felt that Haeckel's evolutionary theories were poetic and religious fantasies rather than valid scientific hypotheses and he therefore attacked Haeckel publicly and unflinchingly. Virchow denied that spontaneous generation, pan-psychism, and Haeckel's other theories were established truths. And above all he questioned Haeckel's desire to make evolutionary religion the ideological and ethical basis of the state and the foundation of all education. He sensed the danger: 'Every attempt to transform our problems into doctrines, to introduce our hypotheses as the basis of instruction—especially in the attempt to dispossess the Church, and to supplant its dogmas forthwith by a religion of evolution—be assured . . . every such attempt will make a shipwreck, and in its wreck will also bring with it the greatest perils for the whole position of science.'[45]

But Virchow's cries for caution were to no avail. Haeckel castigated Virchow's demands for proof of his evolutionary hypotheses as 'perverse' and insisted that further verification was not essential.[46] And it was not only Virchow who experienced Haeckel's wrath. Even those who considered themselves to be Darwinists, but who objected to one or another of Haeckel's ideas, were subjected to frequent verbal abuse and condemned as purveyors of medieval superstition.[47]

It was, therefore, due as much to the extravagance of his ideas, as well as to his real talents as a zoological researcher, that Haeckel was able to attract students from all over Europe and the world to Jena, where he gained enormous fame as a teacher. Haeckel transformed the University of Jena into one of the most exciting centers in Germany for biological study. The University created a chair in zoology especially for him and also maintained an entire Zoological Institution. And he produced some of the most famous names in nineteenth-century biology. Among his students was Hans Driesch, the important theoretician of vitalism in biology, Wilhelm Roux, the creator of experimental embryology, Max Verworn, the founder of cellular physiology, Alexander Kowalewski, the celebrated Russian embryologist, Paul Kammerer, the noted geneticist, Richard Semon, an important neo-Lamarckian, and the brothers Oscar and Richard Hertwig, who figured largely in the development of the science of embryology in Germany.[48] And it is a further measure of the fame which Haeckel achieved in his lifetime that by his eightieth year, he had been accorded membership in more than ninety professional and scientific societies from all over the world.⁴⁹ By his scientific accomplishments, and despite his extravagances and frequent acrimonious disputes, it is clear that Haeckel achieved an aura of respectability, authority, and veneration within the community of German and world science.

At the same time, and although he was of course mainly a zoologist, Haeckel viewed himself as fundamentally committed to the dissemination of Darwinism as a social and political ideology. Therefore, in addition to his work in the classroom and in the laboratory, he lost no opportunity to proclaim the need for a total revolution in German culture. There was, he contended, no reason why evolutionary Monism could not serve as the foundation for a whole new philosophy of life, and he sought not only through his popular writings but also in many public lectures to communicate this idea to the Germans. How well he was received by the general public is suggested by the remarks of an old gentleman who tapped Haeckel on the shoulder after one of his most famous lectures and confided to him: '*Herr Professor, das war keine Rede, das war eine Tat!*'⁵⁰

Thus, during the last decades of the nineteenth century, at a time when even T. H. Huxley, the Darwinian stalwart, was turning aside from the possibility of a social science and an ethics based on evolutionary naturalism,⁵¹ Haeckel continued more seriously than ever to develop and advocate his own evolutionary social Darwinism, applying to society the laws that he perceived in biological and physical nature. He turned his attention increasingly in the 1880's and 1890's to the spelling out of the social, political, and religious interpretations of his conception of Darwinism. His main object came to be the elaboration of a Monistic religion having an evolutionary and naturalistic base, and the enlargement and deepening of the ideas of his earlier days into a complete system of thought. The major statements of his mature philosophical conception of social Darwinism and evolutionary religion are to be found in his famous *Welträtsel* (1899,) and in two other works of the same period: *Der Monismus als Band zwischen Religion und Wissenschaft* (1892), which was an important and authoritative statement of the principles upon which he based his evolutionary religion and his evolutionary ethics; and *Lebenswunder*, published in 1904 as an explanatory sequel to the *Welträtsel*.

Of all these works the most famous was, of course, the *Welträtsel*, the *Riddle of the Universe*. When it was first published in 1899 it immediately became, like Haeckel's earlier popular works, the *Natürliche Schöpfungsgeschichte* and the *Anthropogenie*, one of the most widely read and known books in Germany. It quickly became Germany's most popular philosophical work[52] and during the first year after its appearance it sold more than a hundred thousand copies.[53] It went through ten editions by 1919, was translated into about twenty-five languages, and by 1933 almost half a million copies had been bought in Germany alone.[54]

From the standpoint of scientific accuracy or up-to-date knowledge of science, the *Welträtsel* had little to recommend it and its deficiencies were quickly noted by many scientists and professional philosophers.[55] For example, Haeckel's close friend and colleague, the noted anatomist Carl Gegenbaur, broke off a friendship with Haeckel that had lasted for forty-seven years because of the nature of the book. He angrily told Haeckel: 'I don't approve of such stuff. . . . One doesn't have such things printed.'[56] Or, another typical example, the noted neo-Kantian philospher, Friedrich Paulsen, also condemned the *Welträtsel* in harsh language. 'I have read this book,' he wrote, 'with burning shame over the condition of the general and philosophical education of our people. It is painful that such a book was possible, that it could have been written, edited, sold, read, pondered, and believed by a people who possess a Kant, a Goethe, and a Schopenhauer.'[57] Paulsen seemed to fear that the general reader would be misled by the dogmatic forcefulness of Haeckel's book. He felt that for those unable to judge the scientific accuracy of Haeckel's writings or the true implications of his ideas, a proper evaluation or understanding of the real nature of the book would be out of the question. Paulsen argued that 'Haeckel was not to be taken seriously as a philosopher,'[58] and suggested that he was insensitive to the problematical nature of the questions he was dealing with. '*Was Haeckel fehlt, dass ist überall dasselbe; es ist, was Goethe die Fähighkeit zu sehen, "wo eigentlich das Problem eingeht."* '[59]

However much serious opinion was repelled by what were regarded as the inaccurate and misleading generalizations to be found in the *Welträtsel*, as well as in the other popular works of Haeckel, the book had a vast success among the general reading public. The reason is perhaps not difficult to discover. In the *Welträtsel* the scientific and philosophical 'truths' of the world were seemingly presented in a clear and forthright manner by Germany's greatest biologist. The mysteries of the world and of life were, Haeckel assured his readers, readily explainable and within the grasp of science. For every person wishing some acquaintance with the intellectual world and with the field of science, here was the necessary introduction. In addition, the *Welträtsel* offered a modern religious faith. The science of nature, Haeckel suggested, was not a vast impersonal discipline. On the contrary, it offered the basis for a faith as compelling as traditional religion. Such allurements were well-nigh irresistible, and the peculiar Haeckelian version of social Darwinism became diffused among large segments of the semi-educated masses of the German population. For those who read Haeckel and were convinced, Haeckelian Darwinism assumed the character of a political and religious ideology and faith.

Of course, it was not the semi-educated general reader alone who was attracted to Haeckel and to his ideas. Despite criticism from some professional quarters there were also countless members of the scientific professions and prestigious members of the academic and intellectual community who became deeply attached to Haeckel and to his ideas. Indeed, it is not really possible to understand Haeckel and the role which he played in German intellectual life without being aware of the magnetic hold which he exerted on his adherents. He was regarded by them as a singular religious and national prophet. Thus, for example, among the numerous expressions of admiration for him that characterise the literature of the Haeckelian movement, we find the statement that 'Haeckel is in fact the greatest theologian the world has ever seen.'[60] His disciples took him to be one of the most influential figures in the intellectual history of the modern world. 'One must,' a typical statement ran, 'without being guilty of any exaggeration, maintain that during the most recent years and decades every person who has in some way taken part in human culture . . . has been compelled during his lifetime to take some position in regard to this individual, to his ideas, his strivings and the cultural movement which derives from him.'[61] He was for them god-like. 'This implacable opponent of all dogmatic Christianity revealed himself to me as the best and most advanced "Christ" whom I personally have known.'[62] And still another admirer said of Haeckel: 'I am certain that later decades will honor Haeckel, the artist and the man, to the same extent that priests of all kinds now slander and deride him.'[63] For another Monist it was certain that Haeckel's 'name will become a shining symbol that will glow for centuries. Generations will pass, new ones will arise, nations will fall, thrones will topple, but the wise old genius of Jena will outlast all, and the words of the poet will come true: "The imprint of [his] days on earth cannot disappear in aeons." '[64] But above all, it was Haeckel, his followers admiringly and gratefully recounted time and time again, who was responsible for their intellectual and spiritual emancipation. One disciple wrote: 'I thank Darwin and Haeckel for emancipating my intellect, for my deliverance from the bonds of traditional slavery, to which a great part of mankind is bound for all of their lives. They gave me a key towards an understanding of the great exalted secret of nature and cleared the fog from my eyes which had hindered a clear view of the world.'[65]

It was, however, not only as a proselytizer of a new religion, or as an intellectual giant in the realm of science and biology, that Haeckel was venerated. As Haeckel himself wished, his followers did discover in him also a prophet of the national and racial regeneration of Germany. After having read the *Welträtsel* one Monist recounted how he was able to see clearly for the first time the necessity of standing up for the 'preservation of the individual character of nations and races,' and of promoting the 'unification and common effort of those races which were related to each other, especially the Germanic ones, for they were without doubt at the highest stage of evolution.'[66] And Haeckel evoked among his followers a nationalistic faith that obviously touched the deepest springs of their emotions. Thus, they were consciously inspired by him to write in the following vein of the biological and spiritual continuity of the German people: 'The individual must die, but his blood continues beyond the grave. Blood to blood and bone to bone. . . . The time of national strife is coming. One must not seek to bring nations closer together, but to fathom what one nation must hide from the other. . . . It is good, beautiful, and true that our ancestors did not fear death, and we live that way, we live as Germans.'[67] Haeckel evoked for them the pagan German past. One of his eulogizers recalled that when he met Haeckel for the first time he was certain that he was standing before 'Odhin,' the god of German mythology: 'At that moment I rediscovered my fatherland and my people, and with that I was relieved of all unclarity and anger, of the irony of Heinrich Heine, which is a sign of inner weakness. Rather, there arose the strong feeling of cheerfulness and happiness which is born out of a faith that is sure of itself. In this way Ernst Haeckel returned to me my faith in my people.'[68]

The intensely mystical and romantic nationalism which characterized the life and thought of Haeckel was further expressed by his deep and symbolic attachment to the city of Jena. In the past, Jena had been the home of such intellectual and cultural luminaries as Goethe, Fichte, Hegel, Schiller, Schelling, and Oken, the famous *Naturphilosoph*. Haeckel was keenly aware of the cultural history of this small city in the heartland of Germany and he pictured himself at the head of a grand intellectual and historical tradition. 'What the Wartburg was for Martin Luther,' he wrote, 'what Weimar was for the greatest heroes of German literature, Jena will remain in the future; a mighty fortress of free thought, free scholarship, free teaching—a mighty fortress of reason!'[69]

For Haeckel, therefore, Jena was truly at the center of the world. As he became famous he was, as might be expected, offered new and lucrative academic posts at larger universities. He was approached, for example, by Würzburg (1865), Vienna (1871), Strassburg (1873), and Bonn (1874).[70] But his attachment to Jena and to the University ran much too deep for him ever to consider leaving. He described the city as 'my lovely, small old Jena with its . . . well known advantages and magnetism.' The 'quiet life' of Jena was much better for the pursuit of science than a metropolis like Vienna or Berlin, where the atomsphere was 'agitated,' and 'full of disturbances.'[71] Like many Volkists, Haeckel abhorred the large, modern city.

It was not only the culture and history of Jena and the 'wonderful *Genius Loci*' of 'our Thuringian University'[72] but also its natural setting which appealed very much to Haeckel. It evoked and symbolized for him the unique qualities of German nature. 'The charm with which Mother Nature has in such a unique way endowed our idyllic valley of the Saale, the picturesque forms of our steep limestone mountains, the wonderous red tones and blue shadows with which the glow of the evening sun paints them; our numerous valleys, the charm of our villages crowned with orchards—and then the richness of the flora, which serves to make wandering through the forest so enjoyable for the nature lover'[73] made Jena, for Haeckel, a Volkish symbol *par excellence*, in which history and nature combine to form a perfect unity.

One of the events connected with Jena that was regarded by the Haeckelian Monists as of the greatest significance was a visit by Bismarck to the city in July of 1892. The invitation was proffered by Haeckel at his own initiative and was enthusiastically accepted by Bismarck.[74] When he arrived in Jena, Bismarck 'embraced' Haeckel with 'terrific feeling.'[75] Then the University students unbridled the horses from Bismarck's carriage and pulled it themselves to the hotel. Addressing the assembled crowd from his window Bismarck reminded the inhabitants of the historical significance of Jena. He voiced the fervent hope that Jena would continue her cultural tradition and that in general 'Germany would not sink to the level of France.'[76]

On the following day Haeckel addressed a gathering of the faculty of the University of Jena which had been called to honor Bismarck. Haeckel was effusive in his remarks: 'While the booming of guns at the Battle of Königgrätz in 1866 announced the demise of the old Federal German Diet and the beginning of a new splendid period in the history of the German Reich, here in Jena the history of the phylum [*Stammesgeschichte* or phylogeny] was born.'[77] Haeckel proposed, therefore, on the spot, the creation of an academic degree of Doctor of Phylogeny and enthusiastically suggested that the 'new honorary title should be held for the first time by no one else than the creative genius of modern German history, Prince Bismarck, the deeply perceptive observer and anthropologist of mankind, the far-seeing historical investigator and ethnologist, the practical creator of history.'[78] The faculty seemed to gasp at the devilish unconventionality of Haeckel's method of conferring an honorary degree but he sensed their mood and quickly disarmed them by saying further; 'I assume for myself the diplomatic audacity of our old Reich Chancellor . . . and pose the following question: . . . Do any of those here present . . . have anything against naming Prince Otto von Bismarck Honorary Doctor of

Phylogeny?' Since, of course, no one dared raise his hand, Haeckel then procalaimed Bismarck as the 'first and greatest Doctor of Phylogeny' and added a resounding 'long may he live!'[79]

Haeckel's significance as a romantic figure is also apparent in his widely celebrated reputation as a traveller.[80] In frequent accounts his Monist followers relived the excitement and mystery of his journeys.[81] Haeckel's Odyssean life led him to every corner of Europe, to the tropics, Asia Minor, North Africa, and the Arabian Peninsula. On the surface, his journeys were dispassionate—scientific trips on behalf of naturalistic research. But the underlying tone of his wandering was one of escape from the stifling conventionalities of European life in search of unspoiled nature and primitive and happy man. Like Baudelaire, who sang of *'La Splendeur Orientale'* in his great romantic poem, *L'Invitation au Voyage*, the mystery of far-off places was refracted in the prism of Haeckel's artistic imagination. In his voyages, and in the accounts and paintings which emerged from those experiences, Haeckel dramatized the nostalgia and idealism of those for whom Western Civilization was in a state of fallen grace and for those who hoped to rediscover a lost paradise. In the tropics, Haeckel recounted, 'I might for several months throw off the conventionalities and unnaturalness of our civilized world, and, in the midst of tropical nature's wanton luxuriance, for once yield myself to the full enjoyment of its beauties. Here surrounded by a simple uncultured people, I might hope to form an idea of the imaginary paradisal civilization of our primitive ancestors.'[82] And he gloried in the unspoiled innocence of the natives. 'Fortunate Singhalese!... No political or war-like ambition tortures your soul; no disturbing thought or competition, rise and fall of stocks, drives slumber from your eyes! Those aspirations of higher culture; titles, orders are unknown to you, and yet you rejoice in life!... How comfortably you lie there, dreamily watching the dancing sunlight....' What 'care-burdened' European 'would not covet your innocent nature and your paradisal rest?'[83]

Despite the fact that Haeckel, virtually from the outset of his career, had many highly devoted followers, no formal organization of Haeckelian Darwinists materialized until rather late in his life. There had always been, however, adequate channels of communication for the dissemination of his ideas. In the 1870's and 1880's, Haeckel and a number of other Darwinists edited the widely read journal *Kosmos* which developed into the main forum for evolutionary discussion in that period. At the same time, the noted ethnologist, Friedrich Hellwald, a convert to Haeckelian Darwinism, made available the pages of his journal, *Das Ausland*, to the Haeckelian school of thought. There were also numerous books and pamphlets written and published during the last three decades of the nineteenth century which expressed the broader implications of Haeckelian Darwinism for ethics, politics, and religion.[84] But no formal organization came into existence. It was only after the great popular success which Haeckel achieved with the *Welträtsel* that he began considering the possibility of founding a Monist organization. Most of his closest and ablest followers had already been very active in many branches of the German Free-Thought Movement, which had been founded in 1881 by the famous materialist, Ludwig Büchner.[85] The Free-Thought Movement had, of course, the desire to wean the Germans away from Christianity and it was composed of a broad coalition of diverse cultural groups and individuals of somewhat differing political and social views. They were united in their common opposition to and at times fanatical hatred of Christianity. But during the first years of this century the followers of Haeckel began campaigning for their own organization. They argued that it was not enough to talk about social Darwinism and evolution but rather that the 'deed' of evolutionary thought had to be carried out.[86]

In the autumn of 1904, Haeckel, aghast at what he considered to be the increasingly dangerous rapproachment between the German government and the Catholic Center Party, and sensing, therefore, that the time was propitious for the founding of an organization of Darwinists, presented to the International Free-Thought Congress which met that year in Rome, a program for the establishment of a Monist League.[87] The proposal met with widespread favor among his followers. Then, after more preparatory work, on January 11, 1906, Haeckel succeeded in bringing the Monist League into existence at a meeting in Jena attended by his closest disciples. Haeckel himself was already over seventy years old and was only able to accept the title of honorary president of the new organization, but there was no question that he was to remain its guiding spirit. The first working president of the Monist League was the radical Protestant theologian, Dr. Albert Kalthoff, the pastor of St. Martini in Bremen, a long-time convert to and active supporter of Haeckel's ideas. The first general secretary of the League was Dr. Heinrich Schmidt, a close friend and colleague of Haeckel, who ultimately became one of Haeckel's biographers and the editor of his collected works. Other important participants in the founding of the League were such longstanding followers of Haeckel as the romantic novelists and literary critics Wilhelm Boelsche and Bruno Wille; Dr. Arnold Dodel, an early exponent of Haeckelian Darwinism; R. H. Francé, a noted biologist and Darwinian spokesman and editor; Dr. Johannes Unold, a Munich physician and author of a number of works on evolution and politics, and shortly to become Vice-President of the League;[88] Dr. August Forel, the noted Swiss eugenicist; Wilhelm Schallmayer, one of the founders of the German eugenics movement; Ludwig Gurlitt, the innovating educator and co-founder of the Wandervogel; and lastly Dr. Ludwig Plate, a well-known biologist destined to succeed to Haeckel's chair at the University of Jena. In time, of course, the Monist League acquired other famous names like the sociologist, Franz Müller-Lyer and the novelist Herbert Eulenberg. Perhaps the most notable addition to the membership of the League was the well-known chemist and Nobel Prize winner, Wilhelm Ostwald, who, with Haeckel's assent, assumed the leadership and direction of the Monist League in 1911.[89]

During its first years of existence the Monist League enjoyed a fairly substantial growth. Within five years it could boast a membership of some six thousand and was organized into local groups meeting in about forty-two separate cities and hamlets throughout Germany and Austria.[90] Between 1906 and 1912, the League published a monthly journal, *Der Monismus*. In April, 1912, it was superseded by *Das monistische Jahrhundert*, which soon became a weekly and was published until 1915, when its appearance was interrupted as a result of the War and Ostwald's resignation from the League.[91] In addition, the League also published a number of pamphlets on various problems with which it was especially concerned,[92] and also a small journal for members of its youth movement, *Sonne*. However, its influence went much beyond the membership and publications of the League itself. The Monist League as an organization and many of its individual members participated very heavily in the growing activities of the Free-Thought Movement in the decade or so before the outbreak of the World War. Between 1907 and 1909, a coalition of Free-Thought organizations came together in what was called the *Weimar Kartel*. The *Kartel* directly embraced fourteen organizations and also encompassed five related groups. Its main purpose was to centralize opposition to the Christian churches and to organize systematic departure from the traditional faiths. The Monists were among the leading members of the *Weimar Kartel* and were to be found as the leaders of many of the participating organizations. Thus, through the medium of the *Weimar Kartel*, the Monist League enjoyed the advantage of directly reaching a much larger audience than its own membership would suggest or allow.[93] There also appeared during the first decade of the century a number of semi-official Monist journals. Some of the more famous ones were: *Das freie Wort, Neue Weltanschauung, Dokumente des Fortschritts*, and *Zeitschrift für den Aufbau der Entwicklungslehre*. All of these journals also reached a much larger reading public than that of the official Monist journals themselves.

The main program of the Monist League was taken directly from the social Darwinism of Haeckel. In the *Welträtsel*, and in many earlier works, Haeckel had credited the scientific and technological advances of the nineteenth century and celebrated his own age as one of progress and material accomplishment. On the surface, therefore, he remained a spokesman for progress, optimism, modernism, and science. But there was another, more thoroughgoing, and profoundly different side to his thinking which actually determined the character of his social Darwinism. A moody pessimism was also in evidence in his work and one is struck by the foreboding tone of many of his pronouncements. This darker side of Haeckel's thought was evident in his analysis of the condition of German culture and society in the nineteenth century. When he directed his attention to 'moral and social life'[94] he found society lagging far behind the scientific advances of the age. He thus complained that he felt an 'uneasy sense of dismemberment and falseness' and the threat of 'danger and grave catastrophes in the political and social world.'[95] And he believed that the threat of cultural and therefore of social collapse was imminent. 'To convince ourselves,' he wrote, 'of the truth of this grave indictment, we need only cast an unprejudiced glance at our public life.'⁹⁶ Haeckel, therefore, thundered denunciations of German politics, culture, and society. He recorded his anguish over the ignorance of politicians and of prevalent 'sociological blunders' and 'political nonsense.'⁹⁷ Most branches of the state, he lamented, were backward and corrupt, and Germany's educational system was plagued by medieval learning and church morality. He excoriated the Germans for cultivating false values and wrung his hands over their failure to recognize and realize the truths that were apparent in nature. Disaster was on the horizon, he preached, unless Germany acted radically and forcefully to bring itself into harmony with the laws of biology.

Following Haeckel, therefore, the Monist League did not see itself as a society devoted simply to the discussion and dissemination of scientific thought. It also viewed Germany as standing on the brink of cultural tragedy. Evolutionary science, it asserted, had to become the basis of all aspects of life, both personal and social. Thus, the League conceived its work to be the development and fostering of a complete social, cultural, religious, and political program for Germany. 'The German Monist League,' its official program stated, 'desires to be effective on behalf of a unified *Welt- und Lebensanschauung* based on natural knowledge,'⁹⁸ and it appealed to all segments and social classes of the German people, especially those individuals who felt themselves to be free from traditional clerical beliefs and loyalties. The Monist League, the official program went on, 'strives to bring together all individuals and organizations who no longer rely on the church for their outlook on the world.'⁹⁹ Through ideological change and political action it hoped to create a truly unified nation. But at the same time it was opposed to any fundamental social change. What was needed for Germany, it argued categorically, was a far-reaching cultural and not a social revolution. Germany needed a new ideology, but not a new class structure. The Monists were, therefore, true practitioners of conservative revolution.

The coming of war in 1914 significantly limited the activities of the League. Many of its members were, of course, drafted into the military and many fell at the front.¹⁰⁰ Haeckel himself was in declining health during the war years but he nonetheless continued to write and to take part as much as he could in patriotic activity on behalf of the war. He was, for example, among the signers of the manifesto of German intellectuals appearing soon after the beginning of hostilities, which denied that Germany was responsible for the outbreak of the conflict or that Germany had deceitfully violated Belgian neutrality. In addition, Haeckel also wrote an article in 1914 for the journal *Nord und Süd*, which was revealingly entitled '*Englands Blutschuld am Weltkriege.*' A year later he penned another bitter attack on England and the United States in *Ewigkeit. Weltkriegsgedanken über Leben, Tod, Religion, und Entwicklungslehre*. In 1914, he also had written another work on evolutionary religion, *Gottnatur (Theophysis): Studien über monistische Religion*. And in 1917 he completed a study of the evidence supporting the existence of the properties of soul which were to be found in the inorganic world: *Kristallseelen: Studien über das anorganische Leben*.

By April 25, 1915, when Haeckel's wife died, his own strength was clearly receding. The following August he wrote to his friend, Richard Hertwig: 'Since the death of my beloved wife . . . I have passed an unhappy summer in the midst of the terrible war emergency. Of twelve nephews and great nephews who were at the front, seven have fallen, two are severely wounded. . . . Our diplomacy has not overcome the lies and intrigues of the enemy.'[102]

Despite his personal suffering and the losses to his family, Haeckel remained committed to the achievement of a full military victory for Germany at any price. As late as September, 1917, he was still arguing for the full prosecution of the war effort and fulminated continuously against all movements for peace and compromise with the Allies. Thus, he wrote to Richard Hertwig on September 19, 1917: 'The future now looks very black to me! That the poor Reichstag allowed itself to be misled by two such dumb and frivolous fools as the ultramontane Erzberger and the social utopian Scheidemann to [pass] the stupid peace resolution of July, 1917, is most regrettable. What will peace look like?'[103] And in accordance with his bellicose stand, Haeckel gave his support to the newly created *Vaterlandspartei* of Wolfgang Kapp and Admiral Tirpitz which was opposed to any peaceful termination of the war. Many of the members of the *Vaterlandspartei* found their way into the ranks of the National Socialists after the war.[104]

When the war finally ended with the defeat of Germany in November, 1918, Haeckel was cast into a profound depression and in his letters he expressed confusion and horrified shock. In a letter to a soldier at the front, written one day after the signing of the Armistice, Haeckel complained that peace would only bring about the racial destruction of Germany. 'I fear,' he wrote, 'that the greatly longed for peace will result in a full reversal of modern culture. Our laughing heirs will apparently be the yellow Mongolians.'[105] And at the beginning of December, he wrote of his pessimism in a bitter and sad letter to Richard Hertwig: 'Finis Germaniae!! I see no possible way out any more from the disastrous political situation in which we have been placed by the terrible war. Already today the entire left bank of the Rhine has been occupied by the French.'[106] And he revealed that the German Revolution of November, 1918 left him completely hostile and cynical as to its possibilities. 'The new "German Republic" places its entire hope on the great "national assembly," yet no one knows what kind of new folly will be perpetrated by the ordinary German citizen—the least politically educated [person] in the world!' For the Kaiser, Haeckel expressed nothing but contempt. 'And William II, that swaggering *korps-student*, who in 1890 replaced the creative genius of the new German Reich, in order to lead us to such a glorious future.'[106] But the worst thing, Haeckel complained, was the growing menace of socialism. 'The prettiest role in the whole tragi-comedy is now being played by the new founder of the "Bavarian Republic," Herr Salomon Kuchewski, a Galician Jew, who, under the pseudonym Kurt Eisner has named himself president!'[107] Haeckel continued to fulminate: 'How is it possible for such a degenerate swindler to be able to tyrannise the whole Kingdom of Bavaria for four weeks?'[108] The Bavarians themselves were to blame for this '*Köpernickiade*.' By insisting on a special postal identification under the Second Reich, Haeckel suggested in all seriousness, they had 'drastically weakened the unity of the German Reich before all the world.'[109] And he upbraided the Bavarians for not taking immediate measures against the 'disgrace' of the new socialist republic of Eisner. On the other hand, he also expressed relief that the 'German"November Revolution"' had passed over Jena peacefully. Of Germany as a whole he remarked sadly: 'Who knows what will arise from this chaos'?[110]

Throughout the winter of 1918-1919 Haeckel was severely ill with the grippe. By the summer he confided to Richard Hertwig that the

THE SCIENTIFIC ORIGINS OF NATIONAL SOCIALISM

end was at hand. Five days before his death he complained about a local working-class rebellion that had taken place at the optical works of Carl Zeiss in Jena. He railed against the 'damned' shop committees of the workers and expressed a fear that the University would lose its financial support. Death, he said, would come by early autumn. It came much sooner, on August 9, 1919[111]

NOTES

1. M. Dill, Jr., Germany, *A Modern History* (Ann Arbor, Mich.: University of Michigan Press, 1961), p. 121.
2. Ralph Flenley, *Modern German History* (London: Dent, 1953), pp. 202–203.
3. Ernst Haeckel, *The Story of the Development of a Youth: Letters to his Parents 1852–1856* (New York: Harper, 1923), p. 89. In 1853, Haeckel wrote to his father that he stood up for North German and Prussian superiority in an argument with a pro-Austrian student. 'Never in my life,' he wrote, 'would I have thought that such patriotic sentiments were slumbering in me.'
4. Boelsche, *Haeckel, His Life and Work*, p. 24.
5. *Ibid.*, p. 29. Haeckel's grandfather and father were singled out as two worthy representatives of their age by the nineteenth-century Volkish author, Gustav Freytag, in his book, *Pictures from the German Past*. On the significance of Freytag as a Volkish author, see Mosse, *The Crisis of German Ideology*, pp. 127–28 and *passim*.
6. Quoted in Heinrich Schmidt, *Denkmal eines grossen Lebens* (Jena; Frommann, 1934), pp. 72–74. Schmidt adds that 'Germanic [consciousness] was in the blood of this blond German.'
7. Ernst Haeckel to Hermann Allmers, Freienwalde, September 5, 1860, in Victor Franz (ed.), *Ernst Haeckel. Sein Leben, Denken, und Wirken*, II (Jena: Gronau, 1944), p. 21.
8. *Ibid.*, pp. 16–17.
9. Ernst Haeckel to Hermann Allmers, Berlin, May 14, 1860, in Rudolf Koop (ed.), *Haeckel und Allmers, Die Geschichte einer Freundschaft in Briefen der Freunde* (Bremen: Arthur Geist, 1941), p. 49.
10. Schmidt, *Denkmal eines grossen Lebens*, p. 75.
11. On the political and social aims of Bismarck, see Arthur Rosenberg, *The Birth of the German Republic* (London: Oxford Press, 1931), Introduction.
12. Ernst Haeckel to Rudolf Virchow, Jena, May 24, 1860, in George Uschmann, *Ernst Haeckel, Forscher, Künstler, Mensch* (Leipzig, Urania, 1961), p. 80.
13. Hermann Allmers to Ernst Haeckel, Rechtenfleth, July 8, 1866, in Koop, *Haeckel und Allmers*, p. 108.
14. *Ibid.*

15. Ernst Haeckel to Hermann Allmers, Jena, August 16, 1866, in Franz, *Ernst Haeckel, Sein Leben, Denken, und Wirken*, II, 47.
16. Hermann Allmers to Ernst Haeckel, Rechtenfleth, November 15, 1870, in *ibid.*, p. 56.
17. *Ibid.*, pp. 56-57.
18. Ernst Haeckel to Hermann Allmers, Jena, January 31, 1871, in *ibid.*, p. 60.
19. Georg Uschmann, *Geschichte der Zoologie und der zoologischen Anstalten in Jena 1779–1919* (Jena: Gustav Fischer, 1959), pp. 38-39.
20. Oswei Temkin, 'The Idea of Descent in Post-Romantic German Biology: 1848-1858,' in Bentley Glass (ed.), *Forerunners of Darwin* (Baltimore: Johns Hopkins University Press, 1959), p. 327.
21. See H. Potonie, 'Aufzählung von Gelehrten, die in der Zeit von Lamarck bis Darwin sich im Sinne der Descendenz-Theorie geäussert haben,' *Naturwissenschaftliche Wochenschrift*, V (November 9, 1890), 441-445; and Charles Darwin, *The Origin of Species* (Variorum text, Philadelphia: University of Pennsylvania Press), 1959.
22. Uschmann, *Geschichte der Zoologie und der zoologischen Anstalten in Jena 1779–1919*, p. 41 n.
23. Quoted in Schmidt, (ed.) *Was wir Ernst Haeckel verdanken*, I, 78.
24. *Ibid.*, p. 79.
25. Ernst Haeckel, *The History of Creation: or the Development of the Earth and its Inhabitants by the Action of Natural Causes* (New York: Appleton, 1876), I, 20-23.
26. Ernst Haeckel to Hermann Allmers, Jena, December 15, 1863, in Franz, *Ernst Haeckel. Sein Leben, Denken, und Wirken*, II, 37.
27. Uschmann, *Geschichte der Zoologie und der zoologischen Anstalten in Jena 1779–1919*, p. 44.
28. Ernst Haeckel, 'Ueber die Entwicklungs-Theorie Darwins,' in *Gemeinverständliche Vorträge und Abhandlungen aus dem Gebiete der Entwicklungslehre* (Bonn: Straus, 1902), I, 1-34.
29. Uschmann, *Geschichte der Zoologie und der zoologischen Anstalten in Jena 1779–1919*, p. 48.
30. See letter of Ernst Haeckel to Hermann Allmers, Villafranca bei Nizza, March 27, 1864, in Franz, *Ernst Haeckel. Sein Leben, Denken, und Wirken*, II, 41.
31. For the general significance of Haeckel's biological work on the *Radiolaria*, see Eric Nordenskiold, *The History of Biology* (New York: Tudor, 1928), pp. 508-509.
32. Haeckel, *History of Creation*, I, 1-2.
33. Klemm, *Der Ketzer von Jena*, pp. 116-117.
34. For an assessment of Haeckel's scientific work, see Nordenskiold, *History of Biology*, pp. 508-521; Gavin de Beer, *Embryos and Ancestors* (Oxford: Oxford University Press, 1958), *passim;* and Ernst Cassirer, *The Problem of Knowledge, Philosophy, Science, and History Since Hegel* (New Haven: Yale University Press, 1950), Chapter IX and *passim*.
35. Nordenskiold, *History of Biology*, p. 508.

36. *Ibid.*
37. *Ibid.*
38. Schmidt, H. (ed.) *Was wir Ernst Haeckel verdanken*, I, 134.
39. See Ernst Haeckel, *Die heutige Entwicklungslehre im Verhältnisse zur Entwicklungslehre* (Stuttgart: Schweizerbart, 1877).
40. Nordenskiold, *History of Biology*, p. 518.
41. For more details on the Biogenetic Law and Haeckel's other biological theories, see below, Chapter III, pp. 140–143.
42. Haeckel made much more of his relationship with Darwin than was warranted. Although they did meet a few times and exchanged some letters, Haeckel was not a very important figure in Darwin's life. Darwin recognized Haeckel's efforts on behalf of evolution and in the *Descent of Man*, credited Haeckel's contributions to the study of man's origin. But Darwin mentioned Haeckel only briefly in his *Autobiography*, and in general remained sceptical of what little he knew of Haeckel's broader theoretical speculations. It is probably accurate to say that Darwin had no real conception of the magnitude of Haeckel's commitment to evolutionary religion. Also, Darwin read German only haltingly and died in 1882.

    For the correspondence between Darwin and Haeckel, see Charles Darwin, *Life and Letters of Charles Darwin* (New York: D. Appleton & Co., 1898), and *More Letters of Charles Darwin* (London: J. Murray, 1903).
43. See Cassirer, *The Problem of Knowledge*, Chapter IX.
44. Rudolf Virchow, *The Freedom of Science in the Modern State* (London: J. Murray, 1878).
45. *Ibid.*, p. 57.
46. Ernst Haeckel, *Freedom in Science and Teaching* (New York: D. Appleton & Co., 1879), p. 11 and *passim*.
47. For example, see Ernst Haeckel, *The Evolution of Man* (New York: D. Appleton & Co.,) I, xxvii–xxxvi.
48. For a comprehensive account of Haeckel and his students, see Uschmann, *Geschichte der Zoologie und der zoologischen Anstalten in Jena 1779–1919, passim;* and Nordenskiold, *History of Biology, passim.*
49. For a listing of the organizations which Haeckel belonged to, see Schmidt, H. (ed.) *Was wir Ernst Haeckel verdanken*, I, pp. 170–172.
50. Ernst Haeckel to Bartholomäus Carneri, Potsdam, September 24, 1882, in *Bartholomäus von Carneri's Briefwechsel mit Ernst Haeckel und Friedrich Jodl* (Leipzig: Koehler, 1922), p. 21.
51. On T. H. Huxley's defection from evolutionary ethics in naturalism, see Gertrude Himmelfarb, *Darwin and the Darwinian Revolution* (Garden City, New York: Doubleday, 1959), Chapter 18.
52. Holborn, *A History of Modern Germany, 1840–1945*, p. 396.
53. Ernst Haeckel, *The Wonders of Life* (New York: Harper, 1904), pp. v–vi.
54. Olof Klohr, Introduction, to Ernst Haeckel, *Die Welträtsel* ([E.] Berlin: Akademie Verlag, 1961), pp. vii, viii.

55. Nordenskiold, *History of Biology*, p. 524, writes concerning *Welträtsel*: '... from a scientific point of view it must be regarded as utterly valueless. Its biological section is a rehash of *The History of Creation*, *Anthropogeny*, and the monograph on the plastidule, as little attention as possible being paid to the immense progress made by scientific research since then. As a matter of fact, biology takes up only one quarter of the volume; the rest is devoted to psychology, cosmology, and theology. The cosmological section gives evidence of the author's hopelessly confused ideas on the simplest facts of physics and chemistry.'
    For a detailed critique of Haeckel's science and *Welträtsel*, see Orest Chwolson, *Hegel, Haeckel, und das zwölfte Gebot* (Braunschweig: Vieweg, 1906).
56. Ernst Haeckel, *The Love Letters of Ernst Haeckel* (New York: Harper, 1930), p. 199.
57. Friedrich Paulsen, 'Haeckel als Philosoph,' *Preussische Jahrbuecher*, 101 (1900), p. 72.
58. *Ibid.*, p. 36.
59. *Ibid*
60. Heinrich Schmidt, 'Ernst Haeckel als Theolog,' *Der Monismus*, VI (1911), 119.
61. Schmidt, H. (ed.) Introduction to *Was wir Ernst Haeckel verdanken*, I, 150.
62. Wilhelm Ostwald, 'Was ich Ernst Haeckel verdanke,' in Schmidt, H. (ed.) *Was wir Ernst Haeckel verdanken*, I, 199.
63. Wilhelm Schwaner, 'Der Künstler und Mensch,' in *ibid.*, p. 203.
64. Wilhelm Breitenbach, 'Meine Beziehungen zu Haeckel,' in *ibid.*, p. 214.
65. Friedrich Thieme (no title), in *ibid.*, II, 85.
66. C. H. Thiele, (no title), in *ibid.*, I, 262.
67. Friedrich Siebert (no title), in *ibid.*, p. 351.
68. Eugen Wolfsdorf, 'Odhin und Haeckel,' in *ibid.*, II, 46-47.
69. Schmidt, H. (ed.) Introduction to *ibid.*, I, 59-60.
70. *Ibid.*, p. 58.
71. Ernst Haeckel to Hermann Allmers, Jena, January 31, 1871, in Franz, *Ernst Haeckel. Sein Leben, Denken, und Wirken*, II, 60.
72. Schmidt, H. (Ed.) Introduction to *Was wir Ernst Haeckel verdanken*, I, 58.
73. *Ibid.*, pp. 58-59.
74. Else v. Volkmann, 'Ernst Haeckel veranlasste die Einladung Bismarcks,' in Franz, *Ernst Haeckel. Sein Leben, Denken, und Wirken*, I, 83.
75. *Ibid.*, p. 84.
76. *Ibid.*
77. *Ibid.*, p. 85.
78. *Ibid.*
79. *Ibid.*
80. For an account of Haeckel's many travels, see Boelsche, *Haeckel, His Life and Work*, pp. 256ff.
81. For example, see Hans Wolfgang Behm, 'Haeckel als Forschungsreisender,' *Das monistische Jahrhundert*, II (1913-14), 1309-1316.
82. Ernst Haeckel, *India and Ceylon* (New York: John W. Covell Co., 1883), p. 93.
83. *Ibid.*, pp. 103-104.

84. See, for example, Bartholomäus von Carneri, *Sittlichkeit und Darwinismus* (Vienna: Braumüller, 1871); or Gustav Jaeger, *Die Darwin'sche Theorie und ihre Stellung zu Moral und Religion* (Stuttgart: Hoffmann, 1860).
85. Max Henning, *Handbuch der freigeistigen Bewegung Deutschlands, Österreichs und der Schweiz* (Frankfurt a.M.: Neuer Frankfurter Verlag, 1914, p. 12.
86. Quoted in Schmidt, H. (ed.) Introduction to *Was wir Ernst Haeckel verdanken*, I, 157.
87. Henning, *Handbuch der freigeistigen Bewegung*, p. 16.
88. Unold also edited the first journal of the Monist League, *Der Monismus*, and served between 1910 and 1912 as the President of the League.
89. For a listing of the founders of the Monist League, see *Das monistische Jahrhundert*, I (1912–13), 749.
90. Henning, *Handbuch der freigeistigen Bewegung*, p. 45.
91. *Das monistische Jahrhundert* was superseded by *Mitteilungen des deutschen Monistenbundes*. In 1919, *Monistische Monatshefte* became the official journal of the League.
92. For a listing of the '*Flugschriften*' of the Monist League, see *ibid.*, pp. 61–62.
93. *Ibid., passim*.
94. Ernst Haeckel, *The Riddle of the Universe* (New York: Harper, 1900), p. 1.
95. *Ibid.*, p.2.
96. *Ibid.*, p. 6.
97. *Ibid.*, p. 8.
98. *Ibid.* p. 48.
99. *Ibid.*, p. 54.
100. For the effect of the First World War on the Monist League, see *Das monistische Jahrhundert*, III (1914–1915), *passim*.
101. Koppel Pinson, *Modern Germany* (New York: Macmillan, 1954), pp. 315–316.
102. Ernst Haeckel to Richard Hertwig, Jena, August 30, 1915, in Franz, *Ernst Haeckel. Sein Leben, Denken, und Wirken*, I, 63.
103. *Ibid.*, p. 64.
104. Ernst Haeckel to Richard Hertwig, Jena, December 6, 1918, *ibid.*, p. 66. At about this time Haeckel also became a member of the newly formed *Thule Gesellschaft*, a secret, radically right-wing organization which played a key role in the establishment of the Nazi movement. Other members of the *Thule* included future Nazis like Dietrich Eckart, Gottfried Feder, and Rudolf Hess. Hitler and Anton Drexler attended meetings of the *Thule* as guests. See, René Alleau, *Hitler et les Sociétés Secrètes* (Paris: Grasset, 1969), pp. 247–249 and *passim;* and Reginald Phelps, 'Before Hitler Came: Thule Society and Germanen Orden,' *Journal of Modern History*, XXV (1963), 245–261.
105. Quoted in *Mitteilungen des deutschen Monistenbundes*, IV (1919), 163.
106. Ernst Haeckel to Richard Hertwig, Jena, December 6, 1918 in Franz, *Ernst Haeckel. Sein Leben, Denken, und Wirken*, I, 66.
107–110. *Ibid.*
111. Ernst Haeckel to Richard Hertwig, Jena, August 4, 1919, in *ibid.*, p. 70.

Chapter Two

The Political Assumptions of Monism

IN the tradition of nineteenth-century German romantic nationalism the Haeckelian Monists advanced their general philosophical system and social Darwinism as a critique of the ideological foundations of Western European civilization.[1] Opposed as it was to Western rationalism, humanism, and cosmopolitanism, Monism, despite its links with the international scientific community and its professed attachment to international cooperation and harmony, was a distinctively Germanic movement and ideology. In its essence it represented a conscious and deliberate movement against all attempts to solve the national and spiritual problems of the Germans within the framework of the intellectual, philosophical, social, and political realm of liberal and Christian Europe. The Germans, Haeckel and his followers contended, must either accept a new philosophy based on evolution and science and unite with the forces of nature, or cease, through weakness and deterioration, to exist as a nation.

The theoretical foundations of Monist social Darwinism are to be found in the scientific and philosophical writings of Haeckel. It was his conception of man and man's relation to nature which provided a basis for all Monist pronouncements on social and political questions. For Haeckel, the study of the nature of man was a consuming interest. He sought to solve the riddle of man's existence and he was haunted by what he believed to be man's blind rebellion against his biological origin and biological destiny. For Haeckel, and for his Monist followers, therefore, the most important social consequence of Darwinism and evolutionary biology was its demonstration of the animal origin and nature of man. Man, they argued, was a natural phenomenon and it was this incontestable fact which invalidated all traditional conceptions of his political and social possibilities. Since the decline of the ancient world, the Monists lamented, European civilization had been operating under the illusion and delusion that man enjoyed a unique existence and identity apart from nature. In their minds the main purpose of evolutionary Monism was to dispel this 'reactionary' and 'erroneous' idea.[2]

Haeckel and his followers therefore sought, first of all, to discredit as scientifically untrue all the humanist characteristics which had come to be accepted as peculiar to man in traditional European culture. That man was a unique creature, that civilization represented a distinct triumph over the brutal conditions of an animal and primitive past, that man's spiritual worth was ultimately immeasurable, were all values and assumptions which were called into question by Haeckel and the Monists. Not only did they argue that man was physically 'one and the same in every important respect'[3] with the anthropoids and other lower forms of life—one could observe, Haeckel noted, that the 'milk-producing glands and teats of apes and men are exactly the same in structure and development'[4]—but they especially emphasized that man's powers of reason, his intelligence, his rational consciousness, and his emotions were capacities and traits shared with the lower animals. For Haeckel, man had 'no single mental faculty' which was his 'exclusive prerogative.' Rather, he insisted, man's 'whole psychic life differs from that of the nearest related mammals only in degree, and not in kind.'[5] The love of a mother for its child, for example, which had been 'most nobly expressed in the pictures of the Madonna and Child ... expressing an endless number of works of art,' was to be found 'no less developed among apes than among men.' He therefore mocked and derided man's pretentious beliefs in his own uniqueness: his emotions and physiology were the same as those of the lower animals. Darwinism showed that the more highly developed animals have 'just as good a title to "reason" as man himself, and [that] within the limits of the animal world there is the same long chain of the gradual development of reason as in the case of humanity.'[6]

One obvious implication which the Monists drew from their belief that man's physical and mental characteristics were only 'quantitatively' but 'not qualitatively'[7] different from those of the animals, was that man could lay no claim to a uniquely human soul. Any Socratic or Christian notions regarding the existence of a soul, however casually held, were regarded by them as highly dangerous and unscientific. 'Man is not distinguished from [the animals] by a special *kind* of a soul,' Haeckel maintained, 'or by any peculiar and exclusive psychic function, but only by a higher *degree* of psychic activity, a superior stage of development.'[8] There was, therefore, no spiritual essence which was peculiar to man and any such assumption was a vain and erroneous humanist, Christian, or liberal illusion.

Thus, for the Monists, perhaps the most pernicious feature of European bourgeois civilization was the inflated importance which it attached to the idea of man in general, to his existence and to his talents, and to the belief that through his unique rational faculties man could essentially recreate the world and bring about a universally more harmonious and ethically just social order. While it was undoubtedly true, the Monists admitted, that man was the highest achievement of organic nature, a product of the last stage in the evolutionary process, he was, on the other hand, an insignificant creature when viewed as part of and measured against the vastness of the cosmos and the overwhelming forces of nature.

It was Haeckel who had especially emphasized the insignificance and unimportance of man. 'As our mother earth is a mere speck in the sunbeam in the illimitable universe, so man himself is but a tiny grain of protoplasm in the perishable framework of organic nature.'[9] The magnificence and infinity of the cosmos 'clearly indicates the true place of man in nature, but it dissipates the prevalent illusion of man's supreme importance and the arrogance with which he sets himself apart from the illimitable universe and exalts himself to the position of its most valuable element.'[10] Contrary to what the humanistic tradition teaches, man does not stand at the center of the world, nor are his individual interests and desires necessarily the most important considerations in constructing a social and political philosophy. 'This boundless presumption of conceited man has misled him into making himself "the image of God," claiming an "eternal life" for his ephemeral personality.'[11] Man in general and especially the individual must abandon all illusions concerning his own primacy in the world.

Since man was in all important respects an animal, the Monists argued, it follows that he had to adjust his life and his social ideals accordingly. As early as the 1860's Haeckel had written that it was 'absolutely necessary' that we should 'compare human with extra-human phenomena.'[12] It had to be recognized that 'man is not above nature, but in nature,'[13] and throughout his career Haeckel always taught that 'civilization and the life of nations are governed by the same laws as prevail throughout nature and organic life.'[14] It was fundamental to his position that the 'evolution of man has taken place according to the same "eternal immutable laws," as has the evolution of any other natural body.'[15]

Following the teachings of Haeckel directly, the Monists insisted that for man the 'same laws must be valid today which have regulated the life of other species for millions of years.'[16] and these were to be found exclusively in the natural and not in the historical world. In the construction of any science of society it had to be kept clearly in mind that man could never hope to transcend his animal essence and character and escape into a deceptively idyllic world free from the competition, conflict, and aggression that characterized nature. 'Natural selection in the struggle for life,' Haeckel wrote, 'acts so as to transform human society just as it modifies animals and plants.'[17] There need be no disappointment in recognizing this, for in fact man benefits from unfettered struggle. 'Does not human nature,' Dr. Johannes Unold, the Vice-President of the Monist League pointed out, 'lose its best characteristics and fall into weakness and sonambulism when there is general happiness and a termination of the struggle for existence?'[18] It had to be realized that 'every deviation from natural conditions brings with it inescapably grievous punishment.' Failure to follow the laws of nature directly can lead to the 'crippling' of man and to the 'deterioration of the individual and his family.' For this reason biology had to 'demand' that sociology follow the laws of nature.[19]

It would be difficult to overemphasize the significance of the acceptance in Monist thinking of the literal continuity between the laws of nature and the laws of society. Any comparison which they made between the social and the natural world was in no sense analogical. Just as man was a product of nature so too was the society in which he lived a direct outgrowth of the natural world. Neither history nor its institutions represented a break or departure from nature in any way. And this position was maintained by Haeckel and the Monists with the utmost seriousness and dedication. They held to no Hegelian ideas about history as the process of the unfolding of reason, nor to any Marxian conceptions about the conquest of nature by the social and technological forces of production, nor to any Comtian stages of intellectual development. To the Monists, rather, civilization as a distinctively human creation literally did not exist. 'History,' Haeckel wrote, is 'wrongly taken to mean,' the history of 'civilization, morals, etc.' What he meant was that the ordinary history of the deeds, thoughts, and institutions of men was a pale and insignificant reflection of reality. For him, any consideration of civilization apart from nature and its laws was simply not worthwhile. Real history, he insisted, 'joins what is called the history of the world to the stem-history of the vertebrates.'[20] Sociology as an independent science of an autonomous human realm was to him inconceivable. 'When we take it in its wider sense human sociology joins on to that of the nearest related mammals' and all 'social rules' are ultimately reducible to the 'natural laws of heredity and adaptation.'[21] For Haeckel, therefore, there existed no aspect of social science which could not be understood and expressed in biological terms.

To be sure, the discovery of the animal nature of man and an awareness of its possible implication for society was not limited to Haeckel and the Monists in the decades around the turn of the century. To a large extent they moved along the same paths as those of Sigmund Freud and his psychoanalytic followers, who under the influence of the new biology also turned their attention to the importance of the biological and instinctual nature of man.[22] Whereas Freud, however, sought to caution society against the pursuit of the irrational and of the danger inherent in allowing man's animal and sexual instincts to have free reign, the Monists came to a very different conclusion. Since man is limited, they argued, by his animal nature, he could only weaken himself by attempting to impose upon life an erroneous intellectualism and rationalism.[23] As a humanist, Freud felt that man's rationality could triumph over nature, although it is also true that he became increasingly and pessimistically aware of the high price that would be exacted in human suffering for such a victory. For Haeckel and the

Monists, on the other hand, there could be no humanistic cultural triumph over the forces of man's animal nature and character. And it was this rather pessimistic and cynical conclusion which served to distinguish Monist naturalism from most, if not all, previous naturalistic attempts to explain man as an unique and superior creature of nature.[24]

Thus, in advocating the literal application of the laws of nature directly to society, the Monists believed that they had fathomed the deepest need of theoretical sociology, a scientifically established guide to action and to cultural and social reorganization unhampered by any humanistic illusions. 'Until now,' a leading Monist wrote, 'those who spoke the most about the ideals of mankind, knew the least about the true nature of man.'[25] Thus, the Monists maintained, it was extremely unfortunate that the Christian West had failed to recognize the actual nature of man and instead had inculcated in him deceptive values and beliefs. European civilization, with its inordinate emphasis on the inviolability of the human personality and on the existence of a human soul, had mistakenly protected the weak members of society and had cultivated a false and misleading humanitarianism. This had led, they felt, to the increasing enervation of the individual and to the decline of the natural strength of the most advanced European nations. The 'artificial selection,' Haeckel wrote, 'practised in our civilized states sufficiently explains the sad fact that, in reality, weakness of the body and character are on the perpetual increase among civilized nations, and that, together with strong, healthy bodies, free and independent spirits are becoming more and more scarce.'[26] To be healthy, a society had to be governed according to the absolutely unimpeded laws of nature. Only this literal application of natural law, Haeckel and the Monists argued, would constitute real progress; only under the sway of nature would man finally realize his true capacities and limitations. In effect, the Monists were urging a return to and a cultivation of the elemental and primitive forces of life, as we shall see later on in more detail.

It may be said that for the Monists the recognition of the animal nature of man was far from being simply an interesting academic or intellectual discovery. They contended that knowledge of the natural world provided them with deep insight into the true nature of national problems and they perceived in it the essential clue to a scientifically satisfying program for the social and political regeneration of Germany. For them, Monism was the means of bringing 'all forms of phenomena into a harmonious relationship'; and specifically it could bring about the transformation of the Germans into a 'unified people' with a unified outlook on the world.[27] Monism, they argued, meant liberation from Western Civilization. 'For the fact that our culture can alienate nature to the point of outspoken sickly aversion, we can think a period of human degeneracy that is long since past but whose ideas still rule today, although they are clearly antagonistic to life.'[28] They felt that traditional European civilization was an 'anachronism, a monstrosity' which all along had advocated the harmful '*Weltanschauung* which arose two thousand years ago under the hallucination that the end of the world is imminent.'[29] Monism, on the other hand, was a new vital culture rooted in the natural tendencies and feelings of the nation. Its doctrines expressed the 'warm desire' for intellectual and social emancipation which was 'infusing' the Germans. Monism, they felt, represented an authentic 'longing to be free from medieval ways of thinking, medieval dogmas, and medieval oppression of conscience.' It was an expression of their kind of 'yearning for clarity and truthfulness in thinking and feeling' couched, however, not in the objective and detailed form of rational truths, but launched rather as emotional and pathetic exhortations of a doctrine of national liberation, addressed above all to the reliable patriotic German instincts, and aimed at triggering an enflamed response of herd consciousness. 'Help us German men and women' to fashion a new life and a new civilization they cried out in the same emotional way that Hitler shouted to the Germans less than twenty-five years later.[30]

One important way to make the Germans more aware of their biological ancestry and at the same time to fight the weakness and decay which was inherent in Western Civilization, it appeared to Haeckel and the Monists, was to revamp Germany's educational system. The Monists, therefore, called for a total revolution in the content of the educational curriculum and Haeckel himself became an outspoken pedagogical theoretician and educational reformer. Levelling what were often justifiable objections to many features of education in Germany, Haeckel, along with his Monist colleagues, attacked what they considered to be dead learning on all levels of the school system, ossified curricula, and pedantic and ill-educated teachers and professors. Haeckel, for example, often scorned his academic colleagues as *Dunkelmänner*—men of darkness—and in demanding a revitalization of education often appeared to come close to the criticism of other educational reformers like Jakob Burckhardt, Nietzsche, and Pestalozzi. On the surface, therefore, Haeckel frequently pleaded a justifiable case against narrow and meaningless research, lifeless teaching, and education which neither met the needs of the students nor awakened their creativity. Demanding the secularization of education and the introduction of science into the curriculum, Haeckel sounded like many other naturalistically and progressively inclined thinkers in the nineteenth century. But lurking beneath his progressive sounding phrases and ideas was a theory of education and a program which actively sought to undermine the entire humanistic tradition of general education based upon instruction in the liberal arts. Haeckel saw in the transformation of the school curriculum a way to attack what he believed were the corrupting roots of Western Civilization itself. The West, with its glorification of man, its sense of civilization as representing the development of the human spirit and the ever growing realization of human freedom, were, from Haeckel's point of view, ideas which had to be combatted. By emphasizing the need for science in the new curriculum, Haeckel was at the same time demanding the curtailment or even elimination of the humanities. Instruction in classical civilization, languages, and history, the study of which made the student aware of ties to a common European heritage were deemed by Haeckel to be unnecessary or even downright dangerous. In traditional education, Haeckel wrote, we have an 'immense waste of time over a "thorough knowledge" of classics and the history of foreign nations.'[31] These studies, he felt, had to be supplanted by science so that the new curriculum would place man in the proper biological perspective for the student. And to emphasize his anti-humanistic position, Haeckel wrote in the *Welträtsel* that in 'all education up to the present time *man* has played the chief part [and] the study of *nature* was entirely neglected.'[32] The aim of the new education, Haeckel declared, was the very opposite of this. 'In the school of the future nature will be the chief object of study; a man shall learn a correct view of the world he lives in; he will not be made to stand outside of and opposed to nature.'[33] For Haeckel, therefore, education was not to be based upon a general knowledge of the history of Western Civilization. Through the study of science in general and biology in particular man would learn of his real links to nature. And since he was addressing himself primarily to the Germans, Haeckel hoped that the reform of the educational curriculum would help to disengage them from the traditions and outlook of an erroneous and harmful view of the world which had been the mainstay of the traditional system of education. The new education based upon science would teach the Germans that the universalist assumptions of Western culture had been founded upon religious and metaphysical illusions.]

In organizing their new cultural revolution the Monists came out in opposition to all ideas, religious or secular, which expressed the essential equality of mankind. They argued that men, as primarily biological creatures, were naturally divided into separate, racially determined species. It was their belief that the varied races of mankind were endowed with differing hereditary characteristics not only of color, but also more importantly of intelligence, and that external physical characteristics were a sign of innate intellectual and moral capacity.[34] For Haeckel, for example, 'woolly-haired' Negroes were 'incapable of a true inner culture and of a higher mental development,' and he noted that 'no woolly-haired nation has ever had an important "history".'[35] Rather, the making of real history had to be attributed to the white races, and even more specifically to the Germanic ones. In fact, it was only among the white Germanic races that one could find those individuals who possess a 'symmetry of all parts, and that equal development, which we call the type of perfect human beauty.'[36] Haeckel, in other words, by emphasizing the importance of external physical characteristics, offered to reduce the human individual to a racial type and to equate intelligence and race.[37]

Racial differences, therefore, the Haeckelian Monists contended, were fundamental and significant facts about the actual nature of man and had to influence the development and outlook of any social theory. 'Though the great differences in the mental life and the civilization of the higher and lower races of men are generally known,' Haeckel wrote, 'they are as a rule undervalued, and so the value of life at the different levels is falsely estimated.'[38] For Haeckel, who recorded his support of the ideas of Gobineau,[39] the 'lower' races of mankind were nearer to the animals than to the 'higher' races. The 'difference,' he wrote, 'between the reason of a Goethe, a Kant, a Lamarck, or a Darwin, and that of the lowest savage . . . is much greater than the graduated difference between the reason of the latter and that of the most "rational" mammals, the anthropoid apes.'[40] Therefore, since racial difference was at the core of historical experience it was scientifically incorrect to think of mankind as one. Haeckel voiced his regret that 'most anthropologists dogmatically and firmly hold to the so-called "unity of species" for all the races of Men, and unite them into one species, as *Homo Sapiens*.'[41] This was untenable. 'The unprejudiced and critical inquirer, when carefully comparing [the species of men], cannot rid himself of the conviction that the morphological differences between them are much more important than those by which, for instance, the various species of bears, wolves, or cats are distinguished in the zoological system. Nay, even the morphological differences between two generally recognized species—for instance, sheep . . . and goats—are much less important than those between a Papuan and and Esquimaux, or between a Hottentot and a man of the Teutonic race.'[42] And since the 'lower races (such as the Veddahs or Australian Negroes) are psychologically nearer to the mammals (apes and dogs) than to civilized Europeans, we must, therefore, assign a totally different value to their lives.'[43]

The importance of Haeckel's support for racism obviously transcended the meagre content of the ideas themselves. Haeckel, of course, was far from being the only popularizer of racial nationalism in Germany. Contemporaries, like Ludwig Schemann, the founder of the Gobineau Society, and Houston Stewart Chamberlain, were even more active than Haeckel in disseminating racial propaganda. Haeckel, however, decisively contributed scientific authority to the cause of racism. By bringing biology and anthropology to its support, in works that were widely read and credited, he succeeded in investing the ideas of racial nationalism with academic respectability and scientific assurance. It was Haeckel, in other words, who was largely responsible for forging the bonds between academic science and racism in Germany in the later decades of the nineteenth century.

Following Haeckel, the Monists stressed the political implications which were to be derived from racial knowledge. 'Much of contempo-

THE POLITICAL ASSUMPTIONS OF MONISM

rary research in anthropology may be false and a better knowledge may be lacking,' a leading Monist and a close friend of Haeckel wrote, but the 'enormous significance' of 'racial divisions will remain.' One may observe the importance of race 'when the French Revolution thinks in terms of the battle against German blood in France,' or when 'Bismarck speaks of Slavic moonshine sentimentality,' or when the 'strain of French blood' may be noted 'in the sound of the words of the Rector of the University of Berlin, DuBois-Reymond.'[44] Racial equality, another Monist pointed out, which has been preached in various ways by Christianity and by the ideology of the French Revolution, was really nothing more than an impossible and naive dream.[45] In reality, the different races and nations have profoundly varied needs. Thus, one Monist, who was especially outspoken on the racial issue, wrote: 'Yes, I must even go so far as to say: mankind is [composed] of such varied races, which live in such varied climates and states, that they have no common inward needs.'[46] In fact, he continued, we are 'completely defenseless against these physiological differences and their spiritual consequences.'[47] He claimed further, on the basis of what he believed to be irrefutable evidence, that 'contemporary research in racial science' has shown that there are differences in 'blood, albumen, and in embryology' among the various races.[48] One must admit, he concluded, that there were deep and profound laws of nature which governed the differences between the races, and that these 'rule silently' but effectively.[49]

In general, the Haeckelian Monists readily assumed that nations were themselves representative of either lower or higher racial groups and that in the contemporary world it was the Germans who constituted the most advanced race. In the *Natürliche Schöpfungsgeschichte*, Haeckel had confidently written that it was the Germans who had 'deviated furthest from the common primary form of ape-like men,' and had, therefore, in modern times been able to 'outstrip all other branches [of mankind] in the career of civilization.'[50] He stressed that in the modern world it was the Germans who were 'laying the foundation for a new period of higher mental development.'[51] Since, for Haeckel, it was the discovery of the philosophy of Monism which 'formed the best criterion for the degree of man's mental development,' the Germans were the highest product of evolution, having been the first to recognize, develop, and adopt his theory of evolutionary Monism. The Germans clearly stood at the apex of civilization.

Primarily because the Germans constituted a unique and highly developed race, the Monists sought to impress upon them the concept of the nation as a real evolutionary entity and attempted at the same time to disparage any conception of the state and the community as merely mechanical contrivances of an *ad hoc* political organization. They adopted, in other words, a typically conservative organic theory of society and the state and translated it into racial terms. 'According to the naturalistic way of thinking,' a Monist political treatise stated, 'a people is not an aggregate, a sand-pile of loose equal granules, but is an organic unity.'[52] Germany's future, like that of all biological organisms and species, depended on assuring proper maintenance and continuity of its germ plasm.[53] The nation, they urged, was a total 'community based upon race, spiritual and mental characteristics, language, history and a [territorial] homeland.'[54] The Germans had to eschew cosmopolitanism and realize that significant history can only unfold within the context of the national state. 'It is the concert of nations, not the chaos of individual persons, which comprises mankind.'[55] And since it was the nation which was the sole effective unit in the social evolutionary process, they warned that 'every nation which did not maintain itself and utilize all of its powers for the [advance] of evolution sinned in terms of itself and of mankind.'[56] Germany therefore had an obligation, as the most advanced racial country, to take the initiative and insure its continued supremacy and strength by bolstering its national consciousness. The Germans had to realize that 'all possibility of human cultural evolution rests on the fact that mankind has evolved farther by the continuing accomplishments of gifted individuals, races, and nations.'[57] And after all it had to be recognized that the 'preservation of the culturally capable races appears to be more worthwhile for the progress of mankind than a toilsome and protracted and perhaps unsuccessful raising of less capable and educationally less able human groups.'[58]

This emphasis on the organic racial unity of Germany led some Monists to express nationalistic sentiments of a radically xenophobic kind. To be sure, on the surface, the Monists were not always entirely consistent on this point. At times, especially when participating in or sponsoring international congresses of science, they liked to refer to the inherent unity of the world scientific community and of the urgent need for international harmony and cooperation. But, in reality, internationalism for most members of the German Monist League, was no more than a ritualistic slogan which in no way expressed their true sentiments. Internationalism, for them, was only a residual legacy of the liberalism from which modern science and evolutionary Darwinism had emerged in the nineteenth century. In actual fact, the German Monists were radically and, at times, irrationally nationalistic, despite an occasional obeisance to cosmopolitan ideals.[59]

Thus, in an article appearing in the journal of the Monist League, *Das monistische Jahrhundert*, for example, it was argued that modern civilization had intruded between man and his natural feelings of patriotism and love of country. The author, Ewalt Fincke, a member of the Monist League in Jena, warned that a dangerous tendency was developing in Germany whereby people seemed to be suppressing the natural feelings which they harbored for their own country.[60] He argued that the sense of patriotism which arose naturally from prolonged contact with the natural environment of the nation stood in sharp contrast with the artificially induced attitude of internationalism or cosmopolitanism. 'While patriotism dominates our mind cells through perception and other influences, mostly indirect, it is otherwise with internationalism. What we hear and read of foreign races, nations, states, and countries and see in illustrations does not come into our minds directly but indirectly and indeed artificially.'[61] All of the vehicles and activities of international communication and trade cannot compare in the intensity of their effect with the feelings engendered by contact with the soil and landscape of the homeland. This same Monist further cautioned that international relations were a product of civilization and not of nature, and were therefore cold and false.[62] Thus, to maintain any cosmopolitan or international attitude was to go completely against nature and hence against the logic of existence. 'Only he who neglects the wiser influences of nature which the homeland exerts upon him and attains thereby a kind of impotent thought which derives from civilization, only he will fathom the ultimate magic, how to unlearn patriotism and maintain internationalism.'[63] Germany, therefore, was advised to cultivate a deep sense of the national. 'What we sow is our own and cannot be other than national if we obey nature and if our culture is not used to turn nature upside down and against itself.'[64]

In the Monist ideology, radical racial nationalism was coupled with a profound and aggressive denial of the political and social assumptions of bourgeois liberalism. Such liberal tenets as civil rights, constitutionalism, the separation of the individual and the state, the free and unhindered discussion of political questions, and the desire for a solution to all social problems based upon the compromise of conflicting opinions and interests were all, in one way or another, denied by the Haeckelian Monists. The belief in the possibility of abstract justice, the rule of law, humane relations between individuals, and in the value of personal liberty, and the related convictions that central authority was a threat and that only those societies were truly free where individuals were completely at liberty to pursue a diversity of goals, interests, and activities—these ideas were seriously questioned and even denied outright by the Monists. In opposition to these liberal tenets, the Monists called for the supremacy of the racial community and the state over the individual and his subordination to the impersonal drive of the Volk towards greater power and strength to assure favorable conditions for its continued existence. The institutions and prerogatives of authority were to be wholeheartedly supported. The state is to be seen as a 'product of the human struggle for existence and [of human] striving for organization.'[65] It is the state, it was maintained, which has played the central role in the drama of the 'preservation of the nation,' and thus 'state interests' clearly take 'precedence over those of the individual.'[66] A person who knew the 'value of the state,' Haeckel claimed, also exhibited a 'more highly developed moral sense.'[67] He therefore urged the individual to dedicate and sacrifice himself to the state and to realize that only by complete subordination to it were 'welfare, true happiness, and satisfaction . . . to be found.'[68]

Following Haeckel, therefore, the Monists regarded their ideology as a 'state-preserving and a state-maintaining way of life.'[69] They considered the proper ordering of the state to be the 'largest, most significant task of man and of nature.'[70] It was thus confidentially asserted that 'our planet does not know anything greater or higher than the creation of such a community.'[71] It was in the construction of the state that the 'creative forces of the earth have assumed the greatest role.'[72] No individual can supersede the state and the racial community which it supports and leads. It was Haeckel who pointed out that beliefs like those of the anarchist Max Stirner, or of Nietzsche, which assumed that the state could be dissolved or transcended, were false and dangerous ideas.[73] And Dr. Unold pointed out, with obvious reference to Nietzsche, that that 'which rises above man cannot be a superman but only a well-organized commonwealth.'[74]

Indeed, it was solely in the context of subordination to the organically constituted and centralized Volkish racial community that the individual German could realize his own individuality and effectively be able to assume an appropriate self-fulfilling social role. Dr. Unold pointed out that one of the gravest dangers of liberalism was that it 'exaggerated the formal concept of freedom.' Instead of urging individuals to realize themselves by submitting to the will of the state, liberals 'always strove for freedom from the state' and gave evidence in 'every respect of a fundamental hatred' of it and even wanted to weaken it.[75] Contrary to the assumptions of liberalism, the Monists argued that the individual could not allow himself to stand opposed to and separate from central authority. The individual had, rather, to feel 'grateful'[76] to the state and to work in complete and willing harmony with it. Beyond this, the total resources of the nation had to be mobilized behind the state and discrete interests and conflicts had to be disregarded or subjugated. 'If a man,' Haeckel wrote, 'desires to have the advantages of living in an organized community, he has to consult not only his own fortune, but also that of the society, and of the "neighbours" who form the society.'[77] He had to comprehend his responsibility to the broader community. 'He must realize that its prosperity is his own prosperity, and that it cannot suffer without his own injury.' Haeckel sought to remind the Germans that 'this fundamental law of society is so simple and so inevitable that one cannot understand how it can be contradicted in theory or in practice; yet that is done today, and has been done for thousands of years.'[78]

In urging the Germans to become increasingly devoted servants of the state, the Monists also urged them to acknowledge that 'not enjoyment and happiness, but work is the basis of life.' The community had to absorb the total energies of the individual. To stimulate such devotion the Vice-President of the Monist League proposed the use of the slogan 'everyone a worker!'[80] as the basic principle of Monist social ideology and organization. A person who 'avoids social work,' he asserted, had to be considered a 'parasite' and was to be publicly accused of 'sinning against the essence of life.'[81] To express their total service and dedication to the community, individuals were encouraged to suppress 'greed' and 'lust' and were warned not to try to avoid suffering and sacrifice. The world, it was stated, had to be viewed and understood by the individual 'heroically' and reality had to be embraced in all its unavoidable harshness. The purpose of life was to be defined exclusively in terms of the preservation and strengthening, by what was termed 'social and species morality,' of the racial community as a whole.[82] In the final analysis all considerations of state policy depended solely on whether or not the policy was good for the nation or the race as a whole.[83]

At the same time that the Monists voiced their belief in the efficacy of authoritarian political organization, they were explicitly critical of any doctrine which advocated unhindered personal liberty and freedom. All ideas about human freedom in the liberal or existential sense were anti-evolutionary, they maintained, and were thereby a threat to the well-being of the racial community. As far as the Monists were concerned freedom existed in direct proportion to state power. 'The freedom of all is secured not in the framework of a weak state, but much more in the framework of a strong state.'[84] Freedom, in other words, meant submission to authority. 'The greater the freedom, the stronger must be the order,' they contended.[85] Freedom in the usual sense has never existed in the past and will never completely exist in the future. 'There have never been nations or states in which every person had full freedom and where no one was subordinated.'[86] Monism, it was felt, had to make the Germans aware of this.

Philosophically, Monist distrust of doctrines of political liberty and freedom rested on Haeckel's insistent denial of free will in man. Throughout his career he had strenuously argued that free will was a 'pure dogma based on an illusion.'[87] Neither by will nor by reason, could man triumph over the innate and compelling forces of nature or defy the natural laws of social and political reality. 'The great struggle,' Haeckel wrote, 'between the determinist and the indeterminist, between the opponent and sustainer of the freedom of the will, has ended today, after more than two thousand years, completely in favor of the determinist. The human will has no more freedom than that of the higher animals, from which it differs only in degree and not in kind.'[88] Reason and volition were, rather, expressions of the vital forces of nature which were manifested in the struggle for existence and in the continuing and unavoidable adaptation of the individual organism to its environment. The idea of political liberty, corollary of free will, was also part of the misleading dogma of European culture and therefore had to be strongly combatted. In the *Welträtsel*, Haeckel pointed out that in the eighteenth century the philosophical bases of liberty had been justifiably attacked by the materialistically inclined *philosophes*. Haeckel believed himself to be following in their tradition. He suggested, however, that the thinkers of the Enlightenment had been unavoidably limited in fully developing their negation of the idea of liberty by their inadequate scientific knowledge. But they were on the right road. In the nineteenth century there happily existed 'very different weapons' for the 'definitive destruction' of the idea of freedom. These were, of course, to be found in the 'arsenal of comparative physiology and evolution.'[89] The biological sciences and the concept of evolution had finally and conclusively succeeded in proving that no general principle of freedom could be applied to the individual. Hence there could be no political liberty in the usual bourgeois liberal sense. For Haeckel, man could only adapt to the inner drives of nature and to those laws of society which truly reflected nature; he could not overpower or overturn what is natural and hence irrevocable.

Based thus upon Haeckel's denial of free will and coupled with his general insistence on the insignificance and unimportance of man, the Monists launched an attack on liberal individualism, declaring it to be an enemy of the state and the race. They announced that their theory was 'opposed to exaggerated self-seeking individualism,' and to any way of life which 'tended to ignore . . . connection with the community.'[90] They lamented the fact that under the political conditions which prevailed in Germany, individuals, inspired by liberalism, 'ruthlessly allowed themselves to pursue their own class interests.'[91] As a consequence society gave increasing evidence of decadence while at the same time it tragically continued to allow the dissemination of political philosophies which espouse the unfettered liberty of the individual. Demands for unlimited personal freedom emanated from all stations of the political spectrum, from the clerical forces on the right all the way over to the socialists on the left. But certainly the worst sign of social decadence was the freedom which under the canons of liberalism, permitted the anarchists to preach their harmful doctrines. 'The exaggerated egotistical pretensions among more or less degenerate individuals has reached its climax in the criminal madness of anarchism.'[92] A philosophy which promulgated a weakening of state power to the extent that was demanded by anarchism was seen by the Monists to be nothing less than a pure case of political dementia.

In opposition to unfettered individual freedom, Monism they wrote,, wished to awaken a 'healthy drive for socialisation.' It desired to cultivate an 'insight' into the 'mutual dependence of the individual and the community.'[93] Evolution, it was asserted, demonstrated that everywhere the individual must be placed by an 'inborn drive' at the 'disposal of the species.'[94] Conversely, the survival of the individual was of no importance. Life itself was only of relative value and depended solely upon the usefulness of the individual organism to it own species and to the evolution of life in general.[95] No individual was of unique value in himself and no individual could appeal to a system of absolute ethics which guaranteed the preservation and the sanctity of life. It was Haeckel himself who argued the point: the precepts of moral law, like everything else, 'rest on biological grounds and have been developed in a natural way.'[96] Therefore, there could be no independent, intellectual, objective, rational, or ethically moral order of the world—no Kantian imperatives—which could serve as an absolute guide to mankind. Rather, all values were completely relative and arose only in the context of changing evolutionary needs for survival.

These sentiments of Haeckel's on ethics were enthusiastically echoed by his Monist disciples. 'We have no absolute ethics.'[97] the Vice-President of the Monist League wrote, and another insisted that 'objective good and evil in nature were nowhere to be found.'[98] They proclaimed along with Haeckel that 'heaven and hell are fallen' and that we have 'learned to see true reality.' Man could now be confident that the 'mask of a moral order of the world has dissolved into fog'; absolute morality had been only an ephemeral 'product of human poetry.'[99] Success and survival of the species in the course of evolution was to be the sole and absolute determinant of morality and ethics.

Applying the precepts of their naturalistic ethics, therefore, the Monists felt free to advise the Germans that it was only natural to subordinate themselves to the state and to the race. The individual had to understand and accept the fact that in organic nature 'thousands, indeed millions of cells and individuals are sacrificed' in order that the species itself should be able to survive in the struggle for existence.[100] The main task of politics was to teach the individual how to adapt to existing conditions no matter how harsh or immoral they might seem to be. For the Monists, the challenge of life was clear: 'An organism which cannot adjust to changed living conditions . . . goes under, and an organism which adjusts to new conditions of life too quickly and in a lop-sided way, degenerates.'[101] Politics had to show that the 'entire history of human civilization is in the final analysis nothing else than the sometimes more, sometimes less, conscious and successful process of the adaptation of single races, tribes, and individuals to the existing and to the changing conditions of life.'[102] And no individual could surmount this reality despite the high-sounding claims of liberalism.

On the basis of all this we are now in a position to see what the fundamental ideological presuppositions of Monism actually are. In conceptual terms which were obviously identical with those of fascism and National Socialism later on, Monism wavered between a view of man which, on the one hand, was both disparaging and problematical, and, on the other, spoke of the Germans as belonging to a biologically superior racial community. Like National Socialism, Monism rejected the concept of an 'artificial' and 'mechanical' political community, deriding it as a product of bourgeois liberalism and substituting in its place a program for the organic racial state. Denying the 'superficial' and 'legalistic' claims of liberalism, Monism constantly stressed the need for a deep sense of rootedness on the part of the individual, and for establishing his bond with the larger cosmic and irrational forces of nature and race. Like all fascist ideology, Monism expressed a protest against the atomization and alienation of man in modern life and a hope for the evolution of a more natural, integrated, and harmoniously functioning community. For Monism, as for National Socialism, politics was to be simply the straightforward application of the laws of biology. In the pages of its journals, in its many other publications, and in its frequent public gatherings, Monism proposed that the more quickly Germany separated herself from the Christian West and from bourgeois liberalism, the more certain would its future be and the more successful it would be in the struggle for life and for survival. How Monism sought to disassociate Germany from Christianity must therefore concern us next.

NOTES

1. On Anti-Western ideas in German thought, see Aurel Kolnai, *The War Against the West* (New York: Viking, 1938); Stern, *The Politics of Cultural Despair* and Edmond Vermeil, 'L'Allemagne Hitlérienne et L'Idée International,' *L'Esprit International*, X (1936), 187–206.
2. Haeckel, *The Riddle of the Universe*, p. 11.
3. *Ibid.*, p. 37.
4. Ernst Haeckel, *Eternity. World War Thoughts on Life and Death, Religion, and the Theory of Evolution* (New York: Truth Seeker, 1916), p. 85.
5. Haeckel, *Riddle of the Universe*, p. 107.
6. *Ibid.*, p. 125.
7. *Ibid.*, p. 107.
8. *Ibid.*, p. 201.
9. *Ibid.*, p. 14.
10. *Ibid.*, pp. 14–15.
11. *Ibid.*, p. 15.
12. Haeckel, *The History of Creation*, I, 11.
13. Ernst Haeckel, *The Evolution of Man: A Popular Exposition of the Principal Points of Human Ontogeny and Phylogeny* (New York: Appleton, 1903), II, 456.
14. Haeckel, *Eternity*, p. 116.
15. Haeckel, *Evolution of Man*, II, 458.
16. Johannes Unold, *Der Monismus und seine Ideale* (Leipzig: Thomas, 1908), p. 53.
17. Haeckel, *History of Creation*, I, 280–281.
18. Johannes Unold, 'Vom Sinn des Lebens,' *Der Monismus*, V (1910), 546.
19. *Ibid.*
20. Ernst Haeckel, *The Wonders of Life* (New York: Harper, 1904), pp. 461, 462.
21. *Ibid.*, p. 467.
22. On the importance of the biological side of man in Freud, see Herbert Marcuse, *Eros and Civilization* (Boston: Beacon Press, 1955), p. 21. Professor Marcuse writes, 'Freud traces the development of repression in the instinctual structure of the individual. The fate of human freedom and happiness is fought out and decided in the struggle of the instincts—literally a struggle of life and death—

in which soma and psyche, nature and civilization participate. This biological and at the same time sociological dynamic is the center of Freud's metapsychology.'
23. On Freud's caution against allowing the passions to have free reign, see Alfred Kazin, 'The Freudian Revolution Analyzed,' in Benjamin Nelson (ed.), *Freud and the Twentieth Century* (New York: Meridian Books, 1957), pp. 20-21. Professor Kazin writes: 'For Freud the continuous sacrifice of "nature" that is demanded by "civilization" meant that it was only through rationality and conscious awareness that maturity could be achieved. Far from counseling license, his most famous formula became—"Where id was, ego shall be"—the id representing the unconscious, the ego our dominant and purposive sense of ourselves.'
24. On the general intellectual significance of Freud, see H. Stuart Hughes, *Consciousness and Society* (New York: Knopf, 1958), Ch. IV; and on the history of European naturalism, see John Herman Randall, Jr., *The Career of Philosophy* (New York: Columbia Univ. Press, 1965), I, *passim*.
25. Heinrich Schmidt, 'Die Stellung des Menschen in der Natur,' *Der Monismus*, I (1906), 18.
26. Haeckel, *History of Creation*, I, 172.
27. Artur Hennig, 'Der Monismus und die Kunst,' *Der Monismus*, III (1908), 149.
28. L. Bergfeld, 'Entstehung, Sinn und Ende des Lebens,' *Der Monismus*, IV (1909), 252.
29. Johannes Seidel, 'Das Wesen des Monismus,' *Der Monismus*, VI (1911), 289.
30. Anonymous, 'Ein Heisses Sehnen,' *Der Monismus*, I (1906), 65.
31. Haeckel, *The Riddle of the Universe*, p. 9.
32. *Ibid.*, pp. 362-363.
33. *Ibid.*, p. 363.
34. Heinrich Ziegler, *Die Verebungslehre in der Biologie und in der Soziologie* (Jena: Fischer, 1918), p. 296.
35. Haeckel, *History of Creation*, II, 310.
36. *Ibid.*, pp. 321-322.
37. For a general discussion of the connection that was made in racist thought between external and internal characteristics, see Mosse, *The Culture of Western Europe*, Chapter IV. It is an indication of how seriously Haeckel believed that the physical appearance of a person was a true measure of inward qualities when in 1899 he wrote to his friend, Frida von Uslar-Gleichen, with whom he was having a love affair: 'Because from the moment when our two blond Germanic personalities confronted each other on the morning of June 17, and looked into each other's true blue eyes, I knew that our souls were near akin.' See Ernst Haeckel, *The Love Letters of Ernst Haeckel* (New York: Harper, 1930), p. 63.
38. Ernst Haeckel, *The Wonders of Life* (New York: Harper, 1904), p. 390.
39. *Ibid.*, p. 391.
40. Haeckel, *Riddle of the Universe*, p. 125.

41. Ernst Haeckel, *The History of Creation* (Fourth ed., London: Kegan Paul, 1899), II, 434.
42. *Ibid.*
43. Haeckel, *Wonders of Life*, p. 390.
44. F. Siebert, 'Ueber die Stellung des Menschen in der Natur,' *Der Monismus*, III (1908), 297.
45. Unold, *Der Monismus und seine Ideale*, p. 100.
46. Ewalt Fincke, 'Vaterlandsliebe und Internationalismus,' *Das monistiche Jahrhundert*, II (1913–14), 988.
47. *Ibid.*
48. *Ibid.*
49. *Ibid.*, p. 989.
50. Haeckel, *History of Creation*, 1876 ed., II, 332.
51. *Ibid.*
52. Johannes Unold, *Politik im Lichte der Entwicklungslehre* (Munich: Reinhardt, 1912), p. 125.
53. Otto Juliusburger, 'Gedanken zur Ethik des Monismus,' *Der Monismus*, II (1907), 296.
54. 'Zur Frage- Nationalismus—Internationalismus,' *Das monistische Jahrhundert*, II, 1012. (This statement was submitted by the Krefeld branch of the Monist League. While not objecting to the racism of the statement, the editorial board of *Das monistische Jahrhundert*, cautioned against isolating Germany from the rest of the world by the advocacy of doctrines which unduly emphasized racial exclusiveness).
55. *Ibid.*
56. *Ibid.*
57. Johannes Unold, 'Monismus und Frauenfrage,' *Der Monismus*, VI (1911), 537.
58. *Ibid.*, p. 540.
59. Every once in a while, for example, Haeckel would declare his support for internationalism. Thus, while the First World War was raging he wrote that the 'higher civilized nations should exercise mutual tolerance towards each other and combine for higher common cultural work in the service of true humanity.' But this statement appeared in a book which was at the same time completely devoted to demonstrating the racial superiority of the Germans and which argued for the destruction of Germany's enemies and of the need for international German hegemony. For Haeckel, in other words, international peace and cooperation would come when Germany became the world's greatest power. See Haeckel, *Eternity*, p. 141.

It must also be noted that unless one was familiar with the writings of the German Monists in the publications of the German Monist League then their Volkism might not be readily apparent. Thus, when the German Monist League sponsored an International Congress of Monism in Hamburg, in September, 1911, there were delegates from all over the world including the American freethinker from the University of Chicago, Thaddeus Burr Wakeman, and

Paul Carus, editor of the Chicago based journal, *The Monist*. The deliberations of the Congress centered on the battle against revealed religion and on the need for international scientific cooperation. The Volkish ideas of the German Monists were hardly in evidence and could not be gleaned from the content of their speeches. See the reaction to the Congress of Thaddeus Burr Wakeman, in *Addresses of T. B. Wakeman at and in Reference to the First Monist Congress at Hamburg in September, 1911* (Cos Cob, Conn.: n.p., 1913). To Wakeman and the other Americans who accompanied him to Germany, the Congress represented only an attack on metaphysical and traditional religious ideas.

60. Fincke, 'Vaterlandsliebe und Internationalismus,' p. 987. The *monistische Jahrhundert* did publish one article which took issue with Fincke's racism by the famous geneticist, Paul Kammerer: 'Nationalismus und Biologie,' II (1913-14), 1177-1185. It was probably of some significance that Kammerer was Jewish. After the Russian Revolution, Kammerer settled in the Soviet Union, where he committed suicide in 1926 after falsifying some experiments in genetics. On Kammerer's Jewishness and other biographical details, see S. Winninger, *Grosse Jüdische National-Biographie* (Cernauti: Orient [1928]), III, 392.

The editorial board of *Das monistische Jahrhundert* also took exception to Fincke's article, but not for Kammerer's reasons. They did not seem to object to Fincke's racism, but only to his radical proposal for the isolation of Germany.

61. Fincke, 'Vaterlandsliebe und Internationalismus,' pp. 987-988.
62. *Ibid.*, p. 988.
63. *Ibid.*
64. *Ibid.*, p. 990. Like the Nazis later on, Fincke also denied the international objectivity of science. For him a nation discovered the world in its own way and according to its own national inclinations.
65. Seidel, 'Das Wesen des Monismus,' p. 299.
66. *Ibid.*
67. Haeckel, *Eternity*, p. 129.
68. *Ibid.*
69. Johannes Unold, 'Die Bedeutung des Monismus für Staat und Gesellschaft,' *Das monistische Jahrhundert*, II (1913-14), 739.
70. Unold, *Politik im Lichte der Entwicklungslehre*, p. 74.
71. *Ibid.*
72. *Ibid.*
73. Haeckel, *Eternity*, p. 129.
74. Unold, *Politik im Lichte der Entwicklungslehre*, p. 74.
75. *Ibid.*, p. 168.
76. *Ibid.*, p. 77.
77. Haeckel, *Riddle of the Universe*, p. 350.
78. *Ibid.*
79. Unold, *Der Monismus und seine Ideale*, p. 69.
80. *Ibid.*, p. 75.
81. *Ibid.*

82. *Ibid.*, p. 76.
83. *Ibid.*, pp. 79–80.
84. Unold, *Politik im Lichte der Entwicklungslehre*, p. 168.
85. *Ibid.*
86. Ziegler, *Die Vererbungslehre in der Biologie und in der Soziologie*, p. 320.
87. Haeckel, *Riddle of the Universe*, p. 16.
88. *Ibid.*, pp. 130–131.
89. *Ibid.*, p. 131.
90. Johannes Unold, 'Die Bedeutung des Monismus für das praktische Leben,' *Der Monismus*, II (1907), 287.
91. *Ibid.*, p. 283.
92. *Ibid.*, p. 288.
93. *Ibid.*, p. 287.
94. *Ibid.*
95. Haeckel, *Wonders of Life*, p. 389.
96. *Ibid.*, p. 413.
97. Unold, 'Die Bedeutung des Monismus für das praktische Leben,' p. 297.
98. Herman Kroell, 'Gut und Böse in monistische Beleuchtung,' *Der Monismus*, III (1908), 67.
99. Immanuel Lewy, 'Reformation unseres Gemütslebens,' *Der Monismus*, III (1908), 164.
100. Unold, 'Die Bedeutung des Monismus für das praktische Leben,' p. 287.
101. Seidel, 'Das Wesen des Monismus,' p. 295.
102. Unold, *Der Monismus und seine Ideale*, p. 82.

Chapter Three

Monism and Christianity

HAECKEL and his Monist followers seldom lost an opportunity to criticize established religion. They viewed Christianity as the principal force in the modern world impeding the victory of science, and they accused established religion in Germany of spiritual decay and political reaction. In the place of the Christianity they continually denounced the Haeckelian Monists proposed that a new pantheistic religion of nature be created which would, they felt, more adequately serve and express the spiritual and national needs of the Germans.

The Monist attack on Christianity came at a time when traditional religious beliefs were being forcefully challenged not only in Germany but throughout the rest of Europe as well. As at no other time in the past, revealed religion seemed deeply threatened, and many would have subscribed to the prophecy of T. H. Huxley that 'Christianity is doomed to fall.'[1] For Huxley and other intellectuals and writers who accepted a naturalistic point of view, the impending demise of Christianity was predicted directly on the latest and inescapable findings of science, which explained the nature of man and society in terms of mechanical physics and evolutionary biology. Bolstered by science, they uninhibitedly, even vociferously rejected the notion that man possessed a soul and scorned as the rankest superstition the idea that man could have been directly created by God.[2]

The Haeckelian Monist attack on Christianity and traditional creeds was in one sense a typical nineteenth-century critique of religion as outworn mythology, and it is for this that they are usually remembered. It would, for example, be difficult to discover a general history of nineteenth-century European culture which fails to place Haeckel's name alongside that of Huxley and Tyndall in England, Renan in France, and David Strauss and the other members of the Tübingen School of theologians in Germany. To the extent that Haeckel and the Monists viewed the Judaeo-Christian cosmology as standing directly in the path of advancing scientific knowledge, they may be considered typical naturalistic atheists of the nineteenth century. Throughout all of their writings they expressed the idea that 'where faith commences. science ends,'[3] and espoused a non-miraculous and empirical creation of the world. Science they all explained, must overcome the 'irrational superstition'[4] and false knowledge of mankind's religious past.

The association of Haeckel and the Monists with nineteenth century naturalistic and materialistic atheism reveals, however, only one side of their relationship with Christianity and traditional religion. Undeniably, they belonged to the school of the scientific critics of religion. But at the same time, and even primarily, though this has been overlooked, is that they belonged to the general intellectual movement of nationalistic opposition to traditional Western Christianity which developed in Germany in the last century. The significance of their encounter with religion is to be found in the fact that they played a vital and critical role in the transformation of traditional faith into the pagan, racist, and often occult forms of belief which came to life in Germany in the later decades of the nineteenth century and which continued to flourish later on under National Socialism. The positive Christianity of the Nazis and the even more radical non-Christian sects and cults which existed under their aegis can be traced back directly not only to such rightist nationalists as Chamberlain, Lagarde, Mathilde Ludendorff, and Adolf Bartels, but also to Haeckel and the Monists.[5] Sharing the desire of other radical nationalists for a new Germanic faith, it was they who founded a non-Christian religious movement based on evolutionary Monism which became one of the most important sources for the religious program of Volkism and National Socialism.

It may be said that the vigor with which Haeckel and the Monists pursued their attack on Christianity was, in large measure, rooted in the rapidly changing political and religious history of Germany in the nineteenth century. Especially after the Revolution of 1848, the political importance of both Protestantism and Catholicism in Germany increased immeasurably. Reacting to the attacks which were made upon them by the Liberals in 1848, the Protestant clergy drew ever closer to the Throne and to the feudal aristocracy, and reasserted their traditional conservative stance. Consequently, they came to be frequently associated with the forces opposed to modern culture and, in addition, many complained that the well-springs of faith were close to depletion in the Lutheran Church.

In the second half of the nineteenth century, Catholicism also emerged in Germany as a distinct and separate political force with interests of its own. Condemned to minority status by the exclusion of Austria from the German Confederation in 1866, the Catholics, unlike the Protestants, were unable to identify completely with the Germany of Bismarck. The universalism of Catholicism and its political philosophy which rejected domination of the state over the individual and the church, made it suspect in the eyes of German nationalism. Many came, moreover, to fear Catholicism as an organized political force after the founding of the increasingly powerful Center Party in 1870.[6]

It was Catholicism that felt the major thrust of Monist criticism of Christianity primarily because the Monists alleged that it was estranged from the rising tide of German nationalism. But at the same time the Monists also deeply lamented the political conservatism and intellectual shallowness of German Protestantism. For them Christianity as a whole was a destructive and a superstitious faith and they therefore condemned it as an impediment to a fully satisfying spiritual life for Germany.

The Monist approach to Christianity was, of course, set down and developed by Haeckel. Among his disciples acknowledgement of that fact was unanimous. They all repeatedly and worshipfully testified to the fact that Haeckel had taught them the truth about Christianity and that he was responsible for the intellectual revolution which had taken place in their own lives, their liberation from the bonds of theistic religion. 'All those,' a leading Monist wrote, 'who have experienced that freedom for themselves will first of all thank Haeckel and will thereby celebrate ... as a cultural act of the highest rank his forthright and courageous action in freeing the spirituality of mankind from the chains of dogmatic religion.'[7] It was Haeckel, another Monist wrote, who 'gave me the courage of my faith—others would say: disbelief.'[8]

It was Haeckel, he continued, who destroyed Christianity by 'giving to mankind a better explanation of the nature of the entire world.'[9] It was Haeckel's 'badge of honor that he earned the hatred of the clergy, more so than any of his contemporaries. He carried it with dignity, like one who knows that his final victory is secure. With a clear vision he superintended the entire fight for the enlightenment of science against the teachings of the church and understood the place of his own work within this evolution.'[10] For the Monists, therefore, Haeckel's view of Christianity meant the dawn of a new religious era. His insights into religion were like an 'apple from the tree of knowledge' and were a 'first breach in the fortress of religious belief.'[11]

For the first two decades of his life Haeckel was a convinced Protestant and his early religious life was somewhat typical for those Germans who had rejected the conservative orthodoxy of traditional Lutheranism, on the one hand, and the radical and rational faith of Enlightenment Deism, on the other. His family had come under the influence of the philosophy of Friedrich Schleiermacher, whose theology attempted to transcend the rigid dogmas of revealed faith, emphasized the emotional side of religion, and held to a conception of the divine which clearly bordered on pantheism. My 'pious parents,' Haeckel wrote, 'belonged to the Free Evangelical Church then under the charge of Schleiermacher,' and he described himself as a 'convinced and zealous adherent of that liberal form of Protestantism,' during his youth.[12] He attended church, gave strong evidence of a belief in God, and professed a doctrinal broadmindedness. 'I attach,' he wrote, 'no great importance to the slight distinctions and differences that are to be found among true Christians regarding the opinions concerning the personality of Christ; after all, scarcely two people have quite the same conception of this question; it will always adapt itself and become modified according to the ideas of the particular individual.'[13] Then, however, his university studies in natural science and medicine (1852–1858) and his 'many travels' effected a change of mind after 'heavy moral conflict.' Ultimately, he reached the 'conviction that the mystic faith-teachings of the Christian religion were completely irreconcilable with the certain results of scientific experience.' He subsequently became 'convinced . . . that the Christian religion, as far as the ethical and practical affairs and conduct of life were concerned, gave foundations just as little unassailable, unreliable, and unsatisfactory in every point of view as were those of its theoretic view of the world.'[14] And when he became a physician he noted that he was able to witness at first hand the cruelty and the irrationality of life which also helped to undermine his faith.[15]

Yet, despite his ideological defection from Christianity, Haeckel did remain, technically speaking, a member of the church for most of his life. It was only when he was already close to eighty that he made the final break and at a time when the Monist League was officially campaigning for mass resignation from the traditional faiths. In an article written to coincide with his departure from the church, Haeckel conceded that as a young man 'it would have been only natural to have given proper expression to his conviction outwardly by withdrawal from the Evangelical Church.' But he remained in the church, he wrote, solely 'out of regard for family and friends' to whom leaving would have 'brought heavy sorrow and injury.'[16]

However, even before his conversion to pantheism, and while he was still a convinced Protestant, Haeckel displayed a marked hatred for Catholicism. In letters to his parents written from Würzburg in the 1850's, he made frequent and disparaging references to the strange religious habits of the Bavarian Catholics, to the sinister intentions of the Jesuits, and once to a Catholic procession where 'in the middle of it was the Bishop, or whatever he might have been, a fat, bloated, well-fed priest, vestured in gold and silver.'[17] And in 1859, when he was travelling and studying in Italy he experienced a revulsion against the Catholic south which in its intensity could easily be compared to Luther's reaction to his Italian journey at the beginning of the sixteenth century. Haeckel found Catholicism in Italy to be 'disgraceful,' 'outrageously superstitious,' and a religion which subjected the people to 'papal despotism.' While in Rome he felt that any good Christian must immediately turn into a 'heathen' rather than suffer the oppressiveness and backwardness of the prevalent Catholicism.[18] And about this time even his belief in Protestantism was being quickly eroded away and he wrote to his fiancée, Anna Sethe, that he conceived his mission in life to be the rescue of the Germans from the 'chains of slavery' which had been imposed upon them by the 'priests.'[19]

Haeckel's initial disappointment with Christianity gave way in his writings to absolute hostility and downright hatred. His analysis was direct and uncomplicated. He viewed Christian culture as a deterioration from the more advanced level of development which civilization had reached in classical antiquity. For him, the coming of Christianity initiated the intellectual and spiritual decay of the civilized world. Until its advent the ancient world exhibited a positive and aggressive spirit that was the mark of fundamental social health; subsequently Christianity, with its otherworldly ascetic mentality, had weakened this spirit and destroyed the social fabric of civilization. Thus, for the past two thousand years European culture had been growing increasingly decadent.

Although Haeckel continually and sharply attacked traditional religion in his writings from the 1860's onwards, his most extensive and sharply polemical treatment of Christianity appeared in the *Welträtsel*. No ordinary book, the *Welträtsel* became, by its popularity, the anti-Christian manifesto *par excellence* of the first decades of this century, and, to borrow a phrase, it stood for the final solution of the Christian problem. As serious in its denunciation of prevailing religion as Marx's *Communist Manifesto* was of contemporary capitalism, the *Welträtsel* was even more radical in its approach to religion than the anti-Christian strictures of Paul de Lagarde or Houston Stewart Chamberlain. It admitted to no half-way measures, no compromise with the old faith, no Germanic Christianity. Only a new religion of nature would suffice. Christianity, by inverting the natural hierarchy of the world with its doctrines of equality, submission, and weakness had led the Germans to the brink of biological collapse. The *Welträtsel* therefore did not feature a dispassionate and objective rendering of the nature and history of Christianity. It was an anti-religious tract and it became the chief anti-Christian German primer.

In its historical evolution, Haeckel wrote in the *Welträtsel*, Christianity had passed through four distinctive periods. At its inception 'primitive Christianity' had advanced a few admirable ethical ideals which were, however, only less intelligent restatements of beliefs which had 'existed in theory and in practice centuries before the time of Christ.'[20] The Golden Rule itself was not of Christian origin but was plagiarized from more ancient sources.[21] Christ himself, Haeckel admitted, was a 'noble prophet and enthusiast . . . full of the love of humanity.' However, he was intellectually retarded. Christ, Haeckel pointed out, was 'below the level of classical culture' and 'knew nothing beyond the Jewish traditions.' In any case, none of his writings have survived—a fact that, moreover, creates doubts as to whether he actually lived or not. All that we possess of his teachings was taken from the Gospels of the New Testament, and because they were compiled after his death they are completely unreliable. And, in any event, the Gospels themselves were only the fantastic inventions of the Council of Nicaea.[22]

Once the 'primitive phase' of Christianity passed, dissolution and corruption of the church set in. During its second stage, 'Papal Christianity,' from the fourth to the sixteenth century, Christianity became particularly distorted. In the course of these centuries, Haeckel wrote, the papacy 'tainted the spiritual life of Europe.' Papal despotism darkened the Middle Ages. It brought 'death to all freedom of mental life, decay to science, corruption to all morality.' In contrast with the 'noble height to which the life of the human mind attained in classical antiquity,' it had under 'papal Christianity' deteriorated to a 'level which in respect of the knowledge of the truth, can only be termed barbarian.' Under Catholic influence, all of medieval culture was corrupted. The philosophy, architecture, and poetry of the Middle Ages was 'richly developed' but the conservative principles of their creation did not 'tend to the cultivation' but rather to the 'suppression of free mental research.' Adherence to the essential attitudes of Christianity—the 'exclusive preparing for the unknown eternity beyond the tomb, the contempt for nature, the withdrawal from the study of it'—was enforced as a sacred duty by the Catholic authorities. Frederick the Great was correct, Haeckel concluded in his remarks about the Middle Ages, when he described the period from Constantine to the Reformation as being completely 'insane.'[23]

Having thus disposed of fifteen centuries of European history, Haeckel conceded that the Reformation, the third stage in the evolution of Christianity, had brought a change for the better. He celebrated Luther as a German hero and proposed that the Reformation was the 'commencement of a new epoch.' It represented, he wrote, a 'new birth of reason, the reawakening of science, which the iron hand of the

Christian papacy had relentlessly crushed for twelve hundred years.' It was, in reality, the Reformation which made possible the eighteenth century Enlightenment.[24]

But the victory of science and reason was short-lived. After the eighteenth century religion raised its head once again. For Haeckel, therefore, the nineteenth century, the fourth stage, was a period of 'pseudo-Christianity.' During this last period, he insisted, religion was completely emptied of all content, but still managed to claim the allegiance of millions of people. In the Protestant camp the nineteenth century witnessed a naive attempt to synthesize science and religion. The result was that 'scarcely anything remained of the destructive teaching of faith.' Protestantism failed to recognize that 'dogmatic Christianity has lost every foundation.' Modern Protestantism, he asserted, is a 'religious lie of the worst character.'[25] Its faith is superficial and its fundamental beliefs are scientifically untenable. Neither the orthodoxy of Hengstenberg nor the liberalism of Harnack, Ritschl, or Troeltsch could save it.

Catholicism also, he felt, was bankrupt in the nineteenth century, and he raged against the Catholic church. It had, Haeckel complained, reacted negatively to everything modern. The Doctrine of Papal Infallibility and the Syllabus of Errors demonstrated beyond any doubt its backwardness. It had to be recognized that the history of the papacy 'appears to the impartial student as an unscrupulous tissue of lies and deceit, a reckless pursuit of absolute mental despotism and secular power, a frivolous contradiction of all the high moral precepts which Christianity enunciates.' The great majority of popes were 'pitiful imposters, many of them utterly worthless and vicious.'[26]

Thus, to counteract the Catholic Church the *Kulturkampf* had to be pursued. Haeckel lamented its termination by Bismarck who he felt had misjudged and underestimated the 'unsurpassed cunning and treachery of the Roman *curia*,' and the 'correlative ingratitude and credulity of the uneducated masses.' After 1890, when Bismarck had already fallen from power, Haeckel became increasingly critical of the courting of the Catholics by the government of William II. He reacted bitterly to the important role which was being accorded to the Center Party of the Reichstag. For Haeckel, this could only mean that Germany was in great danger. The Catholic Church, he warned, was gaining too much power partly through the 'unscrupulous intrigues and serpentine bends of its slippery Jesuitical politics, partly through the false church-politics of the German government and the marvellous political incompetence of the German people.' Germany, he fumed, had thus to 'endure the pitiful spectacle of the Catholic "Centre" being the most important section of the Reichstag, and the fate of our humiliated country depending on a papal party, which does not constitute numerically a third part of the nation.'[27] Haeckel's extremist, inflammatory language manifested the complete latent substance of his two statements.[28]

In place of Christianity, Haeckel was prepared to offer the Germans a new religion which was to be derived entirely from science and from the study of nature. He proclaimed to the Germans in ecstatic, poetic, and radically literal terms that *'Alles ist Natur, Natur ist Alles.'*[29] and that the 'goddess of truth dwells in the temple of nature, in the green woods, on the blue sea, and on the snowy summits of the hills.'[30] The old religious world was characterized, by the 'gloom of the cloister' and the 'clouds of incense of the Christian Churches,'[31] but the new religion of Monism would find its faith in the 'loving study of nature and its laws.'[32] He was expressing his most deeply felt belief when he proposed that Germany could literally save itself by religious devotion to nature and to natural law.

When Haeckel spoke of nature it is clear that he meant, of course, 'holy German nature,' which he frequently described as his 'true milieu.'[33] In a letter to his friend, Hermann Allmers, he once remarked that he would not trade German nature for anything that he had seen abroad, no matter how beautiful. 'Admittedly,' he wrote of the south, 'we have no laurel trees and myrtles, no palms and stone-pines, no opuntias and agaves on sun-drenched heights, no eternally blue sky, no immense dark-blue sea. We have, however, in our Germany the unmatched lovely green forest, and we have the freshly swelling moss within it and the bubbling springs and the singing and chirping of birds, and we have the incomparable majestic change of the seasons, the lovely spring, merry summer, graceful autumn, and cozy winter, all of which are lacking in the sad south.'[34] For Haeckel, it was only 'from honest German soil' that it was really possible to 'absorb a love of freedom and life, inner joy in art and nature, and a genuine striving after the true, the good, and the beautiful.'[35]

Haeckel desired, therefore, to be able with his theory of evolution and religion of Monism, to bring the Germans into a satisfying and harmonious relationship with what he considered to be their unique natural surroundings. He sought in his scientific-religious program to link the Germans to their native soil, on the one hand, and to the larger cosmos, on the other. He assumed that the Germans, once freed from Western Christianity, would then be able to give themselves over completely to his new Monist religion. 'It is quite certain,' he wrote, 'that the Christian system must give way to the Monistic.'[36]

Haeckel elaborated his pantheistic religion along the lines of his theory of evolution and his philosophy of nature. Although he considered himself to be a mechanistic materialist, it has long been recognized that in actuality Haeckel's philosophy of nature contained a great many idealist and vitalist assumptions which quite obviously transcended his materialism. Haeckel assumed, for example, in a rather mystical and religious way, the absolute unity and constancy of nature. For him, the cosmos was incontestably an 'all-embracing whole'[37] and he readily preached that the laws of nature were 'absolute' and that they were 'true for the entire universe.'[38] Thus, he piously wrote of the inherent regularity of nature: 'When a stone is thrown into the air, and falls to earth according to definite laws, or when in a solution of salt a crystal is formed, the phenomenon is neither more nor less a mechanical manifestation of life than the growth and flowering of plants, than the propagation of animals or the activity of their senses, than the perception or the formation of thought in man.'[39] In fact, for Haeckel, the entire meaning of evolution was revealed in the unity of the cosmos and in the 'harmonious connection of all the great and general phenomena of organic nature.'[40]

Not only was the cosmos an interconnected whole but Haeckel also insisted on a theory of pan-psychism. For him, there was no difference between the organic and the inorganic. 'The distinction,' he wrote, 'which has been made between animate and inanimate bodies does not exist.'[41] All matter was alive and possessed all the mental attributes which are normally ascribed only to the higher animals. 'Desire and dislike, lust and antipathy, attraction and repulsion, are common to

MONISM AND CHRISTIANITY

all atoms.'[42] All atoms possess, in addition, souls. 'Just as the mass of the atoms is indestructible and unchanging, so also are the inseparably connected atom-souls eternal and undying.'[43] For Haeckel, in other words, the entire universe was alive, and evolution was simply a manifestation of the profound creativity of nature. Indeed, his scientific ideas were far from reflecting ordinary mechanistic materialism.[44]

Having concluded that nature was alive, Haeckel elevated predominant scientific hypotheses of the nineteenth century, such as the theory of spatial ether and the laws of the conservation of mass and energy, to the level of religious dogma and pantheistic faith. Matter, energy, and ether became for him the emanation of some divine spirit and he taught his followers to worship them. 'The Monistic idea of God which alone is compatible with our present knowledge of nature, recognizes the divine spirit in all things.' 'God is everywhere.' 'Every atom is animated, and so is the ether.'[45] Thus, Haeckel presented the universe to his followers as a 'colossal organism'[46] bound together by a 'mobile cosmic ether' which by its universal diffusion 'created divinity'[47] and linked each individual to the divine cosmos. 'Ever more irresistibly is it borne in upon us that even the human soul is but an insignificant part of the all-embracing "world-soul," just as the human body is only a small fraction of the great organised physical world.'[48] And Haeckel attempted to evoke the qualities of this divinely animated world to his followers in terms that can only be described as religious. Equating God with nature he wrote: 'God is almighty; He is the single Creator, the single Cause of all things. . . . God is absolute perfection. . . . God is the sum of all energy and matter'—and Monism alone understands the true 'unity of God and nature.'[49]

Like their mentor, Haeckel's followers spoke of the deep bonds which united them with nature. And like Haeckel they enthusiastically expressed the conviction that 'nature is all soul' and insisted on the necessity and desirability of a deep emotional attachment to the natural world and to the soil of Germany.[50] It was Haeckel, one Monist wrote, who was responsible for 'rooting me once again in the soil of my homeland and thereby establishing for me my moral existence.'[51] The Monists all piously believed that within evolutionary religion the 'cosmos itself becomes God'[52] and they continually expressed their 'unshatterable attachment to *All-Natur*.'[53] In obvious imitation of

Haeckel's style and mode of religious expression, the writing of the Monists was frequently couched also in the language of religious apostrophe. For example, in one of the issues of the official journal of the Monist League, incantatory descriptions celebrate the natural world as origin, substance, and end of human life: 'Nature unites us and holds us together with unbreakable bonds; it is the motherly womb from which we have sprung; it is the ocean in which our lives are absorbed. Innumerable and inseparable are the threads which bind us to the infinite cosmos.'[54]

Thus, for the Monists, evolutionary religion meant the final abandonment of Christianity and the total 'immersion of oneself in nature.'[55] The 'modern individual,' they contended, desires to be 'in and of nature'[56] and wants to 'feel its pulse because he is blood of its blood.'[57] In nature alone man finds his roots. 'The more fundamentally man contemplates nature, all the more deep and exalted is the feeling of interrelatedness with all of organic nature, the more he feels that nature is his homeland and that it can become the basis for his own life.'[58] It is for this reason that biology had to become the queen of modern science. It is from biology that man learns the most about the 'unity of all organic life' and the truth that 'all organisms, from the simplest amoebae and bacteria, to plants and animals, all the way up to man, are similar and equal to each other because they follow the same general laws, have the same characteristics, and are blood relations of each other.'[59] Furthermore, one can find real peace and contentment only in nature. And as one Monist expressed it: 'I must let it be known that the holiest hours for me have been when I have submerged myself in the wonders of living nature and have observed how unconscious life creates forms, performs acts, and expresses needs, just as people do.' It is then that he perceives how the forces of nature 'control my life just as they do plants and animals.'[60] Since the observation of nature produces such revelations, it is essentially a religious activity, and the Monists accordingly cautioned that a person who contemplates nature assumes a great responsibility. 'We may not be trusted to contemplate the basic facts of biology, be it only the life of an ant-hill or the budding and blossoming of plants, without the deepest reverence.'[61] And especially the evolution of man had to be studied in a religious spirit.

'The idea of the evolution of mankind from the animal kingdom not only does not fill us with shame, but rather awakens in us a deep feeling of awe, wonder, and contemplation before the development of nature of which we are a part.'[62]

The new pantheistic religion which Haeckel and his Monist followers developed involved not only the deification of the cosmos but also the revival of many symbols of ancient German pagan religion and mythology. In their religious beliefs the Monists very frequently linked nature worship to the German pre-Christian past. For example, in an article written for the youth movement of the Monist League, it was explained that the word Easter was derived from Ostara, the name of the ancient mythological German goddess of spring. The young members of the League were told how in ancient times the Germans, 'who lived a very hard life,' had celebrated the rebirth of nature in the spring. It was to this concept of rebirth, first developed by their 'blue-eyed, blond-haired' ancestors, that the young Monists were implored to dedicate themselves. Celebrate Easter, they were advised, not by attending church, but by leaving the confining walls of the city, and by going out into the countryside to observe and live in nature.[63] The young Monists were assured that in the spring the countryside and nature would cure them of all unhappiness and would teach them the undeniable truth that only in the northern Germanic climates have the highest cultures been able to evolve. Whereas the tropics have enervated men, the author pointed out, the 'magic' of a 'German spring' would revivify them. Those who sought the joys of German nature would learn that it was 'hardly an accident that culture had evolved to its highest degree in countries that enjoy a changing summer and winter.'[64]

The congenial pure nature religion of the ancient Germanic tribes would survive yet, the Monists often pointed out, had not Christianity been introduced as a corrupting influence. The ancient Germans were in fact justifiably repelled by the teachings of Christianity—teachings which might have been acceptable had they not been warped by the legalistic Jewish framework into which the Palestinian, Christ, cast them.[65] But in this warped form the 'new religion was forced upon them' early in their history by the Franks.[66] With its 'well known cunning,'[67] the Christian church propagated its emphasis on the next world and its passive attitude towards this one, and thus almost completely succeeded in sapping the natural, 'inborn' strength of the healthy 'nordic' people.[68]

The Monists pictured themselves, therefore, as rebelling against an 'oriental religion' which was 'foreign' to themselves and to this world.[69] 'No longer.' they asserted, 'can we allow ourselves to dissipate our strength [in exchange] for the fantasies of a shadowy other world. Our full attention is demanded by this world.'[70] Further adherence to Christianity could only lead to the decline and deterioration of Germany. In fact, the only thing that had saved Germany thus far was the fact that it never really took Christianity seriously in the first place. 'Happily . . . the purely Christian virtues were only practiced by a small minority and among these only fitfully. The forceful German will for life and activity simply pushed aside the weak, other-worldly, culture-destroying aspects of Christian ethics.'[71] Germany had finally to realize that it could no longer be bound up in any way with a 'papal-medieval' past.[72]

Consequently, the Monists campaigned vigorously for the abandonment of the Christian holidays. They pleaded rather for the establishment and acceptance of new 'Volk' holidays which would be based upon nature and which would replace the 'anachronistic'[73] ones of the Middle Ages. In the Christian churches, they complained, one hears only empty sermons, mere phrases, and words which no one really believed anyway. The Germans had to be taught that a holiday could fittingly be celebrated by excursions into the countryside or by the cultivation of one's garden; a winter holiday could be observed by bringing home buds in order to contemplate, at one's own hearth, the life which was potential in them. Simple as such worship might sound, it contributed much more than Christian observance not only to the intellectual life but to the emotional life of man. By turning away from Christianity to worship nature, the new religionist would experience a higher pitch of feeling and spiritual intensity, an emotional release which would enable him to return to his ordinary life inwardly satisfied and refreshed.[74]

The Monist League did try to practice what it preached. It organized excursions into the countryside for religious observance, especially during the bi-annual solstice, June 21st and December 22nd. Given their predilection for the symbolism of rebirth and their mystical attachment to nature, it is not surprising that the Monists were also drawn to the sun as an object of religious veneration. The equinoctial festival had been a part of the old Germanic pagan religious ritual, just as it was part of the cult practices of innumerable other primitive peoples and tribes. In the decades around the turn of the century the Volkish movement as a whole in Germany had revived sun-worship and the Monists were among the most active supporters and enthusiasts of this new pantheistic religion.[75]

As in most other areas of belief and doctrine, the Monists derived their principles of sun worship from Haeckel. In the *Welträtsel*, he had proposed worship of the sun as a higher form of religion than that of Christianity. 'Sun worship,' he wrote, 'seems to the modern scientist to be the best of all forms of theism, and the one which may be most easily reconciled with modern Monism.'[76] The sun is, he pointed out, the source of life and of energy. 'Indeed, the whole of our bodily and mental life depends, in the last resort, like all other organic life, on the light and heat rays of the sun. Hence in the light of pure reason, sun worship, as a form of naturalistic monotheism, seems to have a much better foundation than the anthropistic [sic!] worship of Christians and of other monotheists who conceive of their god in human form.'[77]

Following Haeckel, therefore, the idea of sun worship was taken up with enormous enthusiasm by the members of the Monist League. This was especially true of Wilhelm Ostwald. His famour aphorism, 'Waste no energy; turn it all to account,'[78] was intended not only as an imperative for practical material accomplishment on the part of the Germans but also in the pantheistic sense of utilizing the holy powers given off by the sun. 'The sun is the best thing that we have,' he wrote, in one of the journals of the Monist League. It is the miraculous sustainer of all life on earth. 'The sun is the mother of us all, and we must be grateful to it for everything that we are and do.'[79]

Ostwald's attitudes were echoed everywhere in the literature of the Monist League. In a typical description of a solstice ceremony, we read that prayers to the sun are offered as the central part of the pantheistic ritual. For example, at one such celebration the following incantation to the sun was pronounced:

We are all children of the sun. Out of its womb our planet was born. An eternal law of nature compels us to be within its sphere and influence. The immensity of space is cold, stiff, and lifeless—our luminous mother sun, warming and ripening our fruit, appears as the simple, true element of life. Our ancestors knew this in ancient times. Thus their justifiable joy when the sun made its slow victorious spiral across the sky. They then remembered that all those trees, which concealed their greenness in the winter-time, were consecrated to the god, Wodan.[80]

And a typical poem, one of many worshipping the sun which are to be found in the pages of the Monist League journals, went in part as follows:

Goldene Sonne, des unendlichen Weltalls strahlendes Herz!
Glühend erstehst du aus der dunkeln Nacht.

. . . . .

Du liessest den Menschen werden, du liessest ihm wachsen!
Seinen Geist weckest du; Freude schufest du ihm. . . .

. . . . .

Ach, was wäre ohne dich, was auf Erden ist?

(Golden sun, radiant heart of the infinite cosmos!
Glowing, thou arisest out of the dark night.

. . . . .

Thou hast allowed man to be born, thou hast permitted him to grow!
Thou has awakened his spirit; thou hast created joy for him. . . .

. . . . .

Oh, what would that which is on earth be without you?)[81]

(translated by Daniel Gasman)

But for the Volkists, the sun symbolized more than the life force which the early pagan rituals celebrate, and more than the yearning, in that damp and foggy northern climate, for warmth and light, which the early rituals no doubt also expressed. The sun now symbolized in addition the reawakening of a new national life and communication with the spiritual and energetic center of the cosmos. Thus, for example, in Volkish painting the sun was a constantly present symbol of purity and in countless pictures and drawings created especially for the German youth movement, the rays of the sun were seen as enveloping physically perfect blond Aryan specimens.

The Monists mixed all these symbols of the sun and German pagan religion together with pledges of loyalty to the national regeneration of Germany. For example, in July, 1913, it was reported in one of the accounts of the activities of the League that the Breslau branch of the organization had celebrated the summer solstice in customary fashion by marching out into the countryside. In the speech which one of the speakers delivered, nature and sun were lauded, and then the speaker linked these symbols to the theme of the reawakening of Germany. He cried out:

> Only when we stand for you Oh Volk true in battle and in death, when we seek only you in the strong roots of our moral force, can the humanity which is in us blossom forth to its fullest. Our personality stems from mankind and our individuality from the Volk.[82]

It may be said that in the Monist mind emotional appreciation and religious involvement with nature was linked, in an essential way, to artistic creativity. Very much like the famous Volkish author of *Rembrandt als Erzieher*, Julius Langbehn,[83] the Monists were interested in transforming the Germans into artists. They believed that artistic activity was religious activity and that it could provide one more link to the soil and to the natural landscape of Germany.[84] In their minds painting was a religious experience. For the Monists, artistic-religious sensitivity did not mean unlimited freedom of imagination and creation. The artist, they believed, would have to be bound by the dictates of nature and natural law. Moreover, he would have to immerse himself in nature, become one with the object, therefore proceeding in a manner that was parallel to that recommended by Theodor Lipps, the main theoretician in Germany of the concept of *Einfühlung*, suggesting the idealistic belief that the artist in a mysterious way, becomes part of the contemplated natural model. Their naturalism, in other words, was not to be the product of detached observation, but was to emerge from a kind of mystical empathy with nature which was felt to be alive.[85]

It was Haeckel, once again, who first raised the cry among the Monists for the deliberate cultivation of artistic expression as a means for the veneration of nature. Before becoming a zoologist and a naturalist, Haeckel had been an artist, and had in fact at one time seriously considered painting as a full-time profession. Throughout his life he remained an indefatigable artist and devoted considerable time to sketching and to painting. In his scientific work, wherever possible, he made use of his artistic talents. His drawings, primarily of lower forms of organisms, reflect an enormous enthusiasm for art, and in the course of his life it has been estimated that Haeckel actually executed the impressive number of more than fourteen hundred landscapes, and eight hundred water colors, not to mention numerous drawings and oil paintings.[86]

For Haeckel, nature was, as we might expect, the source of artistic inspiration and the rationale of artistic achievement because he sensed in it the creative demiurge. One admirer recalled his ecstatic reaction to the spectacle of nature: 'I have never seen a person who could become so speechlessly enraptured while viewing a sunset as he. If he has observed a *Radiolar* through the microscope his entire countenance shines with happiness.'[87] For Haeckel there was no distinction between the beautiful in nature and the beautiful in art. There was in effect only one beauty, that of nature. Not surprisingly, therefore, in the *Welträtsel*, Haeckel proposed the introduction of artistic training into the Monist educational curriculum. Observation of nature and artistic study based upon it, he contended, would draw the student away from the harmful otherworldly aspirations of Christianity. Painting was to become a form of religious worship, through the depiction of appearances and through the revelation of the profundity of nature. 'Every pupil must be taught to draw well, and from nature; and, wherever possible, the use of water colors. The execution of drawing and of water color sketches from nature (of flowers, animals, landscapes, clouds, etc.) not only excites interest in nature and helps memory to enjoy objects, but it gives the pupil his first lesson in *seeing* correctly what he has seen.'[88] Haeckel, insisting that art be linked to the real world admitted the need for some 'artistic freedom in the individual treatment and effective composition of the whole picture,' but at the same time demanded the 'conscientious adherence to nature in the reproduction of details.' He believed that for a 'perfect picture' what was needed was the 'synthetic and subjective glance of the artist' as well as the 'analytic and objective eye of the naturalist.'[89]

Very probably, Haeckel's curriculum stressed the need for concentrating on water color painting because the technique required rapid, spontaneous, execution; in this way the spiritual union with nature could be best attained. Thus, water color painting would allow the artist to capture nature, empathetically, to immediately reach its spiritual essence with a minimum of the rational interposition encouraged by the more elaborate medium of oil. By stressing the need to use water colors Haeckel was, in other words, insisting that any rendering of nature had to be a spontaneous and direct reflection of its *Geist*. For him, art was to be a mirror of the external world and a sympathetic echo of its soul. A natural landscape especially, he felt, rendered in water color, would most forcefully bring to expression the artistic structure of nature itself and would link the artist most clearly to his natural German landscape, and would arouse his religious sensitivity.

Haeckel's followers were as enthusiastic about his artistic opinions as they were about his other formulations of Monist belief and doctrine. 'We Monists must become artists'[90] was a statement to be found frequently in Monist literature. Like Haeckel, the Monists insisted on the innate artistic creativity of nature which, they believed, provided the sole material subject matter for art, and especially religious art. 'The artistic drive,' they wrote, 'which is peculiar to all of nature, is alive in every cell'[91] and following Haeckel, they insisted that the 'laws of art are basically natural laws.'[92] With Haeckel, they also pleaded for the introduction and practice of landscape painting. 'From the insight,' they wrote, 'that all of nature is animated, it can be accepted that the landscape is of great importance. Escape into landscape has become a necessity in art.'[93]

In 1899, the same year in which the *Welträtsel* appeared, Haeckel also published another work which was very influential and highly regarded among his followers. It was called *Kunstformen der Natur* and was a collection of large colored plates of cell life, plants, sea organisms, and animals. The Monists believed that the elements of all art forms were to be found in the study of these plates and the book was therefore read and pondered by the Monists with the utmost dedication and seriousness. On the surface, the plates are mainly technical illustrations featuring attractive ornamental designs and patterns composed of detailed, precise, and conventional renderings of botanical and zoological forms.

Yet, they are not quite objectively rendered and the information they are supposed to convey is hardly neutral. Their ornamental lay-out and hypertrophied patterning, and the fantastic and bizarre look of the unfamiliar flora and fauna, transform them in the direction of disquieting, even nightmarish representations that seem to be related to the type of naturalistic mysticism which can be observed in late nineteenth-century Art Nouveau and symbolist artists like Obrist and Redon.[94] (See Plate III.) On the surface, therefore, Haeckel, in *Kunstformen der Natur* was simply the objective, scientific, portrayer of nature. But the essential strangeness of the plates reveal a mystical, decadent, and demonic vision of nature. All this notwithstanding, *Kunstformen der Natur* became for the Monists a kind of illustrated prayer-book of nature and a breviary for the natural forms of art.

As novel and interesting as the Monists' project of transforming the Germans into artists in order to heighten their religious sensitivity may have been, their conception of art and specifically of style was at heart deeply conservative and completely divorced from the revolutionary artistic trends of late nineteenth- and early twentieth-century European painting and aesthetics.[95] Haeckel's formulation of art in the *Welträtsel* and in his *Kunstformen der Natur* revealed an eclectic-retardataire approach to art. Thus, on the one hand, the theory of art put forward in the *Welträtsel* and as illustrated in Haeckel's many watercolors is firmly rooted in the romantic tradition of nineteenth-century landscape painting which included a naturalistic concern. On the other hand, certain of his watercolors and the illustrations for *Kunstformen der Natur*, where the element of naturalism is also preeminent, have, as we have already noted, much in common with contemporary idealistic trends of symbolism and of Art Nouveau. And thirdly, on the whole, his art and above all else his stylistic orientation depended largely on reactionary nineteenth-century academic-naturalistic art and stylistic methods which harked back to the Renaissance and to Aristotle's theory of mimesis.[96] In this way it diverged from the advanced tendencies of romanticism, symbolism, and Art Nouveau. While the avant-garde of romanticism and even more so that of the later symbolism and of Art Nouveau (a number of Art Nouveau artists were initially influenced by Haeckel's zoological drawings)[97] attempted to liberate style from its attachment to appearances, Haeckel remained—consistent with his entire *Weltanschauung*—conservative, in that he clung to academic tenets preaching the subordination of art to nature and of stylistic elements to the visible. Haeckel, despite his yearning for the world-soul, remained imprisoned by the surface appearances of nature and never allowed himself to advance in the direction of abstract painting. In contrast to him, for example, the Art Nouveau leader, Henry van de Velde, who in fact had some passing association with the Monist League, in precisely 1899, the year that Haeckel published his *Kunstformen der Natur*, defended the self-sufficiency and expressiveness of stylistic devices and pointed out as one art historian has noted that abstract 'line derives force from the creator'—rather than from the phenomenal world—'and communicates its energy to the spectator.'[98] By the turn of the century, in contrast to Haeckel's anachronistic inclinations in art, the post-impressionist works of Seurat, Cezanne, Van Gogh, and Gauguin which were already widely known by the Germans and to a large extent German art itself were both gradually conforming to the revolutionary axiom of Maurice Denis, the spokesman for the new art, who, as early as 1890, gave expression to the idea of the emancipation of art from nature. 'Remember,' Denis wrote, 'that painting . . . is essentially a plane surface covered with colors assembled in a certain order.'[99] Thus, for those caught up by the newer trends in Germany or elsewhere, it was the artist, and not nature, who was the source of the new world of autonomous and expressive lines, forms, and colors.

It is therefore quite clear that, as opposed to the Monists, the most advanced European and German aesthetics and art, especially expressionism from the beginning of the twentieth century, was basically anti-naturalistic. Its tenor was irrevocably revealed by Kandinsky, the spokesman of the Munich and European *avant-garde*, in his famous 'On the Spiritual in Art'[100] written in 1910, where he definitely rejected naturalism and preached the gospel of abstract art, which is the very antithesis of the conservative Monist approach.

Thus, despite his own idealistic proclivities, and despite the birth of modern art, Haeckel rather obstinately continued to insist on both the submission of artistic forms and religious emotion to the demands of nature. He did not yield to the new efforts to free the artist and his imagination from the restraints which were imposed upon him by nature and reality. In this spirit, symptomatically foreshadowing the famous Nazi exhibition of '*entartete Kunst*'[101] in 1937, his followers, the Monists, wrote that all of modern art, including abstract art, was 'decadent art.'[102] This could hardly have been otherwise since in Nazi art the romantic, symbolistic, and naturalistic ingredients, which were central to the art of Haeckel and the Monists, played a decisive role, and one may see an uninterrupted line of development from one to the other, still another link between Haeckel, Monism, and Naziism. For the Monists, as for the Nazis, modern 'decadent art' could have place neither in their culture nor in their religion of nature. They insisted that one must regard the latest trends in art as one would an 'unfruitful or degenerate plant.'[103] Art could not and should not attempt to transcend nature. 'It will be clear,' a Monist wrote, 'that in every material there slumbers a regular beauty which must not be killed by the artist, but awakened'[104]—and the contributions of modern art were to be rejected.

In conclusion, therefore, to repeat once again: Haeckel's naturalism was not that of Courbet or Menzel, or of the Impressionists, based upon materialistic and scientific assumptions. Rather, it was a deceptive surface naturalism, which, consonant with Haeckel's general position had, ingrained within itself the fantastic, the bizarre, mysticism, and idealism. Deep down, his naturalism, like that of the Nazis later on, was imbued with romantic and symbolistic mysticism. Despite Haeckel's insistence on objectivity and 'seeing,' and despite his inhibited, precise, and academic-naturalistic style, his watercolors and his purported scientific drawings are much more akin to Moreau's transcendental aspirations and belief in the reality of the 'unseen,'[105] and actually recall more of Redon's brand of mysticism and his realism of the 'invisible,'[106] than they do the materialistically founded realism and impressionism of Courbet, Menzel, Monet, or Liebermann.[107] (See Plate IV)

In the Monist religious program, therefore, neither Christian otherworldly art, nor modern anti-naturalistic or frankly abstract art could serve their purpose. For them 'art could become religion'[108] only by drawing its sustenance from this world and from the 'eternal laws of life.'[109] It was only through naturalism—as tinted with mysticism as

MONISM AND CHRISTIANITY

it was in their view—that the Monists believed that religion, life, and art, could become one.

NOTES

1. Quoted in Hayes, *A Generation of Materialism*, p. 124.
2. For a good general survey of Christianity in the nineteenth century, see Henrich Weinel, *Jesus in the Nineteenth Century* (Edinburg: Clark, 1914); and Julian V. L. Casserley, *The Retreat from Christianity in the Modern World* (London: Longmans, Green, 1952).
3. Haeckel, *The History of Creation*, I, 19.
4. Haeckel, *The Riddle of the Universe*, p. 9.
5. On the general significance of these individuals for the development of Germanic religion, see Paul Banwell Means, *Things That are Caesar's: The Genesis of the German Church Conflict* (New York: Round Table Press, 1935); Stern, *The Politics of Cultural Despair* and Mosse, *The Culture of Western Europe*.
6. On Protestantism in Germany in the nineteenth century, see William O. Shanahan, *German Protestants Face the Social Question* (Notre Dame, Ind.: University of Notre Dame Press, 1951); and on nineteenth-century German Catholicism, see Pinson, *Modern Germany*, Chapter IX.
7. Breitenbach, 'Meine Beziehungen zu Haeckel,' in Schmidt; (ed) I, 211.
8. Ludwig Gurlitt (no title), in *ibid.*, p. 238.
9. *Ibid.*
10. *Ibid.*
11. Walther May, 'Was Haeckel in meinem Leben bedeutet,' in *ibid.*, p. 274.
12. Ernst Haeckel, *My Church Departure* (New York: Truth Seeker, 1911), p. 27.
13. Haeckel, *The Story of the Development of a Youth*, pp. 73-74.
14. Haeckel, *My Church Departure*, p. 27.
15. Haeckel, *The Love Letters of Ernst Haeckel*, p. 29.
16. Haeckel, *My Church Departure*, p. 30.
17. Haeckel, *The Story of the Development of a Youth*, p. 79.
18. Ernst Haeckel, *Italienfahrt. Briefe an die Braut 1859-1860* (Leipzig: Koehler, 1921), p. 8.
19. *Ibid.*, p. 159.
20. Haeckel, *Riddle of the Universe*, p. 314.
21. *Ibid.*, pp. 351-352.
22. *Ibid.*, pp. 311-312.
23. *Ibid.*, pp. 314-315.
24. *Ibid.*, pp. 319-320.
25. *Ibid.*, pp. 321-323.
26. *Ibid.*, pp. 324-325.
27. *Ibid.*, pp. 334-335.
28. Note also the abusive tone of Haeckel's article, 'Die Weltanschauung des neuen Curses,' in *Gemeinverständliche Vorträge und Abhandlungen*, II 342.

29. Ernst Haeckel, 'Energetik und Substanzgesetz,' *Das monistische Jahrhundert*, I (1912–13), 412. It is of some interest that one of Haeckel's most prominent converts to Monist religion was the famous dancer, Isadora Duncan. She was one of Haeckel's most devoted admirers and found in Monism a fitting complement to her exalted vision of life. For details on her relationship with Haeckel, see Allan Ross, Macdougall, *Isadora, a Revolutionary in Art and Love* (New York: Thomas Nelson, 1960), pp. 90, 92, 132, 258.
30. Haeckel, *Riddle of the Universe*, p. 337.
31. *Ibid.*
32. *Ibid.*
33. Ernst Haeckel to Hermann Allmers, Freienwalde, July 13, 1860, in Koop, *Haeckel und Allmers*, p. 52.
34. Ernst Haeckel to Hermann Allmers [Italy, ca. 1859–1860], in Schmidt, *Denkmal eines grossen Lebens*, p. 72.
35. Ernst Haeckel to Hermann Allmers, Berlin, May 14, 1860, in Koop, *Haeckel und Allmers*, p. 44.
36. Haeckel, *Riddle of the Universe*, p. 337.
37. Ernst Haeckel, *Eternity. World War Thoughts on Life and Death, Religion and the Theory of Evolution* (New York: Truth Seeker, 1916), p. 32.
38. *Ibid.*, p. 33.
39. Haeckel, *History of Creation*, I, 22.
40. *Ibid.*, p. 23. Haeckel's belief in the unity of nature and in its regularity is revealingly seen in his famous and now generally defunct Recapitulation Hypothesis (the Biogenetic Law), which held that an individual organism, in its growth and development, retraces the stages or resembles the forms of its ancestors lower down in the scale of being; the idea, i.e., that ontogeny recapitulates phylogeny. According to the implication of the Biogenetic law, when properly investigated, an organism could be brought to reveal its entire biological history and ancestry, even as far back as the origin of life itself.

    Haeckel and the Monists took the idea of Recapitulation to be valid for all of nature. For them, in literal terms, each individual relived and re-experienced the evolutionary process in a heightened and abbreviated form and in this way shared in the eternal cycle and oneness of nature.

    For Haeckel's ideas on Recapitulation, see *History of Creation*, I, 309–311, and for a recent critique of the theory, see Gavin de Beer, *Embryos and Ancestors* (Oxford: Oxford University Press, 1958). A general background for the Biogenetic Law may be found in Arthur O. Lovejoy, 'Recent Criticism of the Darwinian Theory of Recapitulation: Its Grounds and Initiators,' and Jane Oppenheimer, 'An Embryological Enigma in *The Origin of Species*,' in Glass, *Forerunners of Darwin*.
41. Haeckel, *History of Creation*, I, 22. Haeckel's implicit acceptance of vitalism in biology is seen also in his unswerving adherence to the biological theories of Goethe and Lamarck. On Lamarckian influence in Haeckel, see Albert Wigand,

Der Darwinismus und die Naturforschung Newtons und Cuviers, III (Braunschweig: Vieweg, 1877); and Cassirer, *The Problem of Knowledge*, Chapter IX.

42. Ernst Haeckel, 'Ueber die Wellenzeugung der Lebenstheilchen oder die Perigenesis der Plastidule,' in *Gemeinverständliche Vorträge und Abhandlungen*, II, 60.
43. *Ibid.*, p. 61.
44. Haeckel wrote in famous words in his *Generelle Morphologie der Organismen*, I, 11: 'We know of no force without matter . . . and no matter without force. . . .'

Haeckel's description of the soul quality of nature sounded completely theosophical. In fact, Haeckel was one of the major intellectual mentors of Germany's leading theosophist, Rudolf Steiner. In the 1890's both Steiner and Haeckel corresponded with one another and both wrote that they shared a common basic outlook on the nature of the world. See Rudolf Steiner, *Briefe*, II (Dornach: Selbstverlag der Rudolf Steiner Nachlassverwaltung, 1953), *passim*. Haeckel, however, eventually dissociated himself from Steiner, fearing the idealistic implications of the word, theosophy. On the relationship of Haeckel and Steiner, see Hemleben. *Rudolf Steiner und Ernst Haeckel*.

45. Ernst Haeckel, *Monism as Connecting Religion and Science. The Confession of Faith of a Man of Science* (London: Black, 1894), p. 28.
46. Haeckel, *Eternity*, p. 28.
47. Haeckel, *Monism as Connecting Religion and Science*, p. 25.
48. *Ibid.*, p. 16.
49. Haeckel, *Generelle Morphologie*, II, 451-452.
50. H. Michelis, 'Zum Kampf un eine entwicklungsgeschichtliche Weltanschauung,' *Der Monismus*, I (1906), 75.
51. Eugen Wolfsdorf, 'Odhin und Haeckel,' in Schmidt, (ed) *Was wir Ernst Haeckel verdanken*, II, 47.
52. Heinrich Schmidt, 'Gott,' *Der Monismus*, I (1906), 5.
53. Otto Juliusburger, 'Monismus und soziales Wirken,' *Der Monismus*, I (1906), 36.
54. *Ibid.*
55. P. Flaskämper, 'Monismus und Naturgefühl,' *Das monistische Jahrhundert*, II (1913-14), 58.
56. *Ibid.*, p. 64.
57. *Ibid.*
58. *Ibid.*, p. 61.
59. *Ibid.*, pp. 60-61.
60. *Ibid.*, p. 61.
61. *Ibid.*
62. *Ibid.*, p. 63.
63. M. Krische, 'Frühlingsfeier,' *Sonne*, No. 10 (May 9, 1914), 73-74.
64. *Ibid.*, pp. 76-77.
65. Dr. Diesing, 'Der Monismus als die Erfüllung der christlichen Lehre,' *Der Monismus*, III (1908), 394.
66. M. Krische, 'Frühlingsfeier,' p. 73.
67. Anonymous, 'Sonnwendfest,' *Der Monismus*, V (1910), 126.

68. Unold, *Der Monismus und seine Ideale*, p. 89.
69. Johannes Unold, 'Die Bedeutung des Monismus für unsere nationale Entwicklung,' *Der Monismus*, V (1910), 337.
70. Anonymous, 'Sonnwendfest,' p. 127.
71. Unold, *Der Monismus und seine Ideale*, p. 52.
72. Unold, 'Die Bedeutung des Monismus für unsere nationale Entwicklung,' p. 337.
73. Johanna Hennig-Wimpf, 'Einiges über Feste,' *Der Monismus*, III (1908), 245.
74. *Ibid.*, pp. 245–248.
75. On the general significance of sun-worship for the Volkish movement, see Mosse, *The Crisis of German Ideology*, Chapter IV.
76. Haeckel, *Riddle of the Universe*, p. 280.
77. *Ibid.*, p. 281.
78. Wilhelm Ostwald, *Monism as the Goal of Civilization* (Hamburg: International Committee of Monism, 1913), p. 30.
79. Wilhelm Ostwald, 'Die Sonne,' *Sonne*, No. 1 (January 3, 1914), 2.
80. Anonymous, 'Sonnwendfest,' p. 126.
81. Emil Felden, 'An den Sonne,' *Das monistische Jahrhundert*, I (1912–13), 810–812.
82. Anonymous, 'Sonnwendfeiern,' *Das monistische Jahrhundert*, II (1913–14), 388.
83. On the relationship of art and the ideas of Julius Langbehn, see Stern, *Politics of Cultural Despair*, Chapters VIII and IX.
84. On the relationship between art and landscape in Volkish thought, see Mosse, *The Crisis of German Ideology*, pp. 40, 43, 83–86.
85. On Lipps and the significance of *Einfühlung*, see Peter Selz, *German Expressionist Painting* (Berkeley and Los Angeles: University of California Press, 1957), pp. 6–7.
86. Schmidt, *Denkmal eines grossen Lebens*, p. 69.
87. Quoted in *ibid.*, p. 64.
88. Haeckel, *Riddle of the Universe*, pp. 363–364.
89. Haeckel, *India and Ceylon*, p. 14.
90. Artur Hennig, 'Der Monismus und die Kunst,' *Der Monismus*, III (1908), 150.
91. *Ibid.*, p. 152.
92. *Ibid.*, p. 151.
93. *Ibid.*, p. 156.
94. See Robert Schmutzler, *Art Nouveau* (New York: Abrams, 1962).
95. For a good general discussion of the break in tradition which modern art represented, see Werner Hofmann, *The Earthly Paradise: Art in the Nineteenth Century* (New York: Braziller, 1961).
96. On the Aristotelian influences to be found in nineteenth-century Academic Art, see M. H. Abrams, *The Mirror and the Lamp: Romantic Theory and the Critical Tradition* (Oxford: Oxford University Press, 1953), Chapters I and II.
97. For Haeckel's influence on Art Nouveau, see Peter Selz, (ed.), *Art Nouveau* (New York: Museum of Modern Art, 1959), pp. 14, 16, 17.
98. Selz, *Expressionist Painting*, p. 55.
99. *Maurice Denis, Théories* (Paris: Rouart and Watelin, 1920), p. 1.

100. The earliest complete statement on abstract art and its real credo.
101. In 1937, the Nazies organized an exhibition in Munich of so-called 'Degenerate Art,' i.e., modern art.
102. Hennig, 'Der Monismus und die Kunst,' p. 152.
103. *Ibid.*
104. *Ibid.*, p. 155.
105. See Linda Nochlin, *Impressionism and Post-Impressionism, 1874–1905* (Englewood Cliffs, New Jersey: Prentice-Hall, 1966), p. 199.
106. Odilon Redon, *A Soi-même: Journal (1867–1915)* (Paris: José Corti, 1961). pp. 9, 22, 27.
107. See Fritz Novotny, *Painting and Sculpture in Europe, 1780–1880)* (Baltimore: Penguin, 1960), pp. 141ff, 157ff, 194ff, 204, and *passim*.
108. Hennig, 'Der Monismus und die Kunst,' p. 158.
109. *Ibid.*, pp. 153, 160.

Chapter Four

Monism, the Corporative State and Eugenics

THE modern theory of the totalitarian fascist state was adumbrated by the political and social ideology advanced by Haeckel and his followers. Its major assumptions and proposals were in all important respects identical with the political and social program of later twentieth-century National Socialism. It was, in fact, the unique political contribution of the Haeckelian Monists to bring together for the first time into one unified theory, under the auspices of science, the idea of the organically constituted corporative and racial state, of authoritarian state power, and of eugenics as a means of strengthening the political and social structure of Germany.[1]

As in most areas of Monist policy and belief it was Haeckel once again who set down the broad principles upon which his followers were able to elaborate a more complete program of social and political action. In an important and influential address, 'Ueber Arbeitstheilung in Natur- und Menschenleben,'[2] delivered in Berlin in December of 1868, and in his *Natürliche Schöpfungsgeschichte*, published in the same year, Haeckel provided the theoretical basis for the Monist political program. A society's level of culture, he argued, stood in direct relation to the extent of the division of labor in society. Primitive societies were characterized by little division of labor, but in modern, advanced civilization there was a steadily increasing 'differentiation' of tasks.[3] In fact, the enormous productivity and diversity of modern life could be traced to the division of labor itself. In the organization of society men fell naturally into their various occupations, classes, and estates. Their abilities determined their social rank and, given the free operation of natural laws, the actual place a man held in society was a true reflection of his talents. 'It is natural and necessary that the progressive division of labor constantly furthers mankind, and urges every individual branch of human activity into new discoveries and improvements. Thus progress itself universally depends on differentiation.'[4]

Clearly, Haeckel's strong defense and glorification of the division of labor was, in reality, an attack on both bourgeois liberal and socialist conceptions of society. His position implied opposition to the egalitarian individualism of the ideology of the French Revolution and to the Marxian theory of class conflict. Since men, according to Haeckel, were unequal, it appeared to him to be natural for them to participate in society only to the extent of their abilities and to carry out their work in a cooperative and harmonious way for the benefit of the entire community. In place of individual and natural rights and the competition and movement of free and equal individuals, Haeckel stressed the importance of the bonds of community and the mutual obligation of every individual to society.[5] In the same way, he wrote, in which the 'old Golden Rule of morals' has characterized 'narrow personal relations, so too should it become the 'norm within the state' and 'guide the conduct of the different social classes to each other.'[6] For Haeckel, therefore, the division of labor was an accurate reflection of the veritable inequality of all men; at the same time, it was the measure of their integration into an organically constituted society. 'The biologic (sic!) relation of the cells to the tissues and organs' of lower organisms is the 'same as that which exists among the higher animals between the individuals and the community of which they are component parts. Each cell, though autonomous, is subordinated to the body as a whole; in the same way in the societies of bees, ants, and termites, in the vertebrate herds and the human state, each individual is subordinate to the social body of which he is a member.'[7]

Thus, in the development of their social and political program many of the significant followers of Haeckel in the Monist League made a determined effort to reject outright all liberal and democratic political ideologies.[8] At a time when democracy and parliamentary government were increasingly gaining acceptance as a solution for the political and social problems of industrially advanced Western European societies, the Haeckelian Monists launched a systematic attack upon the doctrines of democratic liberalism. To a large extent the tone of the argument was set by the Vice President of the Monist League, Dr. Johannes Unold, who, in a number of books and in the pages of the journals of the League, warned that all of the 'democratic illusions,'[9] of the past had to be dispelled. 'In place,' he wrote, 'of the natural right fiction of free and equal individuals,' one had to recognize the 'true nature of man.'[10] Men were not only social animals but 'predatory' ones as well and within society there was to be found a 'natural inequality of differently talented personalities.'[11] Monism, therefore, could not allow itself to be 'deluded' by the 'phrases and illusions'[12] of liberalism. The 'sharp sense of reality'[13] which Monism possessed revealed the limitations of liberal democracy. 'Brutal reality has awakened us from the pretty dreams of good, free, equal, and happy people.'[14] Rightly considered, reality demonstrates that 'unlimited freedom leads to . . . a lack of regard for the minority and the progressive deterioration of the majority.'[15]

This sweeping criticism of democracy and liberalism was not confined to the writings of Dr. Unold. Professor Heinrich Ziegler, for example, a co-founder of the Monist League, and for a time a colleague of Haeckel, also considered liberalism, equality, and democracy harmful philosophies of political organization. 'Many sociologists,' Ziegler wrote, 'proceed from the idea that men are equal by nature. But day to day experience shows that the doctrine of the equality of men is not correct.'[16] The idea of human equality was an erroneous theory of the Enlightenment philosophers and unfortunately, Ziegler lamented, 'this false theory is still in operation in our own time.'[17] There were, he felt, 'far-reaching differences' between men, and therefore political thinking had to be aware of them.[18] Political theory had to recognize that 'social inequality stands in intimate relation with natural inequality.'[19]

In their program for political organization, therefore, and since men were naturally unequal, the Haeckelian Monists attacked the democratic franchise. In language and concepts that recalled earlier nineteenth-century conservative polemics against democracy, they insisted that government elected by simple majority vote was 'monstrous.'[20] They complained that in a democracy the 'youngest,' the most 'inexperienced' and the 'poorest' have power.[21] Where an equal franchise exists the masses are bound to select their representatives unwisely.[22] 'Won't they,' Dr. Unold cautioned, 'give their approval to those who charm by their eloquence and win over the masses by promises?'[23] The familiar conservative fear was expressed that government by the masses would lead to the triumph of mediocrity. Democracy, it was felt, inevitably led to the 'exploitation of quality by quantity, the best by the majority, the fit and the conscientious by the unfit and the frivolous, the expert by the inexpert, the prudent by the covetous.'[24] Democracy denied the creative talents of the elite who were necessarily small in number. It disregarded 'all differences of understanding and endowment' and mistakenly believed that 'every voter possesses so much insight that he can judge the most important affairs of state and so much common sense that he will be inclined to pay attention only to the common good.'[25] The truth of the matter is, it was contended, that any democratic franchise would submerge those few individuals who really did possess greater intelligence and greater understanding of political problems.[26]

For Haeckelian Monism, democracy had to fail because of the basic irresponsibility of the masses, who, it was insisted, are more conscious of their physical needs than of higher and more desirable spiritual matters.[27] The masses are lazy and are 'always finding' their 'greatest happiness in the least amount of work and in the most amount of enjoyment.'[28] They are incapable of independent and responsible political judgment and generally 'listen more readily to promises and flattery than to proposals which demand difficult performance of duty, self-discipline, renunciation of present pleasures in favor of the future, and respect for others and for the whole [of society].'[29] In addition, those who are elected by equal franchise will support their own political parties before they will see fit to support the nation as a whole. An equal democratic franchise will 'never bring significant men into parliament.' Under it there can be 'no security that the representatives will possess the insight and the knowledge which is necessary for judging the sometimes really difficult questions of internal or foreign politics.' Under an equal franchise representatives will be elected who will possess 'no common sense' and 'no interest in the success of the state.' In fact there is no guarantee that an equal franchise will prevent 'opponents or traitors to the state from entering parliament.'[30] Under an equal franchise it was only the temper and the mood of the masses which controlled parliament. The masses 'think only of their personal advantage and not of the far-off future and so there would always be the danger that in the pursuit of their closest interests—real or imagined—they would neglect to consider the good of the state.'[31] The only conclusion which could be reached therefore was that democracy and mass rule would result in the complete and final deterioration of society. Democracy, these right-wing Monists felt, was the major political danger for Germany.

The Monists suggested that the franchise had to be arranged so that those who possessed greater 'intelligence' would have a better chance of determining the outcome of an election: i.e., the propertied elements of society and the professional classes, As Professor Ziegler pointed out, on the whole, the possessing classes not only had more intelligence but also paid higher taxes and, therefore, had a much better and superior understanding of the needs of the state. The representatives that they elect, he wrote, will inevitably reflect that intelligence and concern. And Dr. Unold queried: 'What person of political or historical experience does not find it highly unreasonable and quite harmful . . . where voting is by simple count that the opinion of a twenty-six-year-old laborer can mean as much as that of a sixty-year-old owner of a factory or that of a tradesman?'[32] Was it not rather clear that the equal franchise was unreasonable in that it 'restrained and excluded' the political power of the 'educated and the property-owning bourgeoisie, the middle class, which was the true backbone of every state?'[33] Is this not most obvious in the large industrial cities? There, the working class 'robs'[34] all the other groups of political influence. 'Who can justifiably explain that cities like Munich, Nürnberg, and Stuttgart should be represented exclusively by members of the workers party? Or who will sanction and who will maintain that it is correct that Social Democratic representatives who are elected by the immigrant working classes should be the true representatives of our Hansa cities?'[35]

As an alternative to democratic liberalism, a number of leading Monists proposed the creation of a corporative state.[36] They saw in the corporative state a non-liberal and non-democratic form of social organization which would guarantee at the same time social and economic stability, harmony between the classes, and national solidarity. Society, they contended, as before, was much more than a simple agglomeration of isolated and atomized individuals. In terms that were once again reminiscent of earlier nineteenth-century political conservatism, the Monists spoke of the organic nature of society and of the mutual interaction and reliance of its various parts on each other. 'What we desire and what we need,' Dr. Unold wrote, 'is neither mass nor class domination, but a forceful, well-ordered, and unified state.'[37]

Monist hankering after the corporative state was not particularly original, but rather reflected an ideological tradition which had been well-established in nineteenth-century German intellectual history. A desire to harness effectively the economic, social, and natural resources of the Reich behind a powerful centralized state and a hierarchically organized society was expressed as early as 1800 in Fichte's *Closed Commercial State*, as well as in Friedrich List's *National System of Political Economy* (1841), and in Ferdinand Lassalle's advocacy of state socialism. And during the first decades of this century, before the rise of Naziism, corporatism often reflected middle class fears of the power of big business, on the one hand, and Marxian socialism, on the other. Attempting to shield the middle class from the pressures and dislocations of modern industrial society, corporative theoreticians advocated a freezing of the class structure of Germany—a form of society which would protect and shelter the various social classes in their respective economic niches. Thus, while not entirely new, the Monist position on corporatism was a restatement in para-scientific terms of a political and social program for Germany which had threatened to become moribund. It was the Haeckelian Monists, together with other social theorists like Othmar Spann, Oswald Spengler, and Moeller van den Bruck, who helped rescue the ideal of corporatism for the modern industrial and scientific era in Germany. And although corporatism was ultimately rejected by the Nazis, it did influence the formation of their ideology. And indeed, corporatism in its Monist form, was often closer to the spirit of National Socialism, than that of Spann, Spengler, or Bruck, both because of its ready acceptance of racism and its willingness to sanction the predominance of the state in all economic as well as in all political matters.[38]

In the new state, as the Monist corporative theoreticians envisioned it, each individual would belong to an occupational or professional corporation. Natural ability would determine occupation, social standing, and rank. In this way a structured and hierarchically ordered society would be created. Each individual would be truly integrated into society and would perform his allotted economic task according to the laws of the division of labor in the framework of his vocational group. The structure of the new society would be shaped by the principle that 'diversity stands higher than equality' and that 'differentiation is higher than unity.'[39]

Neither social equality nor economic equality would be possible or desirable in the corporative state. The Monists denounced economic equality as one more destructive consequence of radical liberalism and its offshoot, socialism. Compensation, they argued, would be given only relative to the amount of work actually done and in terms of its value for the existence and well-being of the entire community.[40] Furthermore, work would be compulsory and would not be left to the 'good will of individual people.' Reality, it was argued, amply demonstrated that people respond only to differential rewards. Where equality of compensation exists no labor is ever performed, and therefore, 'all attempts to establish and justify human equality are shattered by this psychological necessity.'[41] In the corporative state the obligation of labor and different compensation for varied abilities would become social ideals.

But perhaps most significantly, there existed in Haeckelian Monist thinking, as in all later fascist thought, the supposition that corporatism would transform the political life of the nation. For years Haeckel had complained about divisiveness in German life which he believed had been brought on by the existence of diverse political parties. During Bismarck's visit to Jena in 1892, for example, Haeckel proposed the creation of a 'national party' which he said must 'turn its back on the petty squabbles' of the various political factions. All groups which urged the 'undermining of the federal constitution'—and he singled out Catholics, Poles, Guelphs, radical freethinkers, and Social Democrats—where to be excluded from the new party of national unity.[42] Echoing Haeckel, therefore, the Monists asserted that under ordinary parliamentary government political parties had only played a quarrelsome and destructive role, while political creativity had been the achievement of a small elite. Dr. Unold, for example, pointed out that under liberalism 'all the "principal parties"—apart from a few far-seeing, right-thinking, patriotic individuals—have made it especially difficult, if they have not completely thwarted, the political, spiritual, and moral evolution of our nation toward greater political maturity.'[43] Therefore, the main reason for the establishment of the corporative state would be to end, once and for all, the disruptive and destructive character of politics which was inevitable under individualistic liberalism.

The Monists assumed that the corporative state would be more truly representative of the needs and interests of individuals because the focus of the new society would be economic rather than political. The individual would give up his political interests in favor of economic matters, and political parties would be absorbed by and would disappear into the occupational and professional corporations. Men would then see themselves primarily as producers in an integrated society and would no longer be atomized individuals fighting for political expression. In this way the anarchy and confusion of parliamentary democracy would be overcome. Because each corporate group was vital for the maintenance of society no group would be able to supplant or dominate another group. There would be mutual harmony and all would work for the common good of the state. The corporations will 'think of themselves much more as part of the whole, and will learn to pay attention to the legitimate interests of other social groups.' Politics would in other words, become a matter for discussion between noncompeting groups of mutually beneficial economic interests. And 'since it will no longer be a question of winning a majority, or of plundering political power, so too will the so-called "election battles" lose their bitterness and mendaciousness.' Instead of choosing between competing candidates an election would send to the government a 'fit (*tüchtig*) and understanding' representative of his vocational group. Debate in parliament would no longer be waged acrimoniously over remotely abstract issues but would 'assume a much more correct and concrete character, since even though every group will emphasize its own vocational interests, nonetheless, in order to win the votes of others it will become accustomed to proceed with moderation.'[44]

Once liberated from political dissension the state will function more smoothly. With corporative representation the government will be able to 'learn in a much more basic and essential way what the needs and interests of single economic groups are, rather than, for example, when representatives of the Center Party suddenly intervene on behalf of the artisans, the farmers, or the factory workers, or when Social Democracy surrenders the interests of its electorate to its political principles.'[45] In the 'advanced evolutionary state' political differences will iron themselves out and politics will 'be directed along quieter, energy-conserving paths.'[46] Each vocational group will learn the principle of cooperation and will 'carry on only as part of the people as a whole.' In the corporative state 'there can be neither class nor mass domination, nor oppression of quality by quantity.'[47]

At the apex of the corporative structure the Monists envisaged a strong state power which would be controlled by a group of biologically elite individuals. Its main function would be to exercise tight regulatory control over society. Professor Ziegler pointed out that 'whatever great and significant things have been done in the history of mankind, have happened by the interaction of many people under a unified leadership.'[48] But the Monists felt that that leadership might not arise if the proper biological conditions were not maintained.

Thus, along with their fear of democaratic egalitarianism and liberalism the Monists were also haunted by the dread of the biological deterioration of Germany. Throughout all of their writings there was always the sense of time running out, an acceptance of the reality of biological decay which they believed was tragically undermining the health and vitality of the German people. The Monists believed, quite seriously, that each nation and racial group possessed a unique fund of hereditary qualities, the nature of which determined their survival and prosperity. As Dr. Wilhelm Schallmayer, a leading member of the Monist League and one of Germany's foremost pioneers in eugenics, maintained, the cultural and social superstructure of a nation was determined not primarily by social and economic forces but by the condition of the germ plasm of its members.[49] With the threat of Germany's imminent biological deterioration in mind, Dr. Schallmayer pointed out that nations and civilizations have declined in the past solely because they did not know how to avoid biological decay.⁵⁰ The Monists insisted that in human life the organic absolutely determined and had precedence over the cultural. Dr. Schallmayer warned the Germans that any politics which misused and misapplied the hereditary resources of a nation was bad politics and had to be combatted.⁵¹ For him, and for most of the Monists the main task of the state was to insure the survival and reproduction of only the biologically fittest individuals.⁵² Society, they urged, had to recognize that biology alone held the key to the rise and fall of civilizations and races, and that as long as a nation practiced correct biological selection it need never succumb in the struggle for existence.⁵³

In this matter once again it was Haeckel who furnished the theoretical impetus and framework from which and within which his followers and disciples were able to develop a more complete program of eugenics. Successful politics, according to Haeckel, was in reality nothing more than applied biology, and he liked to evoke the memory of the ancient Spartans, who, he maintained, were strong solely because they practiced biological selection. The most 'remarkable' aspect of Spartan history, Haeckel wrote, was their 'obedience to a special law' whereby 'all newly-born children were subject to careful examination or selection.' Then, those children who were 'weak, sickly, or affected with any bodily infirmity were killed.' It was only the 'perfectly healthy and strong children [who] were allowed to live, and they alone afterwards propagated the race.' In this way the Spartans were 'not only continually in excellent strength and vigor,' but they also perfected their bodies and increased their strength with every generation.⁵⁴ Haeckel concluded, therefore, that the 'destruction of abnormal new-born infants' could not be 'rationally' classified as 'murder' as is 'done in modern legal works.' One should regard it rather, he wrote, as a 'practice of advantage both to the infants destroyed and to the community.' Haeckel, therefore, advised the Germans to emulate the example of the ancient Spartans. Was it not, he argued, only a 'traditional dogma' that life had to be sustained under all circumstances.⁵⁵

The Monists themselves were well aware of Haeckel's early contributions to the science of eugenics and were especially struck by his conception of the role which the state had to play in the proper ordering of biological selection. Dr. Schallmayer, commemorating the eightieth birthday of Haeckel, wrote with grateful admiration that he personally was directed onto the path of racial and eugenic analysis by Haeckel and he noted that the master 'did not shrink' from applying eugenics to the problems of mankind. It was Haeckel, Schallmayer pointed out, who taught us that the 'knowledge of the doctrine of evolution should and must be employed in a practical way, and that above all the very least which we aim for is the improvement of our racial, social, and cultural conditions.'[56]

The Monists, therefore, under the guidance of Haeckel, sought to awaken the Germans to the demands of biology and to the danger of physical decline. The arguments which they advanced in support of their objectives in this matter were strongly conservative and frequently puritanical to the point of ludicrousness. The Vice-President of the Monist League, Dr. Unold, warned, for example, in a series of feverishly written tracts that 'many talented civilizations have faltered by degeneration through the pursuit of pleasure.'[57] And almost every Monist author warned of the dangers of alcohol and of illicit sexual relations.[58] Consumption of alcohol, they averred, over and over again, had to be prohibited, and sexual activity and behavior very severely controlled. 'Of what help to a people,' Dr. Unold cried out, 'are all economic, technical accomplishments and progress when its members, in exorbitant egotistical intoxication with life and enjoyment lose interest in the future of their own nation and sentence themselves to die out and bring about racial suicide by underplaying physical fitness.' The pursuit of pleasure, that is, the consumption of alcohol and involvement in illicit sexual relations, weakens the 'force of life in the coming generation and renders it increasingly unfit in the struggle for existence.'[59] And in the same way in which he criticized liberalism for political disruptiveness, so too did Dr. Unold hold it responsible for the threatening biological decay of Germany. He equated liberalism with 'libertinism' and strongly objected to a philosophy which taught that 'that which pleases is permissible.' Dr. Unold singled out August Bebel, the Social Democratic leader, for especially harsh criticism because of his alleged opinion that sexual conduct should be left to the free choice of the individual. Unold was alarmed that Bebel did not seem to be 'aware' of the fact that the 'survival of nations and of humanity itself was dependent upon the regulation of sexual needs' and that he did not understand that 'uncontrolled freedom and desire will lead to impotence and death.' Dr. Unold even found that pornography was the fruit of liberal civilization. He thus self-righteously proclaimed that 'a person who takes a stand against sexually stimulating and scandalous literature which poisons the [minds] of young people through the frivolous use of art, is also setting himself against liberal principles.'[60] Society, according to him, could not be permitted to pursue the liberal goal of the greatest happiness of the greatest number. It had rather to pursue a goal of '*Volkstüchtigkeit*,' the greatest possible biological fitness of the nation. The basis of all political state activity had to be '*Die Bahn frei für die tüchtigsten auf allen Gebieten.*'[61]

To further convince the Germans of the need for eugenic reform, the Monists continually pointed to what they considered to be a dangerous abundance of biologically defective individuals in human society.[62] For them this was the real social problem. There existed, they said, a veritable army of the feebleminded who committed most of the crimes and were guilty of most of the drunkenness. Thus, Professor Ziegler informed his readers that 'most murderers were feebleminded or epileptic.'[63] In addition, he wrote, low intelligence was the cause of most sexual crimes; if one investigated the general situation further it would be discovered that it was principally among the mental defectives that alcohol was consumed in excess: alcohol, sex, and biological inferiority mutually worked to increase the deleterious effect of each.[64] As to less sensational crimes, like robbery, one need only be aware of the fact, as Dr. Ziegler wrote, that criminals seldom need money and break the law merely for the psychological pleasure which crime offers, to see how dangerous defective mentalities can be to society. Crime for the Monists, in short, could not be traced exclusively to social conditions but was also a manifestation of hereditary inborn characteristics.[65]

Although other causes were admitted, the Monists tended to regard poverty, too, as a frequent result of feeblemindedness rather than of economic or social conditions. The impoverished elements of the lower classes were often assumed to be the biologically unfit, whereas economic success was generally taken to signify high intelligence and favorable hereditary characteristics. Professor Ziegler, for example, asserted that the feebleminded made up the 'lowest division' of the wage workers, were the 'poorest paid,' and 'suffered' the most from 'temporary unemployment.' He asserted that individuals on the lowest level of society necessarily showed a 'deficiency in diligence and patience,' were 'untrustworthy' and 'dishonest' and had a predilection for 'drunkenness.' And these less endowed people were a terrible burden for society to support. Since they were the sources of most crime and poverty they were the 'worry children of the state.' Along with poverty went vagrancy and beggary, forms of social behavior which the Monists maintained should be regarded as crimes. Vagrants and beggars were 'inferior,' of 'lower intelligence.' They were the alcoholics and 'vagrancy went together with larceny.'[66]

As for the Monists, therefore, different social classes possessed diverse hereditary characteristics, and they warned that the poor were dangerous because they were a source of civil unrest and opposition to the power of the state. Lower-class neighborhoods were 'hotbeds of moral decay' and 'constant centers of varied infectious diseases, especially infectious sexual sicknesses.'[67] Of course, the opposition to the state which was manifest in the neighborhoods of the poor had much to do with feeblemindedness and drunkenness. Professor Ziegler reported with scientific certainty that in seventy-six percent of the instances where action against the security of the state was concerned, drunkenness was involved and hence the major culprit. It was alcohol which unduly awakened the passions and emotions of the feebleminded lower classes against the state.[68]

The conclusion was accordingly reached that all conditions which could harm the germ plasm of the superior elements of the population or which furthered the reproduction of the inferior had to be eliminated. Thus, the Monists raised grave objections to the modern practice and theory of medicine. It was felt that individuals who were damaged by disease probably should not be permitted to survive and certainly not to reproduce.[69] This attitude was taken over directly from the earliest writings of Haeckel where he had strongly objected to the keeping alive of the chronically ill. 'The progress,' Haeckel wrote, 'of modern medical science, although still little able to cure diseases, yet possesses and practices more than it used to do the art of prolonging life during lingering, chronic diseases for many years.'[70] As a result there is a real danger that hereditary diseases will be transmitted increasingly to succeeding generations. 'Such ravaging evils as consumption, scrofula, syphillis, and also many forms of mental disorders, are transmitted by inheritance to a great extent, and transferred by sickly parents to some of their children, or even to [all] of their descendants.' Medicine practiced in this way, Haeckel asserted, actually aided in the spreading of disease. 'Now, the longer the diseased parents, with medical assistance, can drag on their sickly existence, the more numerous are the descendants who will inherit incurable evils, and the greater will be the number of individuals again, in the succeeding generations, thanks to that artificial 'medical selection,' who will be infected by their parents with lingering, hereditary disease.'[71] It was preferable that life affected by such conditions be terminated. 'We are not bound,' he wrote, 'under all circumstances to maintain and prolong life, even when it becomes utterly useless.' He complained that 'hundreds of thousands of incurables—lunatics, lepers, people with cancer, etc.—are artificially kept alive ... without the slightest profit to themselves or the general body.' He suggested that the number of insane and incurably ill was steadily on the increase and therefore not only was eugenic action necessary for the protection of future generations but the present population of the diseased had to be eliminated. He thus advocated the setting up of a commission which would decide on matters of life and death for the ill and the deformed. Upon a decision of the commission the ' "redemption from evil" should be accomplished by a dose of some painless and rapid poison.'[72]

Haeckel's Monist disciples took up the cry for the scientific and efficient elimination of the diseased and pressed urgently for measures to forestall the reproduction of the sick and the feeble.[73] In innumerable lectures, pamphlets and books they urged that civilization was becoming much too humane. No effort should be made, they argued, to keep the weak and the sick alive by artificial means. 'Our humanitarianism onesidedly considers the well-being and complaints of unfortunate individuals who are alive at present and is extremely indifferent or blind to the suffering which they inflict by their complacency on the next or on later generations.' The weak and the crippled should be denied rather than offered care. 'Instead of always increasing healing and nursing asylums for the spiritually and mentally ill, homes for cripples, etc., it would be a more far-sighted expression of humanitarianism to provide for better human selection by favorable measures so that such unfortunates should not be born so frequently.'[74]

But it was not only the weak and the sick that had to be eliminated from society. The Monists also insisted that the rather large group of criminals, alcoholics, vagrants, beggars, and the very poor be either eliminated or permanently separated from normal society. It was Haeckel once again who early in his career set down the basic propositions on the maximum use of the power of life and death for these groups of people. Haeckel declared himself unalterably opposed to the elimination of capital punishment for criminals. He wrote that 'capital punishment for incorrigible and degraded criminals is not only just, but also a benefit to the better portions of mankind; the same benefit is done by destroying luxuriant weeds, for the prosperity of a well-cultivated garden.' Defend capital punishment, Haeckel argued, and mankind will be incomparably better off. The undesirables would not be able to transmit their hereditary qualities to future generations. 'By the indiscriminate destruction of all incorrigible criminals, not only would the struggle for life among the better portions of mankind be made easier, but also an advantageous artificial process of selection would be set in practice, since the possibility of transmitting their injurious qualities would be taken from those degenerate outcasts.'[75]

Where the elimination of undesirables was not feasible, harsh punishment should be instituted to forestall crime. An accused person, the Monists argued, should not be allowed to plead innocence by reason of insanity or of other causes supposedly beyond his personal control. All must be held accountable for their acts, including the feebleminded and the mentally ill.[76] 'One has the right,' Dr. Ziegler wrote, 'to punish feebleminded and abnormal personalities.' They must be treated as one would discipline an animal. 'When someone maintains that punishment should only be carried out when one believes in free will, then I may inquire of him if he ever had a dog; if this is the case I can show him that he surely often punished the dog without asking if the dog had free will.' If a crime is committed, it is because 'those thoughts and deliberations which should and could have held back the criminal from his deed were not apparent or were too ineffectual.'[77]

Above all the Monists sought to refute the idea that punishment could improve the character of the criminal or that he could be regenerated by education. Since they viewed punishment only as a deterrent against crime, they strongly criticized what they considered to be an erroneous theory stemming from the Enlightenment which held that improvement in the behavior of the criminal is possible given the proper corrective institution or education. Modern theories of education, Professor Ziegler argued, proceed from the 'assumption that the criminal will be bettered.' On the contrary, 'all things show that this is not the rule.'[78] Criminals will always repeat their crimes no matter how long they are held in prison. Once released they must by an inner urge commit their crimes again.[79]

Therefore, the penal code must pay more attention to the personality of the criminal and not worry about the nature of the crime itself. Since the criminal's mental condition could not be altered it was 'hopeless to try to improve those of low intelligence by punishment, because the essence of low intelligence was to be found in the failure to think about consequences.'[80] The more desirable course of action would be to place offenders permanently out of the way in institutions. 'If one wishes, for example, to prevent a drunkard from committing a crime, one must place him in an asylum for drunkards or forcefully prevent him from drinking in some other way.' And the same was true for other varieties of criminals. 'The vagrant must be placed in an institution where he can be put to doing appropriate work.' Other more serious criminals must be permanently isolated from society. 'In regard to feebleminded offenders, especially young murderers and arsonists, human society has the greatest interest in being lastingly protected from such people. The same is true for many categories of moral offenders, especially those who attack children.'[81]

These institutions were to become permanent dwelling places for the undesirable segments of the population. 'Such institutions could be built according to the plan of modern insane asylums and must be provided with farms and workshops, with schools and churches.' To prevent reproduction the men and the women would be separated. Their lives would be free not only of sexual relations but also of alcohol. In this way 'all offences will be prevented which stem from temporary or chronic alcoholism.'[82]

The Monists seemed to be proposing the creation of a well-disciplined sub-culture of inferior beings who would be permanently removed from the affairs of normal life. It was asserted that the inmates themselves would appreciate the value of their confinement. 'For many offenders a lasting internment would not be a hardship because they will be in better circumstances than in their constantly recurring poverty. Many adapt themselves so poorly in human society that they can find no lasting work and can live nowhere in peace. They are pursued by bad luck wherever they are and cannot rise from poverty by their own efforts.' However, in any event, the most important consequence of the asylums was that the 'reproduction of the offender would be halted.' And since the number of criminals will thereby be diminished, there will consequently occur a 'lessening of court costs, prison costs, and expenses on behalf of the poor.' Society will thus be well served.[83]

The Monist program of eugenics was not only concerned with the negative idea of limiting the reproduction of undesirables; it also tried to encourage the upper classes to increase their numbers substantially. The Monists vented their full fury on all neo-Malthusian ideas which suggested the dangers of over-population. Neo-Malthusian ideas, Dr. Ziegler wrote, are 'thoughts which murder a nation' and 'reach out like a spiritual epidemic.'[84] And Dr. Schallmayer warned that 'insufficiency of reproduction is the commencement of the political downfall and the demise of a nation,' while on the other hand, 'a plentiful increase in numbers is the most important condition of the durability of a nation.'[85] While the normal lower classes reproduce for quantity, the upper classes do so for quality.[86] Dr. Schallmayer pointed out that in fact whatever strength the Germans possessed could be traced to their vigorous reproductive capacities. Indeed, all of Europe had to be warned that if it did not take adequate steps to protect its biological inheritance by fruitful reproduction on a large scale, it ultimately would not be able to counter the population explosion of the Orient.[87]

To insure an adequate increase of the desirable elements of the population, the Monists campaigned for new marriage laws. Dr. Schallmayer proposed that childless couples should be required by law to remarry in order to carry out their basic obligation to the nation to have children. To remain unmarried would be criminally illegal. 'For every healthy man and every healthy woman not to marry is a shame and a violation of their obligation to the state.'[88] And Professor Ziegler criticized the practice of late marriage among the upper classes.

This resulted, he warned, in less time for having children. Like Dr. Schallmayer, he pointed out that 'only those nations can play a great role in world history which have a strong capability of increasing; this rests on the supposition that the women may not throw off the burdens which reproduction entails.'[89]

Thus, the Haeckelian Monists were also critical of another liberal demand, the emancipation of women in terms of simple equality between the sexes. To be sure, one of the principal planks in the platform of the Monist League called for the emancipation of women, but this was increasingly understood by the right-wing leadership of the League, in a novel way. Conceiving their program for emancipation in biological, rather than in social terms, great emphasis was placed on the differences between the sexes. Emancipation, they contended, did not mean that women would be free to fulfill exactly the same social role as that of men. 'It is unscientific and unrealistic to view women only according to the ideals and goals which are appropriate to men.' It had to be understood, rather, that there were 'great differences in the inner life of the two sexes.' Women had their own special natures with their own 'desires and feelings.'[90] And the Haeckelian Monists took this to mean that women could best fulfill themselves by having children, by being good mothers, and by helping to maintain the stability of the family so that it could serve the state well. If a woman, they complained, is 'free to disregard the marriage obligations of reproduction there did exist the possibility that she would desire to have no children at all or only one or two.' The full emancipation of women, therefore, based upon exact equality of the sexes, could lead to 'racial death.'[91] Under emancipation of this kind the birth rate will sink and the nation will die out. Women must rather recognize their 'moral obligation' to society. And despite all the talk about emancipation, these Monists went even so far as to maintain that there had to be a return to the 'old-fashioned' point of view which held that the highest obligation of the woman was to her family and that no social or professional obligation could be given priority over family life.[92] In the evolutionary state, it was prophesied, motherhood would be honored and glorified. Birth control would be prohibited. 'Under normal conditions a great number of children should appear as a stroke of good fortune. It will in time be recognized that only those nations that produce a great many children are able to expand and to conquer new territories.' On the other hand, where children are not valued society is bound to be poor and will soon cease to exist. Thus, from the Monist point of view the 'artificial limitation of the number of children is surely a great evil.'[93] Monism had to awaken the Germans to the need for ever increasing their population.

Given all of the Monists' rather macabre suggestions on eugenics as a means of social reform, who can fail to notice the striking similarity of their proposals to the sombre reality of the Third Reich. We shall see a little further on how in fact the continuity between the Monists and the racial eugenicists of Nazi Germany can in fact be readily established.

NOTES

1. On the theory of the corporative state and its meaning for fascism, see Ralph Bowen, *German Theories of the Corporative State* (New York: Whittlesey House, 1947). See also Herman Lebovics, *Social Conservatism and the Middle Classes in Germany, 1914–1933* (Princeton: Princeton University Press, 1969).
2. Ernst Haeckel, 'Ueber Arbeitstheilung in Natur—und Menschenleben,' in *Gemeinverständliche Vorträge und Abhandlungen*, I, 119-167.
3. Haeckel, *The History of Creation*, I, 279.
4. *Ibid.*
5. Haeckel never really explained how it was theoretically possible for a society to exist, based on mutual harmony and cooperation, if at the same time the basic law of life was the struggle for existence. The two ideas are obviously in contradiction. When it suited him, Haeckel referred to the universality of struggle and on the other hand, when it was convenient he spoke of the need for national harmony and unity. At no time did he give any indication that he was aware of a discrepancy in his thinking. In reality, what Haeckel desired was the harmonious cooperation of those individuals within the state, whose survival had already been determined by eugenic selection. All remaining antagonisms would have to be directed outward, away from Germany, thus providing a theoretical justification for imperialism. When stressing national unity the struggle for existence could be accounted for solely as a conflict between nations leaving the individual free to subordinate himself to the national state. For a discussion of the role of imperialism in Haeckelian Monist thought, see below Chapter VI.

It is also to be noted that social Darwinists in other countries attempted to direct the idea of the struggle for existence outward, away from the mother country, and thereby use it, as did Haeckel, as a theoretical basis for imperialism. This was true, for example, of the English 'Social Imperialist,' Karl Pearson. On

Pearson's 'Social Imperialism,' see Bernard Semmel, *Imperialism and Social Reform* (Cambridge, Mass.: Harvard University Press, 1960).
6. Haeckel, *Eternity*, p. 143.
7. *Ibid.*, p. 133.
8. For an isolated expression of support for parliamentary democracy in the Monist League, see Walter Schücking, *Neue Ziele der staatliche Entwicklung* (Marburg i.H.: Elwert, 1913). Schücking, who later played a significant role in drafting the Weimar Constitution, was more representative of the political character of the Monist League after the First World War.
9. Johannes Unold, 'Politik im Lichte der Entwicklungslehre,' *Das monistische Jahrhundert*, I (1912–13), 55.
10. *Ibid.*
11. *Ibid.*
12. *Ibid.*
13. *Ibid.*
14. Johannes Unold *Politik im Lichte der Entwicklungslehre* (Munich: Reinhardt, 1912), p. 125.
15. *Ibid.*, p. 2
16. Heinrich Ziegler, *Die Vererbungslehre in der Biologie und in der Soziologie* (Jena: Fischer, 1918), p. 296. This book was one of the winners in the Krupp essay contest on social Darwinism, For details of the contest, see below, Chapter VII, p. 148.
17. *Ibid.*
18. *Ibid.*, p. 297.
19. *Ibid.*, p. 316.
20. Unold, *Politik im Lichte der Entwicklungslehre*, p. 110.
21. *Ibid.*
22. *Ibid.*
23. *Ibid.*, p. 115.
24. *Ibid.*, p. 116.
25. Ziegler, *Die Vererbungslehre in der Biologie und in der Soziologie*, p. 427.
26. *Ibid.*, p. 428.
27. Unold, *Politik im Lichte der Entwicklungslehre*, p. 116.
28. *Ibid.*
29. *Ibid.*
30. Ziegler, *Die Vererbungslehre in der Biologie und in der Soziologie*, pp. 451–452.
31. *Ibid.*, pp. 454–455.
32. Johannes Unold, *Die höchsten Kulturaufgaben des modernen Staates* (Munich: Lehmann, 1902), pp. 103–104.
33. *Ibid.*, p. 105.
34. *Ibid.*, p. 107.
35. *Ibid.*, pp. 105–106.
36. Although Haeckel himself did not spell out the details of a theory of corporatism, it is nonetheless clear from his writing that he conceived the organization of society and the state along corporative, rather than along individualistic lines.

'The history of civilization,' he wrote, 'teaches us that its gradual evolution is bound up with three different processes: 1) association of individuals in a community; 2) division of labor among the social elements, and a consequent differentiation of structure: 3) centralization or integration of the unified whole, or rigid organization of the community. The same fundamental laws of sociology hold good for association throughout the entire organic world; and also for the gradual evolution of the several organs out of the tissues and cell-communities.' For Haeckel, therefore, individuals were the cells and social classes the organs of society. In the course of evolution and through the division of labor groups arise within society and of necessity fulfill unequal economic and social tasks. 'It is true that within the limits of civilization the differences of the value of life are enormous. The greater the differentiation of conditions and classes in consequence of division of labor, the greater become the differences between the educated and the uneducated sections of the community, and between their interests and needs, and, therefore, the value of their lives. This difference is naturally most conspicuous if we consider the leading minds and the greatest heights of the culture of the century, and compare these with the average man and the masses, which wander far below in the valley, treading their monotonous and weary way in a more or less stupid condition.'

See Haeckel, *Wonders of Life*, pp. 169, 409.
37. Unold, *Die höchsten Kulturaufgaben des Modernen Staates*, p. 87.
38. See Lebovics, *Social Conservatism and the Middle Classes in Germany*, passim.
39. Ziegler, *Die Vererbungslehre in der Biologie und in der Soziologie*, p. 320.
40. *Ibid.*, p. 322.
41. *Ibid.*
42. Quoted in Dietrich Bronder, *Bevor Hitler Kam* (Hanover: Pfeiffer, 1964), pp. 284–285.
43. Unold, *Politik im Lichte der Entwicklungslehre*, p. 195.
44. *Ibid.*, p. 127.
45. *Ibid.*, pp. 127–128.
46. *Ibid.*, p. 162.
47. *Ibid.*, p. 177.
48. Ziegler, *Die Vererbungslehre in der Biologie und in der Soziologie*, p. 320.
49. Wilhelm Schallmayer, *Vererbung und Auslese im Lebenslauf der Völker* (2nd ed.; Jena: Fischer, 1910), p. ix.

It is important to note that Schallmayer attempted to separate himself from most prevailing racial thought in Germany, which he felt to be highly unscientific. For him, eugenics could only succeed where high standards of scientific and biological analysis were employed. It was not, therefore, racial theory *per se* that he rejected, but only what he considered to be its misuse by those whom he contemptuously labelled Germanic '*Schwärmer*.'

For the links between Schallmayer and National Socialism, see Hedwig Conrad-Martius, *Utopien der Menschenzüchtung* (Munich: Kösel, 1955), pp. 74–123.

50. Schallmayer, *Vererbung und Auslese*, p. ix.

Support for this position as stated by Schallmayer can be found throughout Monist literature in the pre-War period. The Monist League issued a shorter version of *Vererbung und Auslese* as one of its '*Flugschriften*' and officially adopted eugenics in its program.

For a further Monist statement on politics and biology, see Heinrich Pudor 'Politik und Sozialbiologie,' *Der Monismus*, III (1908), 452–456.

51. Schallmayer, *Vererbung und Auslese*, p. x.
52. Lutz Hammerschlag, 'Die Drei Ideologien und ihre Synthese: Kulturpolitik,' *Das monistische Jahrhundert*, II (1913–14), pp. 453–454.

Hammerschlag had written: 'The racial hygienicist says quite correctly: Political democracy is a two-edged weapon; wonderful in a community of the fit, dangerous in the hands of the inferior and the corruptible' (p. 453).

The Swiss eugenicist and Monist, Dr. August Forel, wrote: that modern science had to know 'which races can be of service in the further evolution of mankind, and which are useless. And if the lowest races are useless, how can they be gradually extinguished' See *Out of My Life and Work* (New York: Norton, 1937), p. 193.

53. Schallmayer, *Vererbung und Auslese*, p. viii and *passim*.
54. Haeckel, *The History of Creation*, I, 170–171.
55. Haeckel, *The Wonders of Life*, pp. 21, 118.
56. Wilhelm Schallmayer, 'Ernst Haeckel und die Eugenik,' in Schmidt, *Was wir Ernst Haeckel verdanken*, II, 368.
57. Unold, *Politik im Lichte der Entwicklungslehre*, p. 171.
58. See, for example, Forel, *Out of My Life and Work*, pp. 97–98, 145, 193.
59. Unold, *Politik im Lichte der Entwicklungslehre*, p. 199.
60. *Ibid.*, p. 170.
61. Unold, *Die höchsten Kulturaufgaben des modernen Staates*, p. 19.
62. Forel, *Out of My Life and Work*, pp. 190–191.
63. Ziegler, *Die Vererbungslehre in der Biologie und in der Soziologie*, p. 354.
64. *Ibid.*, p. 355.
65. *Ibid.*, p. 352.
66. *Ibid.*, pp. 349–352.
67. *Ibid.*, p. 349.
68. *Ibid.*, p. 355.
69. Schallmayer, *Vererbung und Auslese*, p. 208.
70. This scepticism in regard to medicine was linked to Haeckel's general belief in man's helplessness before the powers of nature. Disease itself was a mysterious, perhaps even a demonic force. 'Among the many absurd opinions,' Haeckel wrote, 'which are daily promulgated in our "cultural circles," certainly one of the most absurd is that "for every disease there must be a remedy." The experienced physician and naturalist, who is familiar with the actual facts, knows that this is of rarest occurrence, and is disposed rather to wonder that a radical remedy exists for certain diseases.' See Ernst Haeckel, *India and Ceylon*, p. 81.

It is of interest that Haeckel's ideas about the limitations of medicine bear a resemblance to the ideas of some of the French decadents in the decades around the turn of the century. J. K. Huysmans, for example, objected to Charcot's physiological explanations of neuroses, and believed rather in a philosophy and art of 'spiritual naturalism' based upon the premise that 'nothing is explained in the mysteries that surround us.' See James Laver, *The First Decadent: Being the Strange Life of J. K. Huysmans* (New York: Citadel, 1955), pp. 124-125.

71. Haeckel, *History of Creation*, I, 172-173.
72. Haeckel, *Wonders of Life*, pp. 118-119.
73. Schallmayer, *Vererbung und Auslese*, p. 208.
74. *Ibid.*, p. 219.
75. Haeckel, *History of Creation*, I, 172-173. It is also of foreboding interest that one of the programs insisted upon by the Monists and by the German Free Thought Movement in general was cremation of the dead. See M. Pauly, 'Die Feuerbestattung in den deutschen Bundesstaaten,' *Handbuch der freigeistigen Bewegung Deutschlands, Österreichs und der Schweiz*, pp. 362-381.
76. For example, Forel, *Out of My Life and Work*, p. 191, had written: '. . . the problem of responsibility, on which the whole of our penal system reposes, is fundamentally a spurious problem; for it is falsely stated. There are no frontiers between irresponsibility and responsibility; there are only different degrees of responsibility. A responsible human being is capable of adapting himself socially, while an irresponsible person is more or less incapable of adapting himself, until at last he becomes a dangerous individual, a criminal or suicide, by reason of his disordered cerebral activity.'
77. Ziegler, *Die Vererbungslehre in der Biologie und in der Soziologie*, p. 358.
78. *Ibid.*, p. 356.
79. *Ibid.*, p. 366.
80. *Ibid.*, p. 380.
81. *Ibid.*, pp. 361-362.
82. *Ibid.*, p. 368.
83. *Ibid.*, pp. 368-369.
84. *Ibid.*, p. 386.
85. Schallmayer, *Vererbung und Auslese*, p. 287.
86. *Ibid.*, pp. 286-287.
87. *Ibid.*, pp. 294-295. The theme of the dangerous consequences of Oriental reproduction was to be frequently found in Monist literature. See, for example, Johannes Unold, 'Die Bedeutung des Monismus für das praktische Leben' *Der Monismus*, II (1907), p. 285.
88. Schallmayer, *Vererbung und Auslese*, p. 358.
89. Ziegler, *Die Vererbungslehre in der Biologie und in der Soziologie*, p. 379.
90. W[ilhelm] B[reitenbach], 'Die Emanzipation der Jugend,' *Das monistische Jahrhundert*, II (1913-14), 298.

91. *Ibid.*, p. 379.
92. *Ibid.*, p. 381.
93. *Ibid.*, p. 383.

Chapter Five

Monism and Marxism

THE relationship of Haeckelian Monism and Darwinism to Marxism and to socialism in general became a politically and ideologically significant issue in Germany as early as the 1860's and 1870's, and the differences between them were heatedly discussed. The relative intensity of the discussion was an indication of the fact that what was at stake was not so much the narrower biological ideas of Darwin or Haeckel or the specific economic theories of Marx, but rather the broader philosophical views of man and history held by the Marxists and the Haeckelian Monists. The essential point, perhaps, which emerged from the entire discussion was the fact that, on the whole, but with notable exceptions, the Marxists were still functioning within the framework of the ethical and humanistic tradition of secularized Christianity and the ideology of the French Revolution, and that the Haeckelian Monists, once again, were committed to a different framework of ideas and to the destruction of all of the values of bourgeois liberalism. And yet, at the same time, Marxian radicalism, with its opposition to many of the features of traditional culture and religion, its sense of mission and belief in the fundamental transformation of society, its materialism and naturalism, often was very close to Monism. Indeed, despite their differences and frequent acrimonious disputes, the Marxists and the Monists were more similar to each other, than either was to the more traditionally minded liberal or conservative parties.[1]

Along with most other materialists of the middle decades of the nineteenth century both Marx and Engels and many other prominent Social Democrats considered themselves to be Darwinists of one shade or another. Within a few weeks of its publication Engels had read *The Origin of Species* and wrote to Marx about the book in December of 1859. Engels praised Darwin for his theoretical triumph over teleology in the organic sciences, but at the same time also cautioned Marx against Darwin's 'clumsy' style and apparent lack of sophistication in philosophical matters.[2]

The following year, Marx himself read Darwin's book, whereupon he immediately accepted the theory of natural selection as a scientific confirmation of his own ideas about human history. Darwin's theory, he felt, with its emphasis on struggle and evolution in the natural world, was the perfect complement to his own theory of class struggle and historical development. Writing to Ferdinand Lassalle in January, 1861, Marx explained that 'Darwin's book is very important and serves me as a basis in natural science for the class struggle in history.' Of course, he added, echoing Engels' comments of the previous year, 'one [had] to put up with the crude English method of development.' But nonetheless, he concluded, 'despite all deficiencies, not only is the death blow dealt here for the first time to "teleology" in the natural sciences but their rational meaning is empirically explained.'[3] And writing to Engels about the same time, Marx noted that *The Origin of Species* 'is the book which contains the basis in natural history for our view.'[4]

It may be said, therefore, that Marx, at least on the surface and initially, seemed to sense in Darwinism the same quest after the automatic and irreversible laws of development and evolution based upon struggle and conflict which had characterized his own work. In Darwinism, he discovered a scheme of development, similar to his own, which excluded the intervention of both God and man. For Darwin, nature evolved inexorably and alone, free of outside interference. For Marx, the course of history was determined largely by the unconscious operation of the forces and relations of material production. And even further, the idea of Darwinian evolution seemed to Marx to serve in cutting away more of the foundations from the static and harmonious vision of the world which he felt had been characteristic of the 'bourgeois' economists and political theorists, as well as the utopian socialists. Among the various socialist doctrines, Marxism had been unique in its studied denial of a theory of harmony of interests as the prime force in social organization and history. And since Marxian economics and historical theory denied the eternal validity of bourgeois society it appears to have been a relief for Marx to discover that change and conflict also seemed to be the fundamental characteristic of the natural world. Thus, in his famous words at Marx's graveside in 1883, Engels, assessing the significance of Marx, said: 'Just as Darwin discovered the law of evolution in organic nature, so Marx discovered the law of evolution in human history.'[5]

At the same time, however, and despite these favorable opinions about the significance of Darwin, it cannot be said that Marx ever seriously accepted Haeckel's misleading extension of Darwin's exclusively biological theory that the laws of nature and history were literally the same. But this was less true for Engels, who had assumed the role of scientific mentor to the Marxist cause, and readily accepted the opinions of Haeckel on scientific and biological questions.[6] To be sure, Engels expressed only contempt for the quality of Haeckel's philosophical and social thought. For him, Haeckel was one of the 'bourgeois materialists,' a thinker who had not advanced beyond crude eighteenth-century materialism. Thus, in his famous essay on Ludwig Feuerbach and his posthumously published *Dialectics of Nature*, Engels took Haeckel to task in philosophy. 'Where does [Haeckel] get his materialism from?' Engels remarked with disdain and complained that Haeckel did not seem to be able to distinguish between inductive and deductive analysis. And not failing to make use of an opportunity to mock the Professors, Engels asserted that Haeckel's errors were to be expected since they were 'characteristic of the thinking... of our natural scientists.'[7]

Yet, it is apparent that Engels carried over more of Haeckel's evolutionary philosophy and science into his version of Dialectical Materialism than he realized or would have admitted. In his philosophical works written during the seventies and eighties of the last century, Engels, in good Haeckelian fashion, stressed continuity between the laws of nature and history and viewed the development of human society in terms of the unconscious operation of the general laws of evolution.[8] Apparently captivated by the tantalizing vision of Haeckelian Monism, Engels felt certain that in combining Marxism with science and Darwinism, one could readily reduce all of nature and society to simple and absolutely decipherable patterns of development. Thus he wrote: 'But what is true of nature which is hereby recognized also as a historical process of development, is likewise true of the history of society in all its branches and of the totality of all sciences which occupy themselves with things human (and divine).' Like nature, therefore, history follows an inexorable course of development which is set down by the laws of evolution. And although Engels conceded that men have consciousness, he nonetheless concluded that this could not alter or transform the fundamental and predetermined course of history. 'Thus,' he wrote, 'the conflicts of innumerable individual wills and individual actions in the domain of history produce a state of affairs entirely analogous to that prevailing in the realm of unconscious nature . . . . Historical events thus appear on the whole to be governed by chance. But where on the surface accident holds sway, there actually it is governed by inner, hidden laws, and it is only a matter of discovering these laws.'[9]

Despite these similarities with Haeckel, the parallel between them should not be overemphasized or carried too far. Admittedly, Dialectical Materialism, as rigidly formulated by Engels, stressed evolution and determinism while at the same time underplaying the importance of man's creative social role in history, a theoretical assumption which had been stressed earlier in Marxian philosophy. But even granting this, Engels nonetheless did not maintain with Haeckel that there existed an absolutely literal and direct connection between the laws of nature and man. Ultimately, for Marx and Engels, and despite the influence of Haeckel, it was the economic forces of production and not the Haeckelian laws of nature which were really the decisive factors in human history. Like most other non-Haeckelian social Darwinists, Marx and Engels conceived of the relationship between nature and history only in broadly analogical terms. In addition, it should be kept in mind that Marx, who often departed from the economic determinism that is the basis for Historical Materialism, tended, especially in his earlier writings, to place much emphasis on the independent role of human consciousness in shaping the course of history. For him, man is related to nature only through the social world and the industry which he *creates*. And unlike Haeckel, who completely rejected free will, and Engels who appeared to deny it, Marx wrote, in a by now famous sentence: 'The philosophers have only interpreted the world in various ways, the point, however, is to change it.'[10] There were also moments when Marx dismissed the social insights of Darwin himself. He once observed, for example, in an amusingly penetrating comment, that all that Darwin had discovered in the natural world was bourgeois society writ large. 'It is noteworthy,' he wrote to Engels, 'how Darwin rediscovers his English society with its division of labor, competition, the opening up of new markets, "inventions," and the Malthusian "struggle for existence," among the animals and plants. It is Hobbes' *bellum omnium contra omnes*, and it reminds one of Hegel in the *Phenomenology* where bourgeois society figures "spiritually as an animal kingdom," whereas in Darwin the animal kingdom becomes bourgeois society.'[11] Implied in Marx's shrewd observation was the understanding that it would be ludicrous to attempt to derive a meaningful ethic from the Darwinian natural world.

If Marx and Engels, therefore, appeared to accept the relationship between their ideas and those of Darwin in a half-serious, half-sceptical way, so too did their followers in Germany attempt to bring Marxian social science into harmony with Darwinism, and at the same time paradoxically to maintain a decided difference from it. For example, such prominent Social Democrats as Heinrich Cunow and August Bebel attempted, in the pages of the chief Marxist journal in Germany, *Die neue Zeit*, to correlate Marxism and Darwinism. And in his highly popular book, *Die Frau und der Sozialismus*, which became a standard handbook of Marxian theory, Bebel devoted much space and emphasis to the relationship between Marxism and Darwinism.[12] Bebel, like Engels unable to escape the allurements of scientific Monism, suggested that all of natural science, Darwinism, social science, and Marxism were really only related parts of one unified theoretical system of the world. 'In order,' he wrote, 'to understand the origin and evolution of the good and bad qualities of sexes and nations, the same methods must be applied and the same laws examined as those by whose help modern science explains the origin and evolution of species and genera with their respective characteristics in the animal world. We refer to the laws named Darwinian.'[13] And his description of the nature of those laws sounded completely Haeckelian. 'Man,' Bebel wrote, 'can form no exception to laws which apply to all organisms in nature; he does not stand outside nature, but is from a physiological point of view nothing more than the most highly developed animal. Unfortunately this is very far from being generally recognized.'[14]

At the same time, however, reflecting the ambiguity of the Marxist position in regard to Darwinism, Bebel could hardly help also pointing to the social and psychological differences between animals and men. The condition of man, he stated, depended not only on his own physical attributes but also on the nature of the prevailing economic and social conditions. An improvement in social conditions would also bring with it an improvement in the general well-being of the species and a mitigation of the harsh laws of nature.[15] As a Marxist, Bebel viewed the goal of social development as involving the termination of the struggle for existence among men and the establishment of a classless society. In classless society men would devote their energies solely to the further conquest of nature and not to fighting with one another. Socialism would bring about an amelioration of the conditions of oppression, exploitation, and wasteful struggle, which were the commonplace products of all class societies. Bebel, therefore, despite his statements in support of the Darwinian laws, concluded his analysis of the relation of Marxism to Darwinism by stating: 'The Darwinian law of the struggle for existence, which finds its expression in nature in the elimination and destruction of lower by stronger and more highly developed organisms, arrives at a different consummation in the human world.'[16] For him as a Marxist, the end of evolutionary struggle and development would have to be the creation of a perfected, egalitarian, and peaceful humanity. Thus, in the socialist society of the future as Bebel envisioned it man would finally be able to transcend his animal origins.

The attempt on the part of the Marxists to share in the prestige of Darwinism and to bolster their own position by attaching themselves to it quickly drew a loud protest from Haeckel and from his followers.[17] In 1878, responding to the public charge of Rudolf Virchow, the radical liberal, that Haeckelian Monism led to socialism and was, therefore, a dangerous doctrine,[18] Haeckel angrily asserted that there was in fact no connection between the two philosophies.[19] Replying to Virchow, Haeckel indignantly wrote: 'I ask myself in surprise, "What in the world has the doctrine of descent to do with socialism?"'

As far as he was concerned, the 'two theories are about as compatible as fire and water.' He explained that the doctrine of evolution and theory of descent taught that the 'equality of individuals which socialism strives after is an impossibility, that it stands, in fact, in irreconcilable contradiction to the inevitable inequality of individuals which actually and everywhere subsists.' The general equality which socialism demands is a chimera based upon a false interpretation of nature. While socialism, he wrote, 'demands equal rights, equal duties, equal possessions, equal enjoyments for every citizen alike,' the doctrine of evolution 'proves, in exact opposition to this, that the realization of this demand is a pure impossibility, and that in the constitutionally organized communities of men, as of the lower animals, neither rights nor duties, neither possessions nor enjoyments have ever been equal for all the members alike nor ever can be.' It had to be understood, rather, that it was the very essence of life to be full of inequalities. Thus, Haeckel actually found that the evolutionary doctrine was the 'best antidote' to the 'fathomless absurdity of extravagant socialist levelling.' Darwinism was 'anything rather than socialist! If this English hypothesis is to be compared to any definite political tendency—as is, no doubt, possible—that tendency can only be aristocratic, certainly not democratic, and least of all socialist.' In short, the political doctrine implied by evolution is elitist. 'The theory of selection teaches that in human life, as in animal and plant life everywhere, and at all times, only a small and chosen minority can exist and flourish, while the enormous majority starve and perish miserably and more or less prematurely. The germs of every species of animal and plant and the young individuals which spring from them are innumerable, while the number of those fortunate individuals which develop to maturity and actually reach their hardly-won life's goal is out of all proportion trifling.' Repeating his oft-stated position, Haeckel declared that the struggle for existence is universal and eternal, and socialism could not bring it to an end with all of its utopian dreams. 'Only the picked minority of the qualified "fittest" is in a position to resist it successfully, while the great majority of the competitors must necessarily perish miserably. We may profoundly lament this tragical state of things, but we can neither controvert nor alter it.' The political principle to be derived, therefore, from evolution is 'aristocratic in the strictest sense of the word.'[20]

In *Die Frau und der Sozialismus*, Bebel sought to answer the anti-Marxist charges of Haeckel. He accused Haeckel of propagandizing and acting in support of the established political and social forces of Germany, and of having abandoned the 'democratic' implications of Darwinism. Bebel did not explain exactly what he meant by 'democratic,' but he wrote that 'it is quite natural that Prof. Haeckel . . . should protest energetically against the fearful accusation that Darwinism plays into the hands of socialism.' This was simply because Haeckel's position represented an unjustifiable extension of the laws of nature to human society. Haeckel's position, he wrote, was 'at best a rude, mechanical application to humanity' of Darwinism. Haeckel, Bebel felt, had failed to understand the difference between the unconscious world of animals and plants, and the conscious existence of human society. He had erroneously assumed that 'because the struggle for existence in nature is carried on unconsciously by animals and organisms without knowledge of laws, that the same thing must take place among men.' Haeckel had overlooked the fact that 'though man is a reflecting animal, the animal is not a reflecting man'; hence his 'false conclusions.'[21]

Although Haeckel continued to make brief and bitter attacks on the Marxists[22] the actual spelling out of the details in the ideological debate with them was left to his Monist followers. In 1893, Haeckel's colleague, the zoologist Heinrich Ziegler, published a book entitled *Die Naturwissenschaft und die sozialdemokratische Theorie*, in which he appraised Marxism from a Monist point of view. In his book, to which Haeckel gave his unqualified support,[23] Ziegler explained that he had found especially disturbing the Social Democratic claim that their interpretation of Darwinism accorded with scientific principles. It was the Monist position, rather, which was closer to nature and to science. It was apparent, Ziegler continued, that Bebel's Marxist approach to Darwinism was utopian in content and, therefore, of absolutely no practical value as a workable political doctrine. Like Haeckel, Ziegler repudiated Bebel's belief in the equality of all men and in the possibility of creating a society free from competition and conflict. He criticized

Bebel for believing that by changing the external conditions of mankind a wholly new individual and a new human nature could be created. Human adaptation and resultant biological change was a slow process, and 'before mankind would have gotten used to the new forms of social organization, any new society would by that time have collapsed.'[24]

In order to demonstrate historically that change among humans and in society took a very long time, Ziegler pointed to the experience of the French Revolution. 'In France,' he wrote, 'in the course of the Revolution there was great opposition to the privileges of the nobility and against "aristocratic sentiment," but no one can now deny that in Republican France a Vicomte is regarded as standing higher than a bourgeois.' Human nature, Ziegler wrote, could be altered only after innumerable generations had elapsed. Denying the inheritance of acquired characteristics, Ziegler proposed that human heredity was 'hard' and therefore that human nature could not be easily altered. Thus, for Ziegler, the 'character of mankind considered in its natural constituents is yet the same as it was at the time of Moses or Homer.' It was these irrefutable facts about human nature which had to be presupposed by any political theory. 'In relation to the establishment of new political and social relationships one can only reasonably take into consideration the next century, and for so short a time the instinctive character of mankind will remain a constant and unchanging one.'[25]

It may be said that the Monists alternated between excessive admiration and profound loathing for the Social Democratic movement. This was as true for Haeckel as it was for his followers.[26] Indeed, some of the Monists were in fact members of the Social Democratic Party, and all of the Monists admired the Party for its successful organizing abilities and for the political power which it had managed to obtain for itself. They felt themselves to be at one with Social Democracy in its anti-clerical activity and in its efforts to improve the condition and to raise the cultural *niveau* of the German working class. In other words, in terms of immediate and practical goals, Monism found much with which to identify in Social Democracy, and admiration for the Marxists was frequently voiced by members of the League. When Bebel died, for example, in 1913, *Das monistische Jahrhundert* eulogized him as one of the greatest German leaders. Bebel was praised for having helped to improve the general material and intellectual level of the German proletariat, an effort which was assessed by the Monists as a 'patriotic attainment of the first rank.' In an 'age of commerce,' they wrote, Bebel had successfully taught the Germans how powerful an idea could be and how necessary it was to cultivate an ideal. The Social Democratic Party and Bebel, therefore, could provide an 'example' for Monism and could show how the 'forces of courage, sacrifice, and perseverance can be awakened in man.'[27]

It was the long range goals of Social Democracy—its desire for violent revolution, nationalization of all the means of production, and the creation of a cosmopolitan world community based upon the power of the industrial working class—which were decisively rejected by the Monists, who nevertheless also considered themselves socialists. In contrast with Marxian internationalism, however, the Haeckelian Monists were 'national' socialists, dedicated to the racial community of the Germans; and their political and social allegiance was to the peasantry and to the lower middle class rather than to the industrial proletariat of the Marxists.[28]

Thus, in the prolific writings of one of the more articulate spokesmen for Haeckelian Monism, Dr. Johannes Unold, expressions of admiration for Social Democracy were to be found in juxtaposition with lengthy and vitriolic attacks upon the 'unhistorical radicalism' of Marxism. In truly conservative fashion Unold argued repeatedly that civilization could progress only under conditions of the strictest social control and organization. Monism, therefore, had to be fully opposed to any 'attempt to bring about progress by a full break with the past and by destroying that which exists.' For new social relations and conditions to be of 'value and durability, the germ of the new must be long prepared,' Unold argued. He felt that the Marxist advocacy of 'forceful revolution' would lead to a 'view of nature and of cultural history which would inevitably result in tragic repercussions.'[29] It was not 'revolutionary radicalism,'[30] that Germany was in need of, but rather a 'strengthening and diffusion of conservative points of view.'[31]

In his criticism of Social Democracy, Unold pointed to what he considered to be the basic ideological errors of the Marxists. He stressed, first of all, that they had irresponsibly advocated the subversion of state power. This negative position, he felt, made Social Democracy, despite some admirable characteristics, a highly dangerous movement from the standpoint of national unity.[32] The Marxists, Unold wrote, were gravely mistaken when they taught that the state had arisen historically by force and thereby had to be overthrown by force in a final revolutionary struggle. On the contrary, reiterating the Monist position, Unold pointed out that the state was created neither by force as the Marxists maintained, nor by voluntary contractual agreement, which was the theoretical assumption of liberalism. Rather, it was a natural organic form of social organization and its continued existence was justifiable and made necessary thereby. The Marxists did not seem to realize that a 'more advanced kind of state could be created' only by 'being true to history and by limiting oneself to that which was possible.'[33]

Unold also found the Marxists to be a disrupting force in the day-to-day life of German politics. They refused, he complained, to participate in and cooperate with the bourgeois parties. Social Democracy, Unold explained, behaved in this way because it naively fought for the attainment of a classless society, which was unrealizable. Therefore, he wrote with the outlandish exaggeration typical of the Monists, 'considered from an evolutionary point of view Social Democracy was the most reactionary of all the political parties. For it was not content, as were some of the conservatives, or [members] of the Center Party, to return to medieval political conditions, but wished rather to impose primitive forms of state and social organization on our richly evolved civilized communities with their densely and highly individualized populations, their many activities, and their diverse needs.'[34] In fact, the only time in history when the Marxist program had ever been fulfilled in any way was at the dawn of civilization when common tribal ownership of land existed. 'At that time there was no classes but only equality of rights and equality of duties for all.' But with social evolution all that has changed and society can never return to the condition of its origin. By its support of common ownership of the means of production, therefore, Marxism simply was advocating a return to the most primitive conditions of mankind's past. 'In the Social Democratic proposals one may observe a deliberate pursuit . . . of evolution in a reverse direction, a complete return to truly original stages, a form of state and

MONISM AND MARXISM

social organization which is similar to the phenomenon of child-like behaviour in old age.'[35]

Having established to his own satisfaction the retrogressive and reactionary character of Marxism, Unold wrote further of the 'torpidity' of Social Democracy and warned of the 'mob domination' which would inevitably characterize a communist victory.[36] Monism, therefore, had to 'work against . . . one-sided brutal communist mass domination or the brutal bureaucratic state.'[37] The real weakness of Social Democracy was that it wished to perpetuate the basic assumptions of liberalism, and had inherited all of its 'weaknesses and shortcomings' in a 'stronger and more vulgar form.' Thus, any victory of the forces of Social Democracy would result in the disregard of the rights of other groups in the nation. It would occasion a 'brutal trampling of remaining classes and interests to realize the mass domination of the proletariat with its communist tendencies.' Under communism there would be oppression of quality by quantity. 'By exaggerating the concept of the "sovereignty of the people" and by mistakenly equating the working class with the people, the Social Democratic Workers' Party wickedly strives to achieve a "free nation," that is, a community, in which a pure numerical majority exploits the community and the state as a means of oppressing those who think differently.' Thus, to allow the Marxian revolution to take place it to court political tyranny and would result in a 'new form of unlimited absolutism.' And all of its objectives were a threat to the well-being of the nation. 'The mass domination which it has striven for for over twenty years, free and equal citizenship, the dictatorship of the proletariat, the socialization of the means of production, direct legislation by the people, election of all officials and judges by majority vote, the establishment of a "people's army" led by citizen-officers, will never lead to a free people's state.' Rather, it would result in a 'terrible despotism' that would 'squander public wealth' and permit the 'exploitation' of the 'honest' and the 'fit.' In the final analysis society would descend into military dictatorship in order to be rescued from the harmful effects of class levelling. Monism had, therefore, to reject all of the political demands of the Social Democrats. Indeed, the goal of Monism should be to curb the 'covetous' and the 'uneducated' masses. The Monists must make Germany aware that once allowed into power Social Democracy would 'awaken among the German working class a monstrous megalomania, an insatiable lust for political power.'[38]

It may be said that if Social Democracy stressed proletarian power and class struggle, the Monists emphasized the need for class harmony—even, we must note, at the price of suppressing all dissident elements. While Social Democracy, the Monists argued, reflected only narrow party interest, Monism stood for 'unity in thought and action.'[39] In his Autobiography, Wilhelm Ostwald recalled that a number of left-wing Monists had urged outright alliance with the Social Democrats. But Ostwald opposed their request and explained that such a merger would have been 'impossible for me, as long as the large contradiction between the concept of socialism and class struggle was not removed. Because a party which is active in class struggle, is without doubt clearly unsocial.'[40] For the Monists it was the nation itself which was superior to any particular class or group. Social Democracy, they complained further, demanded absolute obedience and suppressed differences of opinion as a 'betrayal' of the interests of the working class. As a consequence, Monism had no option but to be 'opposed to such a fanatically inspired party with such a narrow one-sided conception of things' which only expressed the needs and sentiments of a part of the nation. Thus, not only was Monism without 'obligation to [accept] Social Democratic views,' but it also had the 'right and the duty to make the Social Democratic Party aware of the dangers of the "unavoidable evil" which it brings about.' But, of course, once Social Democracy recognized the errors of its ways it would then be free to play a constructive role in German political life. By revising its ideology, Social Democracy and Monism 'will be friends with each other,'[41] they wrote. And revealingly, Dr. Unold, despite his bitter ideological attacks on the Marxists, was still willing to hope that 'German Social Democracy can and will ... advance the evolution of our society once it renounces its radical and doctrinaire fantasies.'[42]

The social and economic program which the Monists advanced as an alternative to that of the Social Democrats represented a kind of middle course between laissez-faire capitalism, on the one hand, and Marxist socialism, on the other. For the Monists, the solution to the economic and social problems of Germany did not consist in the total overthrow of capitalism and the complete nationalization of the means of production. It was to be found, rather, in a social system that would attempt to curb the evils of large-scale free enterprise and at the same time succeed in avoiding the pitfalls of socialist collectivism. Like the Marxists, therefore, the Monists could point out that they were opposed to the traditional privileged groups and classes in society. They claimed to recognize the necessity of combatting the elements of 'capitalism, monarchism, the church hierarchy, and the Prussian landed aristocracy.'[43] And Dr. Unold even openly agreed with the Social Democrats that the working class had truly been exploited by 'plutocratic'[44] capitalism and that the bourgeoisie had always perversely attempted to keep real political power to itself.[45] The Monists emphasized, of course, that a solution to these problems could not be found in Marxism, but that one had to look rather to the writings and the social and economic programs of such social theorists as Adolf Damaschke and Heinrich Wehberg.

Around the turn of the century, Adolf Damaschke and Heinrich Wehberg appeared as potent forces in non-Marxian German social reform circles. Influenced to very great extent by the ideas of the American social critic Henry George and his theory of the single tax, Wehberg and Damaschke, as presidents of the German Land Reform League, proposed a scheme for the abolition of urban poverty, the cessation of the flight of the peasants from the countryside to the city, and the termination of land shortages. Highly critical of capitalist speculation in land and what they regarded as the increasingly excessive cost of ground rents and interest on mortgages, these German land reformers suggested an immediate nationalization of ground rents, a cessation of real estate profiteering, and the ultimate nationalization of all land. It was their intention to make the German peasantry absolutely secure in its tenure of land and at the same time to free as much rural property as possible for resettlement by workers from the urban industrial slums. Apart from land, however, the remaining branches of the economy would be allowed to remain in private hands, their scheme thus representing a compromise between the demands of socialism, on the one hand, and capitalism, on the other. Damaschke and Wehberg envisioned the creation of a revitalized

German peasantry fully enjoying the fruits of its labor and secure from the exploitation of mortgage banks and land speculators.[46]

The Monists were avid supporters of the ideas of Wehberg and Damaschke, and many branches of the Monist League associated themselves with the program of the German Land Reform League.[47] Unlike Marx, who spoke contemptuously of the 'idiocy of rural life,'[48] and his followers, who labored to raise rural life up to a higher cultural level and to involve it within the orbit of the urban center, the Monists envisioned the future of Germany as dependent upon the creation of a rejuvenated countryside, a retreat from the cities, and the establishment of a vital and biologically healthy and vigorous peasant class. Running throughout the writings of Haeckel and the literature of the members of the Monist League was a strong undercurrent of hostility to urban civilization, which they along with many other Volkists, saw as the epitome of the rootlessness and shallowness of modern life.[49] They lamented that the German peasants were being increasingly forced off the land and compelled to migrate to the cities, where they were 'uprooted, homeless,' and 'far from friends and relatives.'[50] For the Monists, it would appear, a nation could well exist without its large cities, but deprived of a peasantry rooted in the land, it would be certain to go under.

Thus, the Monists took the issue of land reform very seriously and argued that the proposals of Damaschke and of the Land Reform League deserved to be put into practice.[51] The disposition of land, they wrote, is the 'basis of all private as well as national existence' and the 'future of our nation depends upon it.' Life is not possible without the land; it is its 'first,' its 'most necessary condition.'[52] In Germany, they asserted, the land once belonged to the people. 'But there came a time when, from mistaken ideas, the land was made an object of speculation, to be bought and sold, like any other article of trade. It was forgotten that land was something different; that it could not be increased according to the need for more; that it is absolutely necessary to all life and labor.'[53] Only proper land reform, therefore, can provide a 'healthy basis for the life of the German citizen.' On the soil of Germany, they said in tones of indignation, there now exists a 'slavery of the many by the few who are in possession of the land.'[54] Therefore, it was in the national interest that the activities of the land speculators and of the landlords should be brought to an end. Landlords and speculators are parasites. 'What was the cause of the great increase in the value of the land? Was it the labor of the few who own it? Did they make any improvements that were of benefit to the community? Oh no, the landlord has done nothing. Without labor, without trouble, or care on his part, his possessions have increased in value.' Rent was only 'tribute' which the peasants payed to the landlords, who 'pocket' the value of the labor of others.[55] The Monists, therefore, urged the nationalization of rent and then ultimately of land itself. Capitalism, with its 'smell of blood and death,' could not be allowed to operate unhindered when it was a question of Germany's very earth. Rather, there had to be an immediate 'cessation of uncontrolled private property in land' and the abolition of the social system which had led to the 'private misuse of the soil of the earth.' It was necessary to 'fight against the Manchester School which has conceived of land and earth as commodities.'[56] And they cried out in ringing terms: 'On to the combat! Let us not superficially remove the withered leaves, but dig at the roots and remove the cause which is eating at the life of the tree! The battle is for a holy cause.'[57]

For the Monists, therefore, Social Democracy was in error when it conceived of capitalism in general as 'exploitative.' Cure the land of the system of speculative free enterprise, the Monists argued, and the economy of Germany would once again be healthy. What was wanted was not the overthrow of capitalism but the institution of a program that would establish 'peace between individualism and socialism!'[58]

And finally, to illustrate further the theoretical hiatus separating the Monists from the Social Democrats, it should be recognized that they not only placed their faith in the rural classes rather than in the urban proletariat, but that there was apparent in their thinking a strong quest after the creation of a rural utopia. In the Monist mind the introduction of land reform was linked to the establishment of utopian-like agrarian communities. At a Congress of the Monist League in 1912, Wilhelm Ostwald announced the launching of a program for the founding of rural Monist cooperatives all over Germany. Although the plan was ultimately not carried out, except for one abortive attempt, *Das monistische Jahrhundert* reported that the proposal itself was greeted by the members of the League with 'enthusiasm and excitement.'

Ostwald's idea was described as an 'audacious' one and the Monists were certain that the 'scientific, economic, and moral preconditions existed' for the successful establishment of such communities.[60] Moreover, they were aware of other contemporary experiments in Germany in utopian living, especially of the colony of vegetarians founded in 1893, which was called Eden. The Monists were very impressed by Eden with its semi-cooperative way of life and an economy based upon horticulture. They recognized in Eden a community which had escaped from the 'decaying influences of the Metropolis' and which provided a life of rootedness in the soil.[61]

This surge of desire among the Monists for a utopian existence is highly revealing. It demonstrates clearly how deep their opposition to and alienation from prevailing German society. For them ultimately, the only real solution to their own and Germany's problems lay in escaping from reality by establishing a perfect life, based upon science, in the midst of decadent industrial society. Thus, as Ostwald outlined his plans to the Congress of 1912, the Monist colonies would 'offer adults a place for the recovery [of their health] and protection against the confusion of contemporary life.' In contrast with the alienated and lonely life to be found in the cities, the colonies would furnish the proper surroundings and atmosphere for the development of 'honest and worthwhile friendships.' And ultimately he expected that these colonies would form a vast and mighty network throughout Germany. 'What I am presenting here in embryonic form,' Ostwald prophesied to the Congress, 'will become a reality for decades and for thousands of years to come.' In these colonies a new way of life and new physical and mental personality—the personality of Monist man—would be created.[62]

Monism, therefore, in the end pictured the social and economic transformation of Germany in terms that were quite different from those of the Marxists. In the next chapter we shall see how the Monists wished to utilize territories outside of Germany for the further realization of their ideals.

NOTES

1. For an analysis of the bond between Marxism and fascism, see Ernst Nolte, *Three Faces of Fascism* (New York: Holt, Rinehart, and Winston), pp. 20-21.

Nolte writes: 'Fascism is anti-Marxism which seeks to destroy the enemy by the evolvement of a radically opposed and yet related ideology and by the use of almost identical and yet typically modified methods, always, within the unyielding framework of national self-assertion and autonomy. This definition implies that without Marxism there is no fascism, that fascism is at the same time closer to and further from communism than is liberal anti-communism, that it necessarily shows at least an inclination toward a radical ideology, that fascism should never be said to exist in the absence of at least the rudiments of an organization and propaganda comparable to those of Marxism.'

2. Engels to Marx, December, 1859, in *Karl Marx–Friedrich Engels: Historisch-kritische Gesammtausgabe (Frankfort-Berlin:* Marx-Engels Verlag, 1927-1932), III, Part 2, 448.
3. Karl Marx to Ferdinand Lassalle, January, 1861, in Karl Marx, *Correspondence* (New York: International, 1942), p. 125.
4. Karl Marx, *Selected Works* (New York: International, 1942), I, 16.
5. *Ibid.*
6. For an analysis of Haeckel by Engels, see his *Anti-Dühring (Herr Eugen Dühring's Revolution in Science)* (New York: International, 1939), p. 80, and *Dialectics of Nature* (New York: International, 1940), pp. 189, 235.
7. Engels, *Dialectics of Nature*, p. 229, and 'Ludwig Feuerbach and the Outcome of Classical German Philosophy,' in Lewis S. Feuer (ed.), *Marx and Engels: Basic Writings on Politics and Philosophy* (Garden City, N.Y.: Doubleday, 1959).
8. For an account of the important influence of Haeckel and his scientific Monism on the development of Dialectical Materialism, see George Lichtheim, *Marxism. An Historical and Critical Study* (New York: Praeger, 1961), pp. 244ff. and *passim.*
9. Engels, 'Ludwig Feuerbach and the Outcome of Classical German Philosophy,' pp. 229–230.
10. Karl Marx, 'Theses on Feuerbach,' in Lewis S. Feuer (ed.), *Marx and Engels: Basic Writings on Politics and Philosophy* (Garden City, N.Y.: Doubleday, 1959). On Marx's conception of the relation of man and nature, see Lichtheim, *Marxism*, p. 251 and *passim*. Lichtheim writes: 'How Marx originally envisaged the relation of nature to history appears plainly enough from his early writings, where the dialectic of human, sensuous, activity and objectified "nature" is described as a process in which man's labour *produces* the external (social) world confronting him. . . . *There is no nature apart from man.'* And he adds a little further on: 'In short, for the early Marx—and in a measure for the mature Marx too—nature and man are complex realities whose interaction is studied in society. This is precisely the reverse of Engel's habit of deducing historical "laws" from the operation of nature conceived as an independent reality external to man.'
11. Marx to Engels, June 18, 1862, in *Karl Marx–Friedrich Engels: Historisch-kritische Gesammtausgabe*, III, Part 2, 77–78.
12. But not without sharp dissent from at least one prominent 'orthodox' Marxist. Karl Kautrsky opposed any attempt to connect Marxism and Darwinism in social

theory, and declared firmly that no bridge could span the two doctrines. See Karl Kautsky, 'Sozialismus und Darwinismus,' *Oesterreichischer Arbeiterkalendar*, XI (1890), 49-54. Kautsky was also critical of Haeckel's racism. See Karl Kautsky. *Are the Jews a Race?* (New York: International, 1926), p. 76.

13. August Bebel, *Woman in the Past, Present, and Future* (San Francisco: G. B. Benham, 1897), p. 54.
14. *Ibid.*
15. *Ibid.*, p. 95.
16. *Ibid.*
17. See Oscar Schmidt, *Darwinismus und Sozialdemokratie* (Bonn: Strauss, 1878), and A. C. Stiebeling, *Sozialismus und Darwinismus* (New York: Schmidt, 1897).
18. Virchow, *The Freedom of Science in the Modern State*, p. 19.
19. The word Socialism may here be equated with Marxism. The Monists also considered themselves to be Socialists, but as we shall see, of a very different kind.
20. Haeckel, *Freedom in Science and Teaching*, pp. 90-94.
21. Bebel, *Woman in the Past, Present, and Future*, p. 96.
22. See, for example, Ernst Haeckel, 'Die Wissenschaft und der Umsturz,' in *Gemeinverständliche Vorträge und Abhandlungen*, II, 374-375.
23. *Ibid.*, p. 375.
24. Heinrich Ziegler, *Die Naturwissenschaft und die sozialdemokratische Theorie* (Stuttgart: Enke, 1893), pp. 19-20.
25. *Ibid.*, pp. 20-22.
26. For example, Haeckel had written in 'Die Wissenschaft und der Umsturz, p. 375: 'I am certainly no friend of Herr Bebel, who has repeatedly attacked me and among other things has indeed slandered me in his book on 'The Woman.' ... I also maintain that the utopian goals of official Social Democracy are unrealizable and that their great ideal state of the future is nothing but a tremendous prison This cannot hinder me, however, from recognizing the justifiable essence of this great social movement.'
27. W[ilhelm] B[reitenbach], 'August Bebel,' *Das monistische Jahrhundert*, II (1913-14), 589.
28. For a political and social defense of lower middle class interests, see Unold, *Politik im Lichte der Entwicklungslehre*, pp. 127-128 and *passim*.
29. Johannes Unold, 'Die Bedeutung des Monismus für das praktische Leben,' *Der Monismus*, II (1907), 288.
30. *Ibid.*, p. 292.
31. Unold, *Politik im Lichte der Entwicklungslehre*, p. 187.
32. *Ibid.*, p. 36.
33. *Ibid.*, p. 65.
34. *Ibid.*, p. 114.
35. *Ibid.*
36. *Ibid.*, p. 121.
37. *Ibid.*, p. 123.
38. *Ibid.*, pp. 174-178.

39. H. Peus-Dessau, 'Monismus und Sozialdemokratie,' *Das monistische Jahrhundert*, II (1913-14), 23.
40. Wilhelm Ostwald, *Lebenslinien* (Berlin: Klasing, 1927), III, 250.
41. H. Peus-Dessau, 'Monismus und Sozialdemokratie,' 23-29.
42. Unold, *Politik im Lichte der Entwicklungslehre*, p. 179.
43. Peus-Dessau, 'Monismus und Sozialdemokratie,' p. 28.
44. Unold, *Politik im Lichte der Entwicklungslehre*, p. 174.
45. *Ibid.*, pp. 175-176.
46. See Adolf Damaschke, *Die Bodenreform* (Berlin: Rade, 1902), and Heinrich Wehberg, *Die Bodenreform im Lichte des humanistischen Sozialismus* (Munich: Duncker, 1913).
47. Lothar Engelberg Schücking, 'Monismus und Bodenreform,' *Das monistische Jahrhundert*, II (1913-14), 1382. For Ostwald's support of *Bodenreform*, see *Lebenslinien*, III, 250.
48. Karl Marx, *The Communist Manifesto* (New York: Appleton Century Crofts, 1955), p. 14.
49. See, for example, Unold, *Der Monismus und seine Ideale*, p. 127: 'How is a healthy, vital, sensitive life possible among people who, like most of our present day inhabitants of large cities, turn night into day and seek their relaxation by staying much too long in damp and smoky places? ... How is a healthy sensitive life possible among over-rushed, over-fed individuals who have poor blood circulation and are enclosed in dark, poorly ventilated shops, offices, and banks and who can hardly digest their over-rich food.'
50. Emil Felden, *The Land of Your Children* (Cincinnati: Fels, n.d.), p. 14. This book is a reprint of a sermon which Felden, a member of the Monist League, delivered at St. Martini, a Monist Church in Bremen, where he was the Pastor.
51. Lothar Engelbert Schücking, 'Monismus und Bodenreform,' p. 1378.
52. Felden, *Land of Your Children*, p. 7.
53. *Ibid.*, p. 11.
54. Max Andler, 'Bodenreform. Wesen und Entwicklung der Bodenreform, *Das monistische Jahrhundert*, II (1913-14), 40-41.
55. Felden, *Land of Your Children*, p. 12.
56. Schücking, 'Monismus und Bodenreform,' pp. 1380-1382.
57. Felden, *Land of Your Children*, p. 22.
58. Max Andler, 'Die Grundbegriffe der Bodenreform,' *Das monistische Jahrhundert*, II (1913-14), 408.
59. Ostwald, *Lebenslinien*, III, 252ff.
60. See the report of the 1912 Congress in *Das monistische Jahrhundert*, I (1912-1913), 418.
61. E. W. Trojan, 'Obstbaukolonie Eden. Eine soziale Siedlungsgenossenschaft,' *Das monistische Jahrhundert*, III (1914-1915), 394.
    For more on Eden, see Mosse, *The Crisis of German Ideology*, pp. 111-112, 121.
62. *Das Montistische Jahrhundert*, I (1912-1913), 418.

Chapter Six

Monism, Imperialism, and the First World War

HAECKEL and the Monists were among the first to formulate a program of racial imperialism and *Lebensraum* for Germany. For them, historical progress was determined not only by the competition of individuals within society, but also by the conflict and struggle of divergent races and nations. At home, they argued, Germany could best gain internal security and stability for itself by fostering class harmony and by attempting to shift the struggle for existence to areas outside the country.[1] Then, once this was accomplished, a strong, united, and biologically superior nation would be free to engage in empire building on a grand scale and progressively subdue the less endowed, backward nations and races of the world for the benefit of the mother country. It was, in other words, the essential contribution of the Haeckelian Monists to bring scientific jargon once again to the support of political and social theory.

Haeckel's vision of German imperialism took in the vast arena of the entire world. Early in his career he advanced the idea of international racial struggle as one of the fundamental characteristics of history. The laws of nature, he urged, taught that some races or nations were destined to surpass and to conquer and destroy others. 'In the struggle for life,' he wrote in the *Natürliche Schöpfungsgeschichte*, 'the more highly developed, the more favoured and larger groups and forms, possess the positive inclination and the certain tendency to spread more at the expense of the lower, more backward, and smallest groups.'[2] An examination of the contemporary world would reveal that 'while the European tribes spread over the whole globe, other tribes or species draw nearer to their complete extinction.'³ Under prevailing racial conditions, while the 'Indo-Germanic' species of men are spreading the 'net of their domain'⁴ over the world, the non-European tribes are destined to be subjected to them. Even if the lower races were to 'propagate more abundantly than the white Europeans, yet they would sooner or later succumb in the struggle for life.'⁵ And Haeckel alluded to the 'American and Australian tribes' and to the 'Papuans and Hottentots' who were, under the inexorable laws of nature, 'fast approaching their complete extinction.'⁶

For Haeckel, therefore, the 'lower' races of mankind were either already on their way to extinction or were, in general, incapable of civilization and were as a consequence very much in need of the leadership and organizing capacity of the Europeans. 'All attempts,' Haeckel wrote, 'to introduce civilization among [the African and Australian tribes] and many other tribes of the lowest human species, have hitherto been of no avail; it is impossible to implant human culture where the requisite soil, namely the perfecting of the brain, is wanting.'⁷ Such species of men cannot be 'ennobled by civilization' which rather only 'accelerates their extinction.'⁸ Haeckel thus concluded that since it 'would be easier to train the most intelligent domestic animals to a moral and civilized life'⁹ than the majority of natives, the interests, needs, and desires of primitive peoples did not have to be reckoned with too seriously and did not have to stand in the way of colonial expansion. Indeed for Haeckel the lives of natives hardly had the same 'value'¹⁰ as that of the white man and therefore colonies could be established and maintained principally according to the needs of the Europeans. In all imperialist ventures, therefore, Haeckel urged a policy of 'realism' based upon the teachings of biology and anthropology, the nature of which, he was certain, had not yet been clearly enough perceived by the Germans as a whole. 'The views on the subject of European nations which have large colonies in the tropics, and have been in touch with the natives for centuries,' he wrote, 'are very realistic, and quite different from the ideas that prevail in Germany.' The Germans could have been much more successful in the gaining of colonies if they had ceased to be bound by the 'idealistic notions' of the existence of an 'abstract ideal-man' whose personality did not at all 'tally with the facts.' Rather, only when there was general recognition of the 'low psychic life of the natives' would Germany's empire really flourish throughout the world.[11]

Haeckel therefore assumed the task of trying to awaken the Germans to the need for colonial expansion. In 1890, in a book describing a journey to Algeria, he noted that he had witnessed the penetration of the French into North Africa, and the overwhelming conviction which he drew from his trip was that Germany, like other European nations, was obligated, for its own security, to acquire new territories. In strong language, he sought to forewarn the Germans that the French—a 'talented' and a 'nationalistically imbued' people—would inevitably wish to regain the 'prestige' which they had lost on the battlefield in 1870. Algeria, he observed, was becoming a powerful hinterland ready to serve the already growing strength of France. Germany therefore had to emulate her and to maintain its own prestige and power. 'A colony like Algeria,' he wrote, 'would inestimably raise our position in the world and our national strength.' Colonies are absolutely indispensable for Germany's survival. He thus proposed the creation of 'agricultural' as well as 'commercial' territories which would serve to absorb Germany's 'overpopulation' and function as trading and coaling centers for its navy and commercial interests. He cautioned that without colonies Germany was losing the best elements of its population through emigration. With colonies, on the other hand, migrants would remain within the orbit of German culture and at the same time would be serving the 'motherland.' Imperialism, Haeckel contended, was only a natural consequence of the 'struggle for existence' among the nations and the sooner the Germans realized how 'vulnerable' their 'geographical position' was in Europe, the sooner would they understand that the acquisition of colonies was a 'question of life itself.' And he called upon 'every German citizen who loves his country' to vigorously support the creation of empire.[12]

In consequence of his overwhelming enthusiasm for the acquisition of foreign territory, Haeckel became one of the principal founders and architects of Germany's most militant imperialistic, nationalistic, and anti-Semitic organizations, the Pan-German League.[13] Riding the crest of support for colonial expansion during the two closing decades of the nineteenth century, the Pan-German League advanced a radically aggressive program in support of German territorial growth. Not only did the lure of new markets and sources of raw materials entice the League to support imperialist adventure, but it also viewed colonialism itself as a stimulus for nationalism and Germanic national pride. The Pan-German League wished for nothing less than the creation of an enormous world-wide German community which would be bound politically and culturally to an enlarged Germany on the continent. It was clearly the underlying assumption of the League that an expanded Germany would have the right and the obligation to rule the world.[14] And, although its membership was comparatively small, consisting for the most part of individuals representing the German academic community, the League was able to exercise enormous influence on both the governmental and private level in the years before and during the First World War. In the words of the famous socialist Kurt Eisner, the Pan-German League 'attained a greater influence on the direction of policy than even the powerful associations of landlords and capitalists. . . . From the first naval measure to the last army bill, all the armaments plans originated in the circles of the Pan-Germans.'[15]

It may be said that the principal role which Haeckel played in the organization and activities of the Pan-German League was to serve as the '*Verbindungsmann*'[16] for the social Darwinism and racial elements of its program. Haeckel's presence gave to the League added weight as a movement espousing a program based upon science and he helped greatly to enhance its appeal not only to the community of the educated in Germany, but also to the general public. And not only Haeckel, but also other Monists were to be found among the active members of the League. For example, Johannes Unold, the future Vice-President of the Monist League, wrote a number of tracts for the Pan-Germans in a series which was headed *Der Kampf um das Deutschtum*. In one pamphlet, *Das Deutschtum in Chile*, Dr. Unold proposed that it was absolutely necessary that there be created a governmental organization which would serve to coordinate the world-wide interests of growing German colonial activities. He suggested that the Germans had a special 'talent' for colonial enterprise and that their 'teutonic drive for expansion' would hopefully lead them to 'fight for an honorable share' in the division of the world, which he considered to be still possible for them.

The Germans, he wrote, had to gather the needed courage for an 'audacious' pursuit of '*Weltpolitik*.'[17] Then, referring specifically to the community of Germans in South America, Dr. Unold suggested that all English, French, and American influence on that continent had to be supplanted. 'Englishmen and Yankees,' he wrote, 'were not liked because of their uncouth ways' and the French were experiencing a 'rapid decline into general corruption' and were 'losing' their capacity for 'leadership.' This left the way open for the Germans, who, by the use of their 'characteristics and capabilities' were in an excellent position to become the 'spiritual, economic, and political teacher and leader' of the South American nations.[18] Unold warned that if the Germans did not assume a role of leadership in South America, then the entire continent would of necessity sink into torpidity, leaving itself open to the 'exploitation and domination' of the United States. And it was not only in regard to South America that the Germans had to look for an opportunity to perform a creative and civilizing role. Unold attempted to remind the Germans that they could not afford to lose sight of their world mission in general, i.e., the cultural and political salvation of mankind. The opportunity to rescue world culture belonged 'incontestably' to the 'German people,' he wrote. Through imperial expansion, Germany would be able to shower the world with its greatness and capacity. And he concluded his pamphlet by warning what a 'loss to humanity' it would be if the Germans failed to emigrate and neglected to insure the creation of a healthy and biologically fit German community in all parts of the world.[19]

The actual extent and depth of convictions supporting imperialism among the leading members of the Monist League did not really become fully apparent, however, until the outbreak of war in 1914. It was this conflict and the issues which it engendered which brought to the surface the real nature of Haeckelian Monist thinking on the need for empire both in Europe and abroad. The First World War revealed the radically aggressive content of their program and shattered all attachment to the superficial and largely illusory pacifism and internationalism which the Monists had often flattered themselves as subscribing to before the war.[20]

It was Haeckel, once again, who gave direction and authority for the position of the Monist League on the war and it was he who clearly set forth a world-wide program of territorial aggrandizement for Germany. In a number of articles and in a more lengthy monograph on the war Haeckel sought first of all to rouse the Germans to support the conflict on the basis of the teachings of evolution. He explained that now, more so than ever before, the Germans had to confront the basic fact of life that 'struggle is the father of all things.'[21] In evolution, it was not only a question of 'competing' peacefully with one's adversary: there were occasions when a struggle had to lead to the 'complete destruction'[22] of the enemy. It was this latter contingency which was demanded by the First World War. To accomplish this annihilation of the enemy, Haeckel admitted, would require much sacrifice, but steeled by the doctrines of evolution and Monism, Germany would be able to prevail in the end. Thus, addressing himself to the German soldier, Haeckel bravely gave assurances that life even under the best of circumstances was uncertain and that in general one had no reason to fear death. Science and evolution, he explained, taught that there was no after-life and that life in general, even in peace time, was purely a matter of chance. Death, therefore, had to be accepted passively. 'The well-educated man of the present,' Haeckel wrote, 'familiar with the teachings of biology, especially one convinced of the truth of the theory of evolution, regards death with rational resignation, as a natural necessity, which must come sooner or later in any circumstances.'[23] The soldier who accepts Monism will 'leave his fate to blind chance, which rules the universe in the absence of a wise Providence.'[24] In this way he will find hardly any difficulty in sacrificing himself for the fatherland. 'If his ethical development is high enough for him to have achieved the proper balance between egoism and altruism, he will also be mindful of his social duty to the state and will gladly offer up his life for the preservation of the fatherland.' And Haeckel was confident that 'thousands of German warriors [would] go into battle' with 'enthusiasm' and would 'sacrifice even their family happiness to the higher interests of their country.'[25]

It was Haeckel's profound belief that England alone was responsible for the outbreak of the war. Of course, there can be no doubt that for Haeckel a war between Germany and England was a deep disappointment. He was attached to England through his friendship with Darwin and had in fact visited Great Britain frequently and had also made a personal contribution over a number of years to a rather large project on the classification of sea organisms which had been sponsored by the British government.[26] Haeckel was, moreover, preoccupied with what seemed to him to be a bitter paradox, that Germany was compelled to enter into battle with a nation that was of the same racial stock as that of Germany. He confided that he would have preferred an alliance of Germany and England, for both, he felt, had a 'common Germanistic culture.'[27] As one racial stock they could have dominated the world. 'Germany's army as the strongest power on land, England's navy as the strongest power on sea, could, when united, bring the gift of permanent peace and progress to the whole civilized world.'[28]

But Haeckel lamented that this entire vision of a racially united Germany and England had vanished as if in a dream. He complained that the 'deep-rooted egoism of the English' had destroyed the possibility of such a London-Berlin axis. Rather, the gulf between the two nations had become so wide that a 'real reconciliation between Germany, who had been attacked, and her treacherous, murderous English brother [was] not to be thought of for some time.'[29] The responsibility for the war, Haeckel wrote, rested squarely on the shoulders of the English, who had started it in their quest after world domination. 'England, the most powerful pirate state in the world, is aiming ... not only to maintain unlimited dominion of the seas and control of all her colonies throughout the world, but also, hand in hand with this, to exploit all the other nations for her own benefit, regardless of their interests.'[30]

It is somewhat amusing that Haeckel's disillusionment with England was expressed in terms that bore rather close resemblance to the irrational plaints of a betrayed lover. In his denial of Germany's responsibility for the war he accused England of entering the conflict solely to carry out her 'long planned attack on the German Reich'[31] and to effect its 'subjection to the British Empire,' or even worse to bring about its complete 'destruction.'[32] The English claim of having become involved in the war because of the violation of Belgian neutrality by Germany was only a smokescreen to cover their long contemplated aggression against the Reich.

Thus, Haeckel felt free to launch a tirade of abuse against the English. He accused them of international 'robbery' and derided their alleged conception of themselves as a '*Herrenvolk*,' which he claimed rested on the 'fancy that England [was] a chosen nation selected by divine Providence in order to bring true culture to all the other nations.'[33] Haeckel was, of course, blindly accusing England of many of the same characteristics which he found to be honorable and acceptable for Germany, but his anger and frustration knew no bounds. 'With astonishing cunning and consistency,' Haeckel fulminated, 'dishonorable England has carried through' its basic self-aggrandizing principles for centuries, 'unmoved by every touch of conscience and feeling of shame.' Its 'effective means have always consisted of making the European nations hate each other' and encouraged them to 'tear each other to pieces' so that it could reap the advantages and augment its 'power and purse.' The English were opportunistic and destructive. They had continually 'violated written agreements, broken promises, terrorized neutral states, destroyed their navies, and bombed their open cities.' They had cleverly wielded their foreign policy to attain their goals of aggression, to make certain that no nation should be 'powerful enough to oppose British tyranny.'[34] They were 'betrayers' and they used 'diplomatic intrigues' to 'cut Germany off from every tie with the outside world.' They had often made 'our postal relations impossible with the world, cut submerged cables, disturbed our short wave telegraphic stations, and plundered our prospering colonies in Africa and Asia.' By the use of propaganda England had 'spread a great systematic net of lies all over the world, through which foreigners were kept in the dark regarding the true circumstances of the war, its causes, course, and significance.'[35] The English foreign secretary, Sir Edward Grey, was a 'murderer of millions' and the world's 'arch liar.'[36] It was Grey who provided the English Parliament with false and misleading documents about the war and thereby confused England's responsibility for it.[37] And finally Haeckel descended rather ludicrously to petty and carping criticism of English national habits. 'We are reminded,' he complained, 'only of the stubborn opposition of England to the metric system, the already generally accepted decimal system, as well as her medieval ceremonies and festival processions, of its rigid habit of dress, or the ridiculous comedy of the suffragettes, something that would not have been possible in any reasonable continental state.'[38]

Perhaps the most revealing and significant aspect of Haeckel's attack on England and his evaluation of the nature of the war was the racial interpretation which he gave to it. In terms that are much more reminiscent of the Third rather than of the Second Reich, Haeckel sought to justify a morally, intellectually, and biologically pure Germany in its fight against an immoral, racially heterogeneous, and hence inferior enemy. He conceived the war as a struggle between the racial cosmopolitanism of the British Empire, on the one hand, and the racially superior Aryan Germans on the other. Even though he admitted that England was of the same racial stock as that of Germany, Haeckel felt that it had nonetheless committed the grievous error of polluting Europe by bringing into battle the inferior races of the Empire allowing them to fraternize with the white and racially superior Europeans. 'Many new and incredible things,' he wrote, 'have happened in the gigantic world war to surprise twentieth century humanity. One of these, fraught with grave consequences, is the way in which England has mobilized all of the different races of man.'[39] And to place in bold relief the perfidy of the English in this matter Haeckel spelled out a long list of the inferior races that were being called into battle. 'First come the yellow, slit-eyed Japanese; then the Mongols from Indo-China, and the brown Malays from neighboring Malacca and Singapore; the dark-brown Austral negroes and Papuans from Oceania, the Kafirs from South Africa, and the Senegal negroes from North African colonies. And that no shade may be lacking in the color scheme of the "inferior" races ... the remnants of the redskins are dragged to the blood-steaming battlefields of Europe.' Frightened by the number of different races that the English were supposedly throwing into the battle, Haeckel warned very seriously that this racial mixture would prove disastrous for the future of Europe. 'Deep students of ethnology and far-sighted statesmen point with anxiety to the grave consequences that are sure to follow this "fraternalization" of all the races both to England herself and the supremacy of the white race as a whole.' The English were tragically oblivious to the fact that the 'cultural and psychological differences that separate the highest developed European peoples from the lowest savages are greater than the differences that separate the savages from the anthropoid apes.'[40]

Even further, for Haeckel the war appeared as a tragedy for the Germans and the Austrians because their 'educational level' was 'much higher on the average than among [their] opponents, and therefore their personal life value [was] also much higher.'[41] He was aghast that on the battlefield they would be subjected to the barbarian practices of the racially inferior troops of the enemy. 'One need but think of the excruciating agony of the wounded soldiers left lying in the turmoil of the international slaughter; one need but think of our noble, finely educated German volunteers tortured and maimed in inhuman fashion by the "hyenas" of the battlefield, the barbarian Indians and the cruel Senegal negroes.'[42] It was also fully apparent that the German soldier showed his superiority by being 'less prejudiced and more capable of arriving at a fair judgment'[43] of the nature of the world than either the English, French, Russians, or Italians. As opposed to the German soldier, the Allied troops had a defective understanding of the world. The outlook of the Englishman was 'obscured by his egoistic megalomania, the Frenchman's by his extravagant national vanity ... the Italian's by his pride in ancient Rome ... the Russian's by his panslavic mania.' All these people, Haeckel was certain, necessarily judged most 'political events very one-sidedly and often quite wrongly.'[44]

Based upon a prognosis of an undoubted German victory, Haeckel was explicit about the territorial gains that Germany was destined to enjoy. He spoke first of all about the most immediate goal of the war as the 'release of the entire world from the insufferable despotism o Great Britain.'[45] In order to smash English power, Haeckel advised the Germans to undertake the 'necessary invasion of the British robber sea state' and with the aid of the 'German navy and army to occupy London.'[46] More fundamentally, however, Germany had to 'make herself a great power on an equal footing with the other great powers.... Like them she should try to acquire colonies and hold her just share in the world's trade.'[47]

It may be said that within Europe, Haeckel envisioned the creation of a vast Germanic *Mitteleuropa*. 'We now hold,' Haeckel wrote, 'considerable territory as valuable security—on the west, Belgium and the north of France; on the east, Poland and the Baltic provinces. These rich countries were formerly German possessions. Antwerp must remain our stronghold on the North Sea and Riga on the Baltic Sea....

At all events, when the treaty of peace is concluded we must demand a considerable extension of the German Empire.'

Haeckel justified the need for territorial expansion on the basis of a theory of *Lebensraum*. 'The German Empire,' he wrote, 'being overpopulated, has urgent need to extend and strengthen its frontiers which before the war were most unfavorable to it.' He pointed out that Germany needed additional territory to stem the tide of emigration and to forestall the Germans from becoming 'cultural manure' for other nations. Of course, an extension of territory would also provide a better line of defense against the possibility of 'future attacks.'[48] It would secure a protected area 'against perfidious England in the west as well as barbaric Russia in the east.'[49]

It was Haeckel's conviction that the new territories of continental Europe that were destined to be incorporated into Germany would also have to be Germanized culturally. Unlike Friedrich Naumann, the famous theoretician and popularizer of the idea of *Mitteleuropa*, who proposed the alliance of a culturally autonomous and a politically and economically interdependent central Europe, Haeckel envisioned the same large area as unified, but subjected directly to German control and culture.[50] 'The new provinces,' he wrote, 'which we are going to annex are energetic and intractable, but with cautious, intelligent treatment they can be Germanized, or at least made accesible to German culture, an important task that is not new for Germany. In former centuries she carried it on over a large extent of territory.'[51]

In addition to the acquisition of territory on the European continent, Haeckel also pointed to the need for a worldwide system of German colonies. 'The German Empire,' he wrote, 'as a world power needs extensive colonies.' In the seventeenth century the 'Great Elector had the far-sightedness to recognize this political necessity.' In the nineteenth century, Bismarck, the 'great founder of the new German Empire, had translated it into action . . . in the face of persistent opposition from many short-sighted politicians.' Haeckel advised, therefore, the creation of a kind of *Mittelafrika*. The Congo would become Germany's possession and its 'immense area of wealth and resources' could for 'centuries to come' be turned into an 'exceedingly profitable field of exploitation.' In Africa, Germany must take special pains to see that England is 'driven out altogether.' England must not be 'permitted to carry out her magnificent scheme of establishing a world-wide empire on land as well as on sea by building direct lines of communication from the Cape to Cairo, and from the Niger to the Irawadi.' Furthermore, the Suez Canal had to be internationalized and Egypt had to revert to her 'rightful owners,' the Turks.[52]

For Haeckel, therefore, the successful conclusion of the war was obviously going to lead to German supremacy in Europe, Africa, Asia, and Asia Minor. Victory would mean the realization of the original dream of the Pan-German League.

Although a number of Monists refused to support the war effort and continued to maintain their pacifism and internationalism, for most members of the Monist League, as for Haeckel, the war was immediately and enthusiastically welcomed as offering the possibility of deliverance from an insufferable historical reality which denied Germany the deserved fruits of empire.[53] The war seemed to them to be a heaven-sent opportunity not only making possible territorial expansion but also providing the requisite conditions for the total transformation of German life and culture according to the Monist program. Thus, many of the leading Monists, like Haeckel, were among the most determined defenders of the righteousness of the conflict. In August, 1914, immediately after the commencement of hostilities, the President of the Monist League, Wilhelm Ostwald, drafted a manifesto which was given prominent display in *Das monistische Jahrhundert*. 'Overnight,' Ostwald proclaimed, 'the German people finds itself in battle against the insidious attack of a neighbor who has for centuries appeared to be only good.'[54] The launching of the war on Germany was an 'attack of barbarism against culture, of hordes against organized life.' Ostwald, therefore, strongly urged the Monists to place all of their strength and property at the disposal of the fatherland.[55]

Ostwald's plea for Monist participation in the war effort was echoed by other Monists. The editorial board of *Das monistische Jahrhundert* declared that the outbreak of the conflict had solved the problem of the relationship between nationalism and internationalism for the Monist League. The only way internationalism could be approached, they wrote, was through a strong and vibrant national state.[56] Still other Monists rallied to the cry of *'Deutschland über Alles'*[57] and the slogan was proclaimed, Monists to the Front!'[58] In ringing articles that attempted to outdo each other in declarations of patriotism it was proclaimed that the 'German nation has arisen, the storm is breaking out.'[59] In *Das monistische Jahrhundert* patriotic poems with a deep Volkish content appeared:

> Unser Glaube—deutscher Glaube! neu gestarkt—
> in alter Form—ward er uns ein neuer Inhalt.
>
> Hundertfach klingt in diesen Kriegestagen, klang
> in diesen Luthertagen, das Wort vom neu belebten
> deutschen Glauben—das Wort vom neu erkannten
> deutschen Gott, von der tiefen neu erwachten Religiosität![60]
>
> (Our faith—German faith! Newly strengthened—
> in its old form—it has for us a new meaning.
>
> There resounds a hundred times in these days of war,
> there has resounded in these Lutheran days, the message
> of a newly revived German faith—the message of a
> newly recognized German god, from the deep and newly awakened religiosity
> *translated by Daniel Gasman*)

Other poems sang of the mass destruction of the enemy:

> Wie mächtig sich über die Grenze schieben
> Die russischen Horden in wildem Triumph,
> Da heisst es einfach: 'Schlachtplan sieben'
> Und den Feind begräbt der masurische Sumpf!
>
> Wie hat der Franzos' sich gebläht und gebrüstet,
> Als lagen wir schön vernichtet da,
> Jah überrannt—wir standen gerüstet
> Und sturmten ihn nieder mit deutschem Hurra![61]
>
> (How powerfully in wild triumph the
> Russian hordes steal over the border,
> Here it is simply called: 'Battleplan Seven'
> And the enemy is entombed by the Masurian swamp!
>
> Oh, how the Frenchman boasted and bragged
> how we were lying here defeated,
> Suddenly overrun—we stood prepared
> and stormed him down with a German Hurrah!
> *translated by Daniel Gasman*)

MONISM, IMPERIALISM, AND THE FIRST WORLD WAR

As Haeckel had done, the Monists also insistently disclaimed any responsibility on the part of Germany for the war. They referred repeatedly to the Kaiser as a leading 'pacifist' and were certain that the conflict was a defensive one for Germany.[62] 'The German people, Kaiser, and army did not want the war; it was forced upon them'[63] was a typical Monist position. Germany, they argued, was the innocent victim of half-civilized and backward nations. 'Russia and Serbia,' a Monist wrote, 'have not yet joined the ranks of the civilised nations. They are still robber states consisting of a band of thieves in the guise of a state.'[64] And like their mentor Haeckel, the Monists lost no opportunity in attempting to awaken the Germans to the threat which England posed for the future of Europe. Not only, they contended, were the English highly aggressive but they had malevolently instituted the calamitous policy of calling upon the inferior races of the Orient and of their Empire to fight in Europe.[65] 'Japanese, Indians, and Egyptians'[66] were to be found among the British soldiers. This was a calamity; it had allowed the inferior races to witness first-hand a European civilization divided within itself and it had provided the 'Negro with a view of a war of whites against whites.'[67]

The Haeckelian Monists were among the most constant supporters of the idea which equated Germany with civilization itself. They asserted in self-righteous and arrogant terms that Germany was the bearer of all that was truly worthwhile in world culture. 'We have to maintain,' wrote Wilhelm Breitenbach, a leading Monist, 'that universal values are bound up with our own existence, values which stand or fall with us, and objectively speaking, if we go under, the world will be much poorer in its essential qualities.'[68] Thus, from the Monist point of view, through the war Germany was actually confronting her ultimate historical destiny. 'We did not want this war,' another leading Monist wrote, 'and have never conceived of such an involved fate for the Germans. However, we must! Either it casts us into the abyss or it exalts us to world historical greatness and leadership.'[69] Were Germany to be defeated, he contended, there would be total 'chaos.'[70] A British victory would mean that Europe would be 'lacerated for another half century by useless wars.' Then the leadership of humanity would 'pass to the Americans or to the East Asiatics,' which would, of course, subject the world to racially inferior elements.

Unquestionably, the Germans had to 'triumph, in order to save for the future of mankind something of German fitness, inwardness, chivalry, and the art of organization.'[71]

It was taken for granted by the Monists, following Haeckel, that Germany would annex territory both in Europe and in other parts of the world after the war. 'The aim of victory,' they wrote, 'is for Germany and Germanic culture to arrive by struggle at a leading position in the world, which it deserves; and the most important goal which lies behind victory is obviously Germany's security for the future and the realization of a lasting peace in Europe.'[72] One of the most vociferous advocates of territorial and economic aggrandizement for Germany was the President of the Monist League, Wilhelm Ostwald. His radical pan-German ideas are revealed in a number of speeches delivered at gatherings of the Monist League, and in an interview with a Swedish journalist in December, 1914, while on a trip to Stockholm to persuade Sweden to come into the war on the side of Germany. In both his speeches and in his remarks to the Swedish journalist, Ostwald defended Germany's role in the war by first of all maintaining that since its '*Kultur*' was 'above that of the rest of Europe' it was obligated to 'bring its neighbors up to its own standards of civilization, even if force had to be employed.'[73] For Ostwald, therefore, the war was a kind of blessing because it offered Germany the opportunity to convey her talents to Europe and even to the rest of the world. 'It is war,' he uninhibitedly remarked, which will 'make the other nations participate ... in our higher form of civilization.'[74] He contended that Germany's enemies were at a very low level of culture and therefore were sorely in need of German know-how. 'Among our enemies at present,' he said, 'Russia has in fact reached only the stage of the hordes while the French and the English are now where the Germans were more than fifty years ago.' A victory for Germany would open up Europe to German investment and economic activity which would serve to raise the level of the other continental nations. 'In view of our immense force of expansion . . . we shall profit so greatly from the relations with our neighbors that war will be impossible in the future. It is under this form, that of the right to hold property, that we look forward to a conquest.'[75]

At the end of the war, Ostwald further suggested, there would have to be a complete 'rearrangement of the map of Europe.'[76] Borders would be so drawn that the possibility of all English influence and threat of intervention in the affairs of other nations would be eliminated. The era of English ascendancy was at an end, he prophesied. 'It is the last of a barbaric epoch. If we want lasting peace... England's maritime power must be destroyed; for it has been the source of all wars for centuries.'[77] In the redrawing of the map of Europe 'equilibrium will not be attained by having a conglomerate of absolutely equal states, something which hitherto England has used for its own advantage. With the exception of Russia, which belongs to Asia and not to Europe, Europe will be an organized whole, in which every nation would be assigned a special significance and position, in order to advance the common well-being of all European nations.' Of course, the actual leadership of the newly formed Europe would devolve exclusively upon Germany.[78] There would be a confederation of states, a United States of Europe, with the Kaiser as president. It did not matter in the least whether the smaller nations desired such a political union with Germany or not. Ostwald insisted that they would be compelled to participate even against their will.[79]

As we have noted before, part of the Monist dream was to reconstitute Germany as an organic state free of political or class hatred and directed towards a common national and racial goal. Interestingly enough, the Monists felt to a very large extent that they had attained at least the beginnings of such a harmonious social structure for Germany with the *Burgfrieden* which had come into existence at the outbreak of the war. In their articles and speeches during this early war period the Monists frequently contrasted the harmony and bonds of German life with the weakness and alienation of Western capitalist and liberal society. Ostwald, for example, stated that 'while among the English and the French individual personal freedom stood highest, we Germans have achieved a higher stage of organization by bringing together highly evolved personalities for common work.'[80] The ideal of an integrated nation was being reached and he happily noted that the war had served to 'remove party differences' in Germany. He was of the opinion that 'this accomplishment reached immeasurably far' and that the 'deep rift which rent our nation, has been removed, hopefully for all time.' Ostwald was especially impressed by the fact that the Social Democrats had become loyal citizens, and he was confident that the Marxists would now finally abandon their adherence to a theory of class struggle and would seek to work in harmony with other groups of a unified nation. With this unity the 'preconditions existed for the German people to take over the organization of Europe.'[81]

Contentment with the *Burgfrieden* and assessment of its deeper meaning for Germany came also from other Monists. For example, in a speech to the Monist League, the famous Volkish theologian, Dr. Max Mauerenbrecher, explained to his audience that the structure of the modern Western state as it was developed by France during the Enlightenment and the French Revolution had a fatal flaw. France had not been able to 'discover any way to bind the atomised individual; it had elan and spirit, but not organization. It broke up the old, but could not create the new, neither in state or society, nor in the rearing of character and religion.'[82] England also, Mauerenbrecher said, suffered from an 'inner weakness.' She was the victim of her capitalism and her mercantile social system. In becoming a nation representing exclusively the interests of the bourgeoisie, England had substituted crass money making for 'knighthood,' 'heroism,' and the 'old English ideal.'[83] Thus it had no real strength or desire to fight. It could only devote its energies to making money. It was necessary, Mauerenbrecher argued, for Germany to 'melt in an intense flame the spirit of capitalism which reached us from England and to grasp old English pride and heroism for our own temper of life.'[84]

For the Monists, therefore, the war was finally going to allow them to fashion a new civilization that would be free of the atomized individualism of the French liberal state and the commercial huckstering spirit of the English bourgeoisie. As Dr. Mauerenbrecher preached to the Monist League: 'In a word, the German period of humanity cannot simply signify the continuation of French Democracy or English capitalism. New forces are appearing . . . which guarantee a newly created culture.'[85] With a German victory, he prophesied, a new world would arise. 'When an old Europe breaks up in convulsions and a new one arises in the flames then indeed sacrifice is necessary.'

MONISM, IMPERIALISM, AND THE FIRST WORLD WAR

But he assured the Monists that the 'value and greatness' of the new civilization would have made the price worthwhile.[86]

NOTES

1. For a general discussion of the role of 'Social Imperialism' as a foil for class struggle in Germany, see Naumann, *Behemoth*, Chapters V, VI.
2. Haeckel, *The History of Creation*, II, 324.
3. *Ibid.*, I, 256.
4. *Ibid.*, II, 324.
5. *Ibid.*, I, 256.
6. *Ibid.*, II, 325.
7. *Ibid.*, 363.
8. *Ibid.*
9. *Ibid.*, 366.
10. Haeckel, *The Wonders of Life*, p. 390.
11. *Ibid.*, pp. 390-391.
12. Ernst Haeckel, *Algerische Errinerungen*, in *Von Teneriffa bis zum Sinai* (Leipzig: Kroner, 1925), pp. 84-85.
13. Otto Bonhard, *Geschichte der Alldeutscher Verband* (Leipzig: Weicher, 1920), p. 3. Haeckel was also a member of the *Deutschen Flottenverein*, the *Kolonialgesellschaft*, and the *Verein für das Deutschtum im Ausland*. See Schmidt, *Denkmal eines grossen Lebens*, p. 76.
14. For an analysis of the program of the Pan-German League, see Mildred S. Wertheimer, *The Pan-German League 1890-1914* (New York: [Colombia University Press], 1924). For the Volkish significance of the Pan-German League, see Mosse, *The Crisis of German Ideology*, Chapter XII.
15. Quoted in Pinson, *Modern Germany*, p. 311.
16. Bronder, *Bevor Hitler kam*, p. 287.
17. Johannes Unold, *Das Deutschtum in Chile* (Munich: Lehmann, 1900), pp. 3-4.
18. *Ibid.*, p. 62.
19. *Ibid.*, pp. 65-66.
20. As we have already noted (Chapter II, 42-43) the Haeckelian Monists occasionally expressed perfunctory support for internationalism. Similarly, one could also encounter declarations supporting pacifism which seemed to bear no relation to their belief in the universality of struggle. Thus Haeckel wrote: 'I am on principle a pacifist.' But he was also quick to point out that pacifism could only succeed when the laws of evolution were adhered to—when the racially superior nations were free to triumph over and dominate the weaker ones. 'As I myself,' Haeckel wrote further, 'have for many years taken part in work for international conciliation, having been a member of "arbitration societies" in England, France, and Italy, I know from my own experience what great 'practical obstacles are put in the way of these ideal endeavors. It is my conviction that here too permanent progress can be attained only when the fundamental principles of

evolution, of genetic anthropology and sociology, and of the monistic philosophy based thereon, are better understood and more generally recognized.' See Haeckel, *Eternity*, pp. 141, 155.
21. Ernst Haeckel, 'Weltkrieg und Naturgeschichte,' *Nord und Süd*, CLI (1914), 440.
22. *Ibid.*, p. 142.
23. Haeckel, *Eternity*, p. 45.
24. *Ibid.*, p. 46.
25. *Ibid.*
26. For material Haeckel prepared in cooperation with the English see Great Britain, Challenger Office, *Results of the Voyage of H.M.S. Challenger During the Years 1873-76*, Edinburgh, 1880-95.
27. Haeckel, *Eternity*, p. 156.
28. *Ibid.*
29. *Ibid.*, p. 157.
30. *Ibid.*, pp. 157-158.
31. Ernst Haeckel, 'Englands Blutschuld am Weltkriege,' *Das monistische Jahrhundert*, III (1914-15), 540.
32. *Ibid.*, p. 545.
33. Haeckel, 'Weltkrieg und Naturgeschichte,' p. 144.
34. *Ibid.*
35. *Ibid.*, p. 145.
36. *Ibid.*, p. 146.
37. *Ibid.*
38. *Ibid.*, p. 144.
39. Haeckel, *Eternity*, pp. 106-107.
40. *Ibid.*, p. 107.
41. *Ibid.*, p. 36.
42. *Ibid.*, p. 42.
43. *Ibid.*, p. 154.
44. *Ibid.*, pp. 154-155.
45. Haeckel, 'Weltkrieg und Naturgeschichte,' p. 140.
46. Ernst Haeckel, Letter to Otto Juliusburger (no date or place), in *Das monistische Jahrhundert*, III (1914-15), 657.
47. Haeckel, *Eternity*, p. 158.
48. *Ibid.*, pp. 168-169.
49. Haeckel, 'Weltkrieg und Naturgeschichte,' p. 147.
50. For a general discussion of the ideas of Friedrich Naumann, see Henry Cord Meyer, *Mitteleuropa in German Thought and Action 1815-1945* (The Hague: Nijhoff, 1955), Chapter IX.
51. Haeckel, *Eternity*, p. 169.
52. *Ibid.*, pp. 169-170.
53. Some Monists, outside of Germany, however, protested against the expansionist and pro-War sentiments of Haeckel and the German Monist League. See, for ex-

ample, a letter of protest to Haeckel by August Forel, in *Out of My Life and Work* (New York: Norton, 1937), pp. 303-304. Forel objected especially to a poem written by one of Haeckel's followers which asked for the slaughter of Germany's enemies by the millions. Another Swiss Monist objected to the pro-war sentiments of the German Monist League and wrote that Monism as he understood it had nothing to do with nationalism. See Otto Borngräber, 'Ein offnes Wort an den Deutschen Monistenbund,' *Das monistische Jahrundert*, III, 926-930. Ostwald replied to Borngräber by stating that in fact Monism could be equated with German culture and he denied that Monism and German nationalism were incompatible. See Wilhelm Ostwald, 'Antwort,' *Das monistische Jahrhundert*, III (1914-15), 930-933.
54. Wilhelm Ostwald, 'Monisten!' *Das monistische Jahrhundert*, III (1914-15), 497.
55. *Ibid.*
56. Anonymous, 'Vertagung der Hauptversammlung,' *Das monistische Jahrhundert*, III (1914-15), 499.
57. August Kahl, 'Der Krieg und die Kunst. Nach einem Vortrag von Herbert Eulenberg, gehalten am 14. Dezember in der Ortsgruppe Hamburg,' *Das monistische Jahrhundert*, III (1914-15), 801.
58. W[ilhelm] B[reitenbach], 'Der Krieg', *Das monistische Jahrhundert*, III (1914-15), 502.
59. Erich Dombrowski, 'Die Vorgeschichte des europäischen Krieges,' *Das monistische Jahrhundert*, III (1914-15), 511.
60. Käte Schäfer-Gerdau, 'Unser Glaube,' *Das monistische Jahrhundert*, III (1914-15), 746.
61. Dr. M. von der Porten, 'Was wir aus den Siegen lernen wollen,' *Das monistische Jahrhundert*, III (1914-15), 587.
62. Breitenbach, 'Der Krieg,' p. 500.
63. F. M., 'Der Krieg,' *Das monistische Jahrhundert*, III (1914-15), 592.
64. *Ibid.*
65. Max Mauerenbrecher, 'Das neue Europa und die neue Kultur,' *Das monistische Jahrhundert*, III (1914-15), 794.
66. *Ibid.*, p. 795.
67. *Ibid.*
68. Breitenbach, 'Der Krieg,' p. 500.
69. Mauerenbrecher, 'Das neue Europa und die neue Kultur,' p. 828.
70. *Ibid.*, p. 795.
71. *Ibid.* It is revealing in this connection that in his *Eternity*, Haeckel refused to call the United States by its name and dubbed it 'Columbana' instead. For him the United States was a racial mixture, and hence a disunited country. See Haeckel, *Eternity*, pp. 70-71.
72. F. Müller-Lyer, 'Das Problem eines "Kontinentalbundes,"' *Das monistische Jahrhundert*, III (1914-15) 753.
73. Wilhelm Ostwald, interviewed in *The Eagle*, Brooklyn, New York, December 20, 1914.

74. *Ibid.*
75. *Ibid.*
76. *Ibid.*
77. Wilhelm Ostwald, 'Deutschlands Zukunft,' *Das monistische Jahrhundert*, III (1914–15), 622.
78. *Ibid.*
79. Wilhelm Ostwald (no title), *Das monistische Jahrhundert*, III (1914–15), 657.
80. Ostwald, 'Deutschlands Zukunft,' pp. 621–622.
81. *Ibid.*, pp. 622–623.
82. Mauerenbrecher, 'Das neue Europa und die neue Kultur,' pp. 793–794.
83. *Ibid.*, p. 795.
84. *Ibid.*, p. 827.
85. *Ibid.*
86. *Ibid.*, p. 753.

Chapter Seven

Monism and National Socialism

IF one surveys the origins of the Volkish movement in Germany during the three or four decades prior to the First World War it is apparent that Haeckel played an influential, significant, indeed a decisive role in its genesis and subsequent development. An impressive number of the most influential Volkish writers, propagandists, and spokesmen were influenced by or involved in some way with either Haeckel or his Monist followers. In the development of racism, racial eugenics, Germanic Christianity, nature worship, and anti-Semitism, Haeckel and the Monists were an important source and a major inspiration for many of the diverse streams of thought which came together later on under the banner of National Socialism.

Probably the most important and far-reaching influence of Haeckel may be found among the leading racial anthropologists and eugenicists who lived and wrote in the decades around the turn of the century. Apart from such writers as Wilhelm Schallmayer, Heinrich Ziegler, and August Forel, whom we have already noted as active members of the Monist League, the fact is that nearly all other leading figures in the field of eugenics and racial science in Germany were deeply and consciously indebted to Haeckel for many, if not for most, of their ideas. It was this group of individuals, both within and outside of the Monist League, who as it were published the banns for the marriage of racism and eugenics which took place a few decades later on under the Nazis.

One of the most influential authors in the field of racial anthropology and eugenics was the physician Ludwig Woltmann (1871–1907), who has been described as the 'most important representative of the Gobineau theory of the Nordic race' in Germany at the turn of the century.[1] Woltmann studied under Haeckel and in 1900 submitted a manuscript, 'Der politische Anthropologie,' to an essay contest in which Haeckel, Heinrich Ziegler, and another Monist, Professor J. Conrad, were the judges. The contest itself, which ultimately led to the publication of ten volumes of influential social Darwinist tracts, was sponsored by the industrialist, Alfred Krupp, and its theme was: 'What can we learn from the principles of Darwinism for application to inner political development and the laws of the state?'[2] The first prize was won by Haeckel's disciple, Wilhelm Schallmayer, for his manuscript, 'Vererbung und Auslese'; Woltmann, who won fourth prize, hotly rejected the decision of the judges and withdrew in anger from the contest, which served to alienate him permanently from Haeckel.[3] Nonetheless, as a result of the contest and the publicity surrounding his dispute with the committee of judges, Woltmann gained a great deal of popular recognition and in 1903 published the contest-essay on his own. A year earlier, in 1902, he founded a racist journal, the Politisch-anthropologische Revue, and in its pages campaigned for the forceful biological maintenance of the Nordic race. Also, in a number of books written during the seven or eight years before his premature death in 1907, Woltmann attempted to effect a fusion of the ideas of Haeckel and Marx.[4] Although he criticized Haeckel's negative attitude towards socialism he accepted his fundamental idea that there was an exact parallel between the laws of nature and those of society. A member of the Social Democratic Party, Woltmann transformed the Marxist concept of class struggle into a theory of worldwide racial conflict.[5] He described the Germans as the highest species of mankind and contended that the perfect physical proportions of the Nordics expressed an inner superiority and a heightened spirituality. Like Haeckel, he argued that any mixture of the races would lead to the biological deterioration of the Germans. Woltmann, like Haeckel, taught that life was a constant struggle for existence and for racial purity, and he sought to forearm Germany against biological decay.[6]

Even closer than Woltmann to Haeckel's social theories was Otto Ammon (1842–1916), another leading social Darwinist and racial anthropologist.⁷ Ammon was among the authors recommended for additional reading in the *Welträtsel*,⁸ and in three influential books, *Die natürliche Auslese beim Menschen* (1893), *Der Darwinismus gegen die Sozialdemokratie* (1893) and *Die Gesellschaftsordnung und ihre natürlichen Grundlagen* (1895), Ammon very closely paralleled Haeckel's social Darwinism. For Ammon, predictably, the laws of nature were also the laws of society. Struggle for existence and the inequality of all men, he wrote, were permanent aspects of life. Bravery, cunning, competition were all parts of the eternal scheme of things and it would be foolish to wish them away.

In obvious imitation of Haeckel, Ammon taught that Darwinism had to become Germany's new religion. It had to be accepted as a complete *Weltanschauung* and its ideas had to be encouraged in every facet of life. With a triumph of evolutionary Monism, he contended, religion and philosophy would no longer be in mutual contradiction.⁹

Ammon also repeated the well-worn racial arguments. He suggested that the lower races of mankind had to succumb in the struggle for existence. Racial struggle itself was a 'necessity for mankind.'¹⁰ Only when weak individuals and races perish is mankind as a whole able to reap the benefit. Ammon believed, of course, that it was the Germans who possessed superior racial and biological characteristics and he appealed for a return to the values and attitudes of the primitive Germanic tribes, who had led lives of natural bravery unencumbered by the errors and weaknesses of Christian civilization.¹¹

The ideas of other prominent social Darwinists like Alexander Tille and Alexander Ploetz who also began writing in the decades around the turn of the century, may also be linked with Haeckel.¹² In 1893, Tille published a book entitled *Volksdienst. Von einem Sozialaristokraten*, which was highly praised by Haeckel.¹³ Tille freely borrowed Haeckel's conception of the 'aristocratic' character of nature and he argued that social inequality was biologically determined. His defense of social inequality won for him the appreciation and support of a number of German industrialists, who appointed him director of public relations for German industry in Berlin and in Saarbrücken. Like Haeckel, Tille attached enormous importance to the animal origin and character of man and he felt that a general acceptance of this fact would lead to spiritual and ideological changes both necessary and desirable in German cultural life. And in another influential and widely read book which also received the approbation of Haeckel, *Von Darwin bis Nietzsche* (1895), Tille, who acknowledged his debt to Haeckel, explained the impact which the discovery of biological evolution had made on ethics, and agreed with Haeckel that all absolute ethical values had been obliterated by the discovery of evolution. Tille argued that only the unimpeded laws of nature could be the source of morality.[14]

Dr. Ploetz was vitally interested in the problem of achieving proper biological selection and became one of the more important workers in the school of racial hygiene in Germany.[15] Interested primarily in maintaining the vigor of the Germans, who he believed were threatened with biological decay, Ploetz advocated sending the biologically unfit to the battlefield, so that biologically superior individuals could be preserved for reproduction. He demanded that married couples be required to submit to the state an affidavit of their intention to have children. A medical board would then determine if they were biologically and materially fit to procreate. If, despite this precaution, children were born with physical or mental defects, they would have to be eliminated.

In 1904, Dr. Ploetz became one of the principal founders of the racially inspired eugenic journal, *Archiv für Rassen- und Gesellschaftsbiologie*. Among the editors were not only such future Nazi scientists as Eugen Fischer and Fritz Lenz, but also Ludwig Plate, a close colleague of Haeckel, a member of the Monist League, and the successor to Haeckel's chair in zoology at the University of Jena. The first issue of the *Archiv* was dedicated to Haeckel and to August Weismann. In the articles of the journal, Haeckel's name was constantly referred to; it is clear that the contributors regarded him as Germany's major prophet of political biology, and one cannot avoid noticing the great weight which at all times was attached to his scientific authority, and to his ideas on politics and eugenics. The *Archiv*, which continued to be published right up through the Nazi period (until 1944), became one of the chief organs in Germany for the dissemination of eugenic ideas and provided a respectable scientific framework for Nazi writers. Many of its contributors expressed racist and Nazi-like eugenic ideas long before the existence of the National Socialist Workers' Party.

After 1933, therefore, no need was found by the new regime to disband the *Archiv*, to alter its general point of view, or to change its board of editors. On the contrary, it may be said, that the *Archiv für Rassen- und Gesellschaftsbiologie* had anticipated events by over a quarter of a century.[17]

In regard to the racial theory of the Germans as Aryans, one should take note of the famous colleague of Haeckel, Ernst Krause (pseudonym Carus Sterne).[18] Together with Haeckel, Krause edited the journal *Kosmos*, the chief organ of the Darwinian movement in Germany in the 1870's and in the 1880's. In addition, Krause had been the noted author of popular biographies of Erasmus and Charles Darwin. In these books he had attempted to demonstrate the continuity which he believed to exist between English and German Darwinism, and he became one of the most widely read popularizers of Darwinian ideas in Germany. But Krause was also at the same time an imposing figure in the Volkish movement. In the early 1890's, and shortly before his death, he wrote two influential books in defense of Aryanism and Germanic ideology. In his *Tuisko-Land, der arischen Stämme und Götter Urheimat* (1891), he undertook to locate the place of origin of the Aryans, to trace their migrations, and to assess their impact on the racial development of Europe. And in a second work published two years later, *Die Trojaburgen Nordeuropas: ihr Zusammenhang mit der indogermanischen Trojasage von der entführten Sonnenfrau (Syrith, Ariadne, Helena), dem Trojaspielen Schwert- und Labyrinthtänzen zur Feier ihrer Lenzbefreiung*, Krause involved himself in all kinds of historical and literary gyrations to prove that the Greeks were really Aryans and were consequently the racial forebears of the Germans.

The individuals whom we have mentioned thus far in our discussion wrote and worked, more or less, generally within the precincts of scientific and intellectual respectability. But it is important to recognize that Haeckel and the Monists also influenced and inspired a number of important Volkists who may be grouped among the more radical and eccentric figures in the racial and eugenic movement. For example, there were some Volkists who forcefully advocated the immediate establishment of racially-pure, rural utopian communities. Rebelling, as did the Monists, against urbanism and the unhealthy life of the industrial center, their avowed purpose was to help maintain and foster the purely Nordic qualities of the Germans. These communities were to provide a stable and convenient framework for the breeding of large numbers of Aryans. And one of the most persistent and famous advocates of such breeding communities was the youth movement leader and well-known novelist, the author of *Varuna* (1907), Willibald Hentschel.

Hentschel, who was born in 1858, studied and completed a degree in zoology under Haeckel's direction.[19] However, after leaving the University of Jena, Hentschel declined to accept an academic position and instead became involved in many Volkish and anti-Semitic pursuits. He became a close friend and ideological collaborator of Theodor Fritsch, the well-known anti-Semitic publicist, and his works were published by Fritsch's *Hammer Verlag*.[20] But the most influential aspect of Hentschel's career and the *leitmotiv* of his thinking was the propaganda which he disseminated in support of a plan for the establishment of a breeding colony for pure Nordics which was to be called Mittgart, after the name of the legendary home of the Aryans. In this community as Hentschel envisioned it, an Aryan elite would be created by scientific methods of procreation and he was certain that in short time it would be able to boast a membership of the best racial elements in Germany. The cities, on the other hand, would become centers for the biologically unfit who would be allowed to quickly die off.[21]

After the First World War, Hentschel's ideas bore practical fruit when he became the ideological mentor of the *Artamanen*, a right wing youth movement. The name of the organization itself was Hentschel's invention, which he derived from the name of the god of the Aryans, Artam. Under the leadership of Wilhelm Kotzde and Bruno Tanzmann, the *Artamanen* became the most influential racial-utopian and proto-Nazi youth movement in the Weimar Republic. Following Hentschel, they propagandized for the creation of a racially pure Germanic peasantry to be fashioned upon the nobility of German blood. *Lebensraum*, for an expanding population, could be attained by the exclusion of the Poles from the eastern territories, and the newly acquired land resettled by racially acceptable Germans rescued from urban industrial slums. For the *Artamanen* the perfection of the race could only take place in intimate connection with the soil of Germany.

They therefore took up residence in rural communities and worked as agricultural laborers. It was their aim to accumulate capital and settle down as peasants forming the nucleus of racially pure communities.

From the start there were close ties between the *Artamanen* and the Nazis and many of the individuals who first received their ideological and social training in this movement later on became officers and leaders in the SS.[22] Among the charter members of the *Artamanen* are Heinrich Himmler, the leader of the SS, Rudolf Hoess, the Commandant of Auschwitz, and Walther Darré, Hitler's minister of agriculture and architect of Nazi resettlement policy in the east.[23] Through Hentschel, therefore, and the *Artamanen*, Haeckel's racial eugenics found one more way to practical expression in the Third Reich.

On the lunatic fringe of the social Darwinist movement one might also place the contribution to Volkism of the Viennese racial philosopher and publicist, Dr. Georg Lanz von Liebenfels.[24] Liebenfels was a frequent contributor to the semi-official Monist journal, *Das freie Wort*, and was himself the editor and publisher of a notoriously anti-Semitic and crackpot racist magazine, *Ostara, Zeitschrift für Blonde*. His main idea was that only blond Aryans were truly human and he sought to warn the Germans that their innocent young Nordic maidens were in constant danger of being ravished by men of the inferior races, whom he likened to animals. In books with such exotic titles as *Theozoologie oder Die Kunde von den Sodoms-Äfflingen und dem Götter Elektron*, or, *Anthropozoikon: Der Vormensch, Affen und Tiermensch in der Bibel*, Liebenfels wrote that true *homosapiens* had ethnological roots only in Germany and that the sole bearers of culture in the modern world were the Aryans.[25]

One might also, in this regard, take notice of Hermann Rohleder, a member of the Leipzig branch of the Monist League, who published a volume on racial anthropology in 1918 called *Künstliche Zeugung und Anthropogenie*.[26] Rohleder dedicated his book to Haeckel 'with deepest honor.' As Fritz Bolle has pointed out, Rohleder's thesis was quite simple and provides one with a good example of the brutal tendencies of social Darwinist thought in Germany. Rohleder proposed the mating of man and ape in order to demonstrate once and for all the animal character of man and his derivation from the anthropoids.²⁷

It was not only in the realm of eugenics and racism, however, that Haeckel and the Monists profoundly influenced the rise of the Volkist ideology. Their far-reaching impact may be observed in the outlook and organization of the highly influential Bohemian literary circle of Friedrichshagen, which began meeting around the turn of the century.²⁸ The Friedrichshagen Circle, which was named after the suburb of Berlin in which it met, was the gathering place of a truly outstanding number of Germany's leading Volkist intellectuals in the decade and a half prior to the outbreak of the First World War. The leaders and founders of the Circle were two important Monists: Bruno Wille and Wilhelm Boelsche.²⁹ Both were life-long fighters for Darwinism and nature worship, and their novels, essays, and literary criticism were vere widely known and read in Germany. Both had been very close to Haeckel, had written biographies of him, and were among the founders of the Monist League. Among other important Volkists who were attached to Friedrichshagen was Fidus (Karl Höppner), the famous illustrator whose drawings for the youth movement were especially known; the celebrated author Gerhardt Hauptmann and his brother Carl, who was an active member of the Monist League and had been a student of Haeckel; and the proto-Nazi writer, Moeller van den Bruck, the author of the influential book *The Third Reich*. Bruck's first wife was Hedda Eulenberg, an active member of the Monist League, and a frequent contributor to Monist journals on cultural topics.³⁰

Haeckelian Monist influence may also be observed in the highly important Volkish circle of the publisher and author Eugen Diederichs. In a very real sense it was Diederichs who actually brought Volkish ideas into widespread respectability during the first two decades of this century. Through the medium of his publishing house, which incidentally was located in Jena, Diederichs presented the ideas of Monism to the German reading public in scores of books and brochures. In 1912, Diederichs founded the highly influential journal *Die Tat*, which Haeckel himself recognized as a Monist publication.³¹ In addition, Diederichs also organized a cultural circle in Jena, the *Sera* group, which, as the name suggests, was dedicated in Monist style to sun-worship and Germanic mythology and pagan religion. The influence of Diederichs extended into the 1920's and through *Die Tat* influenced the formation of the National Socialist ideology. And after 1933, many of the members of the *Tat* Circle enthusiastically entered the ranks of the Nazi party.[32]

It is perhaps one of the more persistent generalizations of modern German history that the youth movement arose in Germany largely as a reaction to the materialism of Haeckel and to the mechanistic culture which he is reputed to have encouraged.[33] In actual fact, the very opposite is true. Haeckel and his Monist followers were at the very center of the formation of the *Wandervogel*, Germany's modern youth movement.[34] It was Haeckel's very close and dedicated follower, and co-founder of the Monist League, the famous educator, Ludwig Gurlitt, who, together with men like Karl Fischer, brought the German youth movement into existence for the first time in Steglitz, a suburb of Berlin, during the early years of this century.[35] Gurlitt, who had already written widely on the need for educational reform and had been expelled from the staff of the Steglitz *Gymnasium* for his innovating ideas, was also the mentor of Karl Fischer, who is ordinarily regarded as the founder of the youth movement.[36] It was Gurlitt who actually conveyed to Fischer the educational ideas of Paul de Lagarde and Julius Langbehn, the chief nineteenth-century prophets of the Volkish movement.[37] And once the Wandervogel was established, Gurlitt himself became the first chairman of the advisory council of the organization.[38] A few years later when the Monist League was formally organized, a Monist youth group was also created, *Sonne*, which affiliated itself with the larger German youth movement.[39]

In addition, it should also be recognized that Haeckel had other channels available to him to reach the younger generation. For example, one of his closest followers was Georg Hirth, a co-founder of the Monist League, and the editor of the romantic youth magazine, *Jugend*. In the pages of *Jugend*, which was one of the most widely read publications for youth in Germany at the turn of the century, Haeckel's ideas about nature worship received wide coverage from Hirth. In February, 1904, to celebrate Haeckel's seventieth birthday, an entire issue of *Jugend* was devoted to him. Haeckel was presented as the romantic prophet of nature worship and the illustrations and designs accompanying the articles evoked in typical *Jugendstil* the imagery of the mysterious and of far-off places.⁴⁰ German youth, therefore, had every opportunity to become familiar with the true content of Haeckel's social Darwinism, and his ideas of the need for a return to nature and for the cultivation of a life within nature.

Even further, Haeckel's influence is to be noted in the Germanic Faith movement, an organization founded by Wilhelm Schwaner and Ludwig Fahrenkrog, which unquestionably accelerated the development of an anti-Christian pagan religion in Germany. Schwaner was one of the original founders of the Monist League,⁴¹ and in 1913 wrote the *Germanenbibel*, a rather popular collection of patriotic writings derived from famous German literary figures. Another popular book which he wrote was a work for educators which was entitled *Unterm Hakenkreuz*, a collection of essays from a radically Volkist point of view. Schwaner was also a leader in the *Volkserzieher*, an organization which played an active role in the famous *Wandervogel* convention at the *Hohe Meissner* in October, 1913. Called on the centenary of the Napoleonic wars in Germany, the meeting at the *Hohe Meissner* sought unsuccessfully to unite the entire German youth movement. At the convention the *Volkserzieher* urged the *Wandervogel* to adopt a radical Volkish program and they proclaimed that they 'regard Germany, not Palestine, as the promised land.'⁴² In addition, Schwaner was also an active Pan-German and wished that the frontiers of Germany should encompass, not only Austria, but also Switzerland, Luxemburg, Holland, and Belgium.⁴³ This, he argued, would prepare Germany to meet any combination of powers that might be thrown against her.

It was in 1908 that together with a friend, the artist Ludwig Fahrenkrog, another disciple of Haeckel,⁴⁴ Schwaner founded the *Germanische Glaubens Gemeinschaft* (GGG). By means of the organization both Schwaner and Fahrenkrog sought to apply the pantheism of Haeckel towards the formulation of a completely pagan religion rooted in the festivals of pre-Christian German life.⁴⁵ The organization became part of the general Free-Thought Movement in Germany and gained a significant following. In fact, many of the ideas of the GGG were carried over into the Germanic pagan religious movement of Mathilde Ludendorff in the 1920's, which in turn directly influenced the religious program of the Nazis.⁴⁶

In yet another sensitive area, the Jewish question, one may detect the influence of Haeckel and the Monists. In his attitude towards the Jews, Haeckel once again revealed the radical nature of his thinking and demonstrated agreement with the prevalent anti-Semitism of many of his Volkist colleagues. Haeckel was one of the most vociferous opponents of the Jews, and his importance for the history of anti-Semitism in Germany is that he did much to bring the Jewish question into the realm of biology. As in all questions the Jews were subjected by Haeckel to 'scientific' analysis and he, along with his other anti-Semitic contemporaries, discovered that the Jews possessed inborn racial characteristics which apparently were resistant to change. Haeckel made his anti-Semitism widely known and lent his authority to it in the *Welträtsel*, where he asserted that Christ's merits derived from the fact that he was only half Jewish. Like his contemporaries Houston Stewart Chamberlain or Paul de Lagarde, Haeckel sought in the *Welträtsel* to uphold the reality of an Aryan Christ. He therefore asserted that Christ's true father was a Roman officer who had seduced Mary. The proof of this was that Christ exhibited positive traits of personality which could not, according to Haeckel, have been Jewish. 'The characteristics which distinguish [Christ's] high and noble personality, and which give a distinct impress to his religion, are certainly not Semitical; they are rather features of the higher Arian [sic!] race.'[47]

In 1893, the novelist, essayist, and journalist Hermann Bahr, himself a Monist, conducted a series of interviews among outstanding German personalities in order to ascertain their attitude towards the Jews and anti-Semitism.[48] Haeckel was among those interviewed and his response, as we might expect, betrayed strong feelings of anti-Semitism.

In a callous and at times flippant response, Haeckel charged the Jews themselves with generating anti-Semitism. Shrugging off all responsibility on the part of the non-Jewish world, Haeckel told Bahr that the very durability of anti-Semitism throughout history led one to the inescapable conclusion that the Jews were in fact the source of their own misfortune and were themselves to blame for the sentiments that were often expressed against them. 'I cannot believe,' Haeckel said, 'that such a powerful, enduring, and great movement could have been possible without adequate cause.'[49] He found, rather, that anti-Semitism arose from an inner justification and was not to be considered the product of a pathological state of mind. Approvingly aware of its pervasiveness, Haeckel acknowledged the existence of anti-Semitic feelings among many of his students and this seemed to him to be completely normal and predictable.

In offering further observations on the Jewish question, Haeckel asserted that he considered anti-Semitism to be a 'national' and 'racial' problem rather than a religious one. And evoking the spectre of intrinsic Jewish cosmopolitanism, Haeckel contended that the Jews were alienated from German life and society and that the Germans therefore felt ill at ease among the Jews. In addition, the problem, he explained, was exacerbated by the fact that Germany was in the midst of a national renaissance. Since nationalism and not internationalism was the prevailing political current not only in Germany but throughout all of Europe, it was therefore to be expected that anti-Semitism would continue to grow and develop. '*Vorderhand ist das Nationale Gefühl im Wachsen, im Erstarken*,'[50] he observed, and anti-Semitism was an inevitable and justifiable by-product of this movement.

A possible way of resolving the conflict between the Germans and the Jews, however, was total assimilation into German life and culture. Assimilation, Haeckel contended, had to be demanded of the Jews, even compelled if necessary. 'It must be understood that the [German] people will no longer tolerate the strange ways of Jewish life, and their desire is to deprive the Jews of all that is specifically Jewish and to convert them to German habits and customs so that they will resemble the people among whom they live in all respects.'[51]

As far as the anti-Semitic movement itself was concerned, Haeckel expressed the belief that its continued existence was needed because it performed the necessary function of compelling the Jews to assimilate. It served to make them aware of their own condition and was therefore a healthy social movement. 'Anti-Semitism is a justifiable idea because it [seeks to] free the Jews from their separatist behavior, and desires that they assimilate with us completely.' And only by disappearing as a separate group could the Jews demonstrate their patriotism and at the same time serve the national interests of Germany.[52]

Hermann Bahr also asked Haeckel if anti-Semitism might not in reality have the opposite effect and encourage the Jews to isolate themselves from the Germans. Haeckel replied by saying that every social movement had its successes and also its dangers. As for himself, he felt that, on the whole, the anti-Semitic movement had served to awaken the Jews and the Germans to the existence of a Jewish question. It had helped to show that the continued emigration to Germany of Jews from eastern Europe had to be stopped. The Russian Jews, Haeckel argued, were absolutely incapable of imbibing German culture, and it was even in the interest of the German Jews themselves to have the easterners excluded. 'In this matter false humanitarianism can only be harmful and I think that we have to energetically protect ourselves from the Russian Jews.' In attitudes that were very close to Hitler's view of the Russian Jews whom he viewed so myopically in Vienna, Haeckel described them as a 'filthy' people with an 'outlandish' appearance. Indeed, the impression he conveyed to Bahr was that they could hardly be considered to be human at all.[53]

As far as the Monist League was concerned, although it was not officially anti-Semitic and even though some Jews were to be found in its ranks,[54] there were frequent expressions of uneasiness about the 'Jewish question.'[55] The problem of the Jews, they wrote, was 'one of the most difficult'[56] that Germany had to face. It was their feeling that the Jews had to renounce all ties to Judaism and to world Jewry so that they could cease to exist as a separate group.[57] With the renunciation of Judaism, they wrote, the Jews would happily 'disappear for all time as an individual nation.'[58]

But beyond anti-Semitism and the other links that have been established, certainly the most significant and heretofore largely unnoticed and unrecognized influence of Haeckel and the Monists on the development of National Socialism is to be found in Hitler himself. It has only relatively recently been observed that a relationship appears to exist between, on the one hand, the general outlook of Hitler and the framework in which he cast his ideas and, on the other hand, the social Darwinism of Haeckel and the Monists.[59] However, these insights have thus far not been developed or elaborated upon to any great extent. More intensive probing into the ideological framework of Hitler's thinking, especially as intimately recorded in his *Tischgespräche*, reveals a critical, general and also a specific relationship with the ideas of Haeckel. Indeed, rightly considered, a number of Hitler's conversations and the content of some of his writings emerge as an extended paraphrase and at times even plagiarism of Haeckel's *Natürliche Schöpfungsgeschichte* and the *Welträtsel*. The first question that should be answered, therefore, is whether or not it is likely that Hitler read the works of Haeckel or was in a position to know of his ideas or the beliefs of any of the Monists.

There appears to be at least two significant contacts that can be established between Hitler and members of the Monist League. Hitler was familiar with the ideas of Wilhelm Boelsche, the literary critic and guiding spirit of the Friedrichshagen literary circle, who was, as we have already noted, also a close disciple and biographer of Haeckel and a co-founder of the Monist League. Boelsche did much to popularize the ideas of Haeckel in Germany and influenced Hitler mainly through his widely known book, *Vom Bazillus zum Affenmenschen*. From Boelsche Hitler had direct access to the major ideas of Haeckelian social Darwinism.[60] Secondly, Hitler himself stated that in his youth he had been profoundly influenced by the famous Norwegian explorer of Greenland and the Arctic, Fridtjof Nansen.[61] Nansen was a member of the Monist League and recognized Haeckel as one of the most decisive intellectual influences in his life.[62] What Hitler could discover in Nansen's writings was a glorification of nature, especially of the ice-bound north, and a stress on the original and distinctive elements which were to be found in pre-Christian northern European culture. Apart from Boelsche and Nansen, to discover other exposures of Hitler to the ideas of Haeckelian Monism we must rely mostly on inference.[63]

In the decade and a half prior to the outbreak of the First World War, Hitler was in his late teens and early twenties. As part vagrant, part bohemian artist in Linz, Vienna, and Munich between 1900 and 1914, Hitler made his first wider contact with the outside world and with higher culture.[64] According to his own accounts he became an avid, even voracious reader during this period and sought to educate himself, especially after failing to gain admission to the Academy of Fine Arts in Vienna. Although it is doubtful that Hitler was as disciplined or as comprehensive in his reading as he claimed,[65] it is nonetheless apparent that whatever smattering of culture he possessed was gained primarily during those years before the war. Even as an undisciplined

MONISM AND NATIONAL SOCIALISM

reader there is every reason to suppose that the young Hitler would have had some contact with Haeckel's *Welträtsel*, which, as we have seen, was one of the most read and popular books in Germany during the first decade of the century. A work like the *Welträtsel* would have especially appealed to a pseudo-educated mind like that of Hitler, as it had to so many others without much sophistication who had sought an authoritative yet simple account of modern science and a comprehensible explanation of the world. Thus, it may be taken as likely that Haeckel's ideas filtered down to Hitler in one way or another. This is supported by the fact that in the 1930's, when Hitler had assumed power, in one of his conversations with Rauschning he referred specifically to Haeckel's opposition to Christianity, giving evidence of understanding the context in which Haeckel had cast his thinking. Thus, at least some of Haeckel's focal ideas were clearly known by Hitler. To identify Darwin, instead of Haeckel, as the matrix of Hitler's social Darwinism, as is generally done, is to ignore, in addition to the enormous success of the *Welträtsel* and Hitler's reference to Haeckel, the obvious reality that since the publication in 1866 of Haeckel's *Natürliche Schöpfungsgeschichte*, the Germans understood Darwin and Darwinism through the distorted lenses of Haeckel. When the Germans refer to Darwin, more often than not they in fact mean, not Darwin, but Haeckel and his Monist philosophy.[66]

Hitler's indebtedness to Haeckel lies in the underlying ideology at the heart of significant parts of his conversations, speeches, and writings. They show a basic kinship with the principles and even with some of the formulations of Haeckelian social Darwinism and with Monism. Hitler's views on history, politics, religion, Christianity, nature, eugenics, science, art, and evolution, however eclectic, and despite the plurality of their sources, coincide for the most part with those of Haeckel and are more than occasionally expressed in very much the same language. Naturally, this is not to deny the influence on Hitler of many other writers and Volkish intellectuals, for it is apparent, that Hitler's views were far too heterogeneous a compilation to be limited to a single source. Yet, the evidence does seem to show parallels and affinities between Hitler and Haeckel that so far have not been satisfactorily explored and determined. In the thought of Hitler, as in that of Haeckel, social Darwinism was brought together under the rubric of evolutionary religion and it is this common feature of their thought which indissolubly binds them together and makes them part of one intellectual tradition. Both Hitler and Haeckel shared a common sense of mission in regard to man and to his relationship to nature. In his general outlook on the world Hitler protested as much as Haeckel did that the great defect of modern Western society was that man was in constant violation of nature. As Ernst Nolte has expressed it, Hitler was in 'dread' of the forces of 'antinature.' He believed that there were 'certain basic structures of social existence' which were 'threatened' by the 'transcendence' in man, by his quest for freedom and equality, and by his uncalled for rebellion against the dictates of nature. In his *Weltanschauung*, therefore, Hitler was 'afraid *of* man *for* man' and defended human culture as he understood it against the Western tradition. Like Haeckel he sought to curb the 'germs of disintegration' within society by returning to the paths marked out by nature. For Hitler, therefore, social Darwinism was not simply the idea of struggle. It was the holy conception of nature and understood in this way his idea of the world was indistinguishable from that of Haeckel.[67]

In the *Tischgespräche*, one of the words and concepts most frequently employed by Hitler was W*issenschaft*, science.[68] From the content of his conversations it is patently clear that he thought of himself as rooted in the rational and scientific tradition of modern European civilization and that he was certain that there was a basis in science for all of the beliefs and policies which he espoused. But it was as true for Hitler, as it was for Haeckel, that science, as one historian has observed, 'did not mean ... a special application of rational culture, the by-product of a free ranging imagination coupled with a disciplined outlook on the world.'[69] It consisted rather of a literal reading of nature, a discovery of the absolute, irrevocable, and incontestable laws of the world. Thus, as far as Hitler was concerned, it was not necessary to grasp the *meaning* of nature. One had only to *describe* the world and to accept its laws and its phenomena unquestioningly and with devotion. 'As for the *why* of these laws, we shall never know anything about it. A thing is so, and our understanding cannot conceive of other schemes.'[70] Thus, in the same awe-inspired way that Haeckel had taught that we cannot know the impenetrable and 'innermost character of nature' and had urged deference to the 'great eternal iron laws'[71] of the universe, Hitler spoke of the necessity of becoming familiar with the laws of nature which he was certain would 'guide us on the path of progress.'[72] He urged that it was 'useful to know the laws of nature—for that enables us to obey them. To act otherwise would be to rise in revolt against heaven.'[73]

Hitler applied his belief in nature to the world of man in the same resolute and literal way that had been characteristic of Haeckel. He argued that in human affairs 'as in everything, nature is the best instructor.'[74] He insisted, as Haeckel had, that 'one must start by accepting the principle that nature herself gives all the necessary indications, and that therefore one must follow the rules that she has laid down.'[75] And for Hitler, as for Haeckel, this was especially true in regard to the laws of society. Hitler, like Haeckel, lamented the tragedy that 'man, alone amongst the living creatures, tries to deny the laws of nature.'[76] It was nature that had to provide absolute guidelines for the total organization and direction of society.

Like Haeckel, Hitler conceived of man's lot on earth as 'characterized by an eternal struggle . . . against beasts and against men themselves.'[77] History was nothing less than 'an eternal struggle for existence,' and politics had to be based therefore upon the direct application of the laws of nature and struggle. 'The earth continues to go round, whether it's the man who kills the tiger or the tiger which eats the man. The strongest asserts his will, it's the law of nature.'[78] One must recognize the radical bond which united man and society with nature. It was true that 'men know as little why they live as does any other creature of the world.'[79] But they were subjected to the conditions of life whether they liked it or not. 'Nothing that is made of flesh and blood can escape the laws which determine its coming into being. As soon as the human mind believes itself to be superior to them, it destroys the real substance which is the bearer of the mind.'[80]

Like the Monists, Hitler was concerned with preserving and maintaining the biological prowess of Germany: just as weaker animals were weeded out by natural selection or struggle so too must weaker human beings be eliminated. And he evoked the memory and tradition of the eugenic practices of the ancient Spartans in language virtually identical to Haeckel's. It is to be recalled that Haeckel had written:

'Among the Spartans all newly born children were subject to a careful examination and selection. All those that were weak, sickly, or affected with any bodily infirmity, were killed. Only the perfectly healthy and strong children were allowed to live, and they alone afterwards propagated the race.'[81] Similarly Hitler wrote: 'Sparta must be regarded as the first folkish state. The exposure of the sick, weak, deformed children, in short their destruction, was more decent and in truth a thousand times more humane than the wretched insanity of our day which preserves the most pathological subject.'[82]

Not only his eugenics but also the manner in which Hitler formulated his racial ideas seem to have been freely borrowed from Haeckel. Like Haeckel, Hitler believed that mankind was divided into separate races that were as sharply divided from each other as species in the animal and plant kingdom. In the struggle for existence the lower and weaker races were bound to die out, and here again Hitler appears to plagiarize Haeckel. One need only compare their definitions of racial difference. For Haeckel, the 'mental differences between the lowest men and the animals are less than those between the lowest and the highest man.'[83] Similarly for Hitler the 'difference which exists between the lowest, so-called men and the other highest races is greater than that between the lowest men and the highest apes.'[84] For Haeckel, the difference between the reason of a Goethe, a Kant, a Lamarck, or a Darwin and that of the lowest savage . . . is much greater than the graduated difference between the reason of the latter and that of the most "rational" animals.'[85] Similarly, for Hitler 'there is less difference between the man-ape and the ordinary man' than there is between the latter and a 'man like Schopenhauer.'[86] These nearly identical passages would appear to suggest that Haeckel's ideas and characteristic formulations did somehow reach and affect the mind and thinking of Hitler.

Highly revealing is the fact that Hitler not only conceived of social problems in general in the light of biology but also treated the special Jewish question in the same way. For this, too, there was a tradition in Monism. As we have noted above, Haeckel regarded the Jews as a race with unenviable characteristics and described them in biological terms. And other Monists had on various occasions repeated an idea which was gaining popularity in Germany in the last half of the nineteenth century that the long survival of the Jews could be explained in terms of natural selection. By no means implying it as a compliment, they developed the notion that through persecution and difficult conditions the Jews had become extraordinarily strong. Their powers of survival, it was implied, were somehow rooted in their physical makeup.[87] But this idea can also be found in Hitler, who had explained in the *Tischgespräche*, that '*Der Jude ist der klimafesteste Mensch der Erde*,' the Jew is the 'only human being capable of adapting himself to any climate and of earning a living just as well in Lapland as in the tropics.'[88] Thus, he warned, it would be all the harder to eliminate them. In planning for their destruction one had to take into account their special biological characteristics, and Hitler linked the discovery of the 'Jewish Bacillus' to the same kind of work which had been performed in the nineteenth century by Pasteur and Koch.[89] For Hitler, since the 'Jewish virus' caused disease it was only *natural* that the Jews had to be eliminated. The need was objective, natural, and scientific. 'Whose fault is it when a cat devours a mouse? The fault of the mouse, who has never done any harm to a cat?'[90] Once a 'people is rid of its Jews' then it can 'return spontaneously to the natural order.'[91] And while Haeckel did not himself advocate the physical elimination of the Jews, nonetheless the idea of using physical force against the Jews could be found in at least one Monist author, Heinrich Pudor.[92]

Hitler's conception of history was likewise tied to his acceptance of the literal supremacy of nature. Very much like Haeckel and the Monists, Hitler argued that Western Civilization had obscured the true relationship between man and nature. Somewhere along the line man's knowledge and understanding of himself had gone awry. Not surprisingly, for Hitler, as for Haeckel, the culprit was Christianity. For two thousand years Europe had been trying to convince itself that man was not really part of nature, and that had led to the continual decline of civilization after the fall of the ancient world. Consequently, in the *Tischgespräche*, Hitler dwelt inordinately on the evils of Christianity and offered the Germans a new faith which was to be rooted in nature. Once again the content of the *Welträtsel* is manifest.

Yet even the most recent studies of the mind of Hitler describe his notion of the decadence of Western Civilization as some sort of lunatic, but nonetheless original theory. For example, the English historian, Norman Cohn, has recently written the following:

.... Hitler arrives at a whole philosophy of history, an interpretation of human existence from the beginning onwards, which has a certain crazy originality. As Hitler sees it, human history forms part of nature and follows the same laws as the rest of nature. If it has gone wrong, that shows that some force is at work to frustrate nature's intention, and that has in fact been the case for thousands of years. There follows an outline of history which portrays it as one long degeneration. Nature demands inequality, hierarchy, subordination of the inferior to the superior—but human history consisted of a series of revolts against this natural order, leading to ever greater egalitarianism.[93]

But this conception of history was hardly the fruit of Hitler's 'crazy originality.' It was only a simple repetition of Haeckel's historical views which had been widely disseminated in Germany since the 1860's and had already become the property of countless Volkists. For Hitler, as for Haeckel, since its inception Christianity had preached against the laws of nature, and this had led to the decline of society. It was Christianity which had destroyed the natural hierarchical order of the world. This was essentially the thesis which we have seen Haeckel advancing in his *Natürliche Schöpfungsgeschichte* and in the *Welträtsel*, and it was also the major historical assumption of Hitler. Let us therefore have a closer look at Hitler's opinion of Christianity and see to what extent a parallel can be established with Haeckelian Monism.

There was first of all a common historical appraisal of the effect which Christianity had had on civilization. It might be recalled that Haeckel had written of the 'barbarism' which Christianity embodied in contrast to the 'noble height to which the human mind had attained in classical antiquity.'[94] For Hitler, too, the 'heaviest blow that ever struck humanity was the coming of Christianity.'[95] The history of the world, he felt, had been fundamentally disturbed by its appearance. 'But for the coming of Christianity, who knows how the history of Europe would have developed? Rome would have conquered all of Europe, and the onrush of the Huns would have been broken on the legions. It was Christianity that brought about the fall of Rome— not the Germans or the Huns.'[96]

For Hitler, as for Haeckel, the worst period in the history of Europe was the time of the ascendency of the Papacy. For Haeckel it was the 'despotism of the papacy that lent its darkest character to the Middle Ages; it meant death to all freedom of mental life, decay to all science, corruption to all morality.'[97] For Hitler the 'period stretching between the middle of the third and the middle of the seventeenth century [was] certainly the worst humanity has ever known; blood-lust, ignominy, lies.'[98] If it hadn't been for Christianity, the 'Roman Empire under Germanic influence would have developed in the direction of world domination, and humanity would not have extinguished fifteen centuries of civilization at a single stroke.'[99] For Hitler 'Christianity [was] the worst repression that mankind can ever have undergone.' It had 'promulgate[d] its inconsistent dogmas' and had 'impose[d] them by force.' One had finally to realize that 'such a religion carries with it intolerance and persecution. It's the bloodiest conceivable.'[100]

Further, as we recall, it was Haeckel who had denounced Christianity for showing 'contempt . . . for self, for the body, for nature, for civilization, for the family, and for women.'[101] He derided its morality of weakness[102] and its fantastic belief in the next world.[103] Likewise, Hitler saw 'Christianity as a rebellion against natural law, a protest against nature.' Did it not represent, he contended, the 'systematic cultivation of human failure?'[104] It was a 'catastrophe' to be 'tied to a religion that rebels against all the joys of the senses.'[105] Christianity, Hitler said, was an 'invention of sick brains; one could imagine nothing more senseless, nor any more indecent way of turning the idea of God-head into a mockery. A Negro with his tabus is crushingly superior to the human being who seriously believes in transubstantiation.'[106] And Hitler concluded as Haeckel had done that there was 'something very unhealthy about Christianity.'[107] Its pessimism had to be overcome.

Hitler mocked the articles of Christian faith as much as he lamented their deleterious effect on history. And here once again he expressed ideas which sound very Haeckelian. He asserted that Christ was not Jewish and was illegitimate—an argument directly from the *Welträtsel*.[108] 'Galilee,' Hitler said, 'was a colony where the Romans had probably installed Gallic legionnaires and it's certain that Jesus was not a Jew. The Jews, by the way, regarded him as the son of a whore— of a whore and a Roman soldier.'[109] In the same way that Haeckel mocked all conceptions which conceived of God in man's image,[110] Hitler joked that 'if the mental picture that Christians form of God were correct, the God of the ants would be an ant, and similarly for other animals.'[111] In the spirit of Haeckel, Hitler termed Heaven and

Hell 'nonsensical' ideas.[112] Hitler even repeated the same scientific arguments which Haeckel had originally advanced against Christianity. Time and again Hitler spoke of the affront to science which Christianity represented. And, most significantly, like Haeckel, he stressed and singled out the idea of biological evolution as the most forceful weapon against traditional religion and he repeatedly condemned Christianity for its opposition to the teachings of evolution.[113] For Hitler evolution was the hallmark of modern science and culture, and he defended its veracity as tenaciously as Haeckel.

Thus, for Hitler, as for Haeckel, Christianity had to be abandoned. Hitler even criticized Houston Stewart Chamberlain for supposing that there were some spiritual values in Christianity that were worthwhile.[114] Nor did he feel that a return to the worship of pre-Christian Germanic cults was possible.[115] Rather, Hitler's solution of the religion problem was completely Haeckelian. 'We shan't be able to go on evading the religious problem much longer. If anyone thinks it's really essential to build the life of human society on a foundation of lies, well, in my estimation, such a society is not worth preserving. If, on the other hand, one believes that truth is the indispensable foundation, then conscience bids one intervene in the name of truth, and exterminate the lie.'[116] For Hitler, as for Haeckel, the only alternative to Christianity was a religion of nature and science. The form of the new religion which Hitler proposed was nothing less than an exact duplication of Haeckel's evolutionary Monism. 'Man,' Hitler said, in a passage that might easily find a place in Haeckel's famous essay, *Der Monismus als Band zwischen Religion und Wissenschaft*, 'has discovered in nature the wonderful notion of that all-mighty being whose law he worships. Fundamentally in everyone there is the feeling for this all-mighty, which we call god (that is to say, the dominion of natural laws throughout the whole universe).'[117] Man, Hitler believed, is of nature and must immerse himself in it—a direct parallel to the credo of the Monist religion. 'The elements of which our body is made belong to the cycle of nature.'[118] If man conforms to nature then in the 'long run' he will 'triumph over [Christian] religion.'[119] In the new nature religion, he argued, it would be realized that nature was a unity 'From now on in, one may consider that there is no gap between the organic and the inorganic world.'[120] Salvation was to be found in the study of nature and in the worship of its diverse forms and beauties.[121] 'I think that the man who contemplates the universe with his eyes wide open is the man with the greatest amount of natural piety; not in the religious sense, but in the sense of [possessing] an intimate harmony with things.'[122] It is 'possible to satisfy the needs of the inner life by an intimate communion with nature.'[123]

Hitler described the satisfaction to be derived from the worship and study of nature in purely Monist terms. There was that same belief in its power of redemption. 'Even in raging winter, one knows that spring will follow. And if, at this moment, men are being turned to blocks of ice, that won't prevent the April sun from shining or restoring life to these desolate spaces.'[124] Man had to stand in awe before the infinity of the cosmos. Just as Haeckel had taught as one of the articles of Monist faith that the '*extent* of the universe is infinite and unbounded' and that the '*duration* of the world is equally infinite and unbounded'[125] Hitler believed that the 'cosmos is infinite in all senses' and that this truth about nature had to be disseminated among the masses and 'expressed in an accessible fashion.'[126] Like Haeckel, Hitler suggested that the infinity and magnificence of nature had to be studied with aid of the microscope and the telescope.[127] As a counterweight to Christianity he proposed the construction of astronomical observatories all over Germany. They would be the principal weapon, he believed, for changing the religious sentiments of the entire German people. With Haeckel and the Monists, therefore, Hitler preached his cardinal religious idea: observe nature and 'you destroy the world of superstition.'[128] For Hitler, as for Haeckel, nature was salvation.

And finally, one last illustration of how seriously Hitler had accepted the idea of evolution in the Haeckelian sense, and the literal reading of nature. In the final days of the war, rejecting all pleas on the part of his advisors to arrange a compromise peace with the allies in order to spare Germany further destruction, Hitler ordered instead the destruction of the factories, bridges, railroads, and all utilities. When it was protested that this would harm Germany more than it would the advancing armies, Hitler said to Albert Speer: 'If the war is lost, the German people will perish too. There is no need to take any heed of the industrial plant and artifacts which the Germans might need to continue a primitive existence. On the contrary, it is better to destroy these things ourselves. This people have shown themselves to be the weaker, and the future belongs to the stronger people of the East exclusively. Those who survive this battle are the less worthy anyway, for the best will have fallen.'[129] Hitler ended his life as an evolutionary Monist in the deepest sense.

After 1933, many prominent Nazis who apparently were more aware than Hitler of their intellectual predecessors had no hesitation in expressing their deep debt to Haeckel and freely described him as a major prophet of National Socialism. In February, 1934, to commemorate the Centenary of Haeckel's birth, celebrations were held at the University of Jena. In an address prepared for this occasion, the zoologist, Professor Victor Franz, suggested that the idea of evolution had become an intellectual treasure for the new Nazi state and he linked the spirit of Darwinism to a poem which appeared in one of Gottfried Feder's pamphlets, *Was Will Adolf Hitler? Das Programm der N.S.D.A.P.*[130] Franz described Haeckel as a 'mighty nordic type' and proudly related that Haeckel had pursued a life of action and physical accomplishment. Haeckel, Franz continued, was aware of the racial uniqueness of the Germans, and he recounted a trip which Haeckel had made when he was a young man to the island of Heligoland, where he had reported finding the 'superb, nordic, primitive German *Kernvolk.*'[131] Franz also found much to admire in Haeckel's political beliefs. He explained that Haeckel opposed the Social Democratic concept of the equality of man, and that he understood that Darwinism was an aristocratic and not a democratic ideology. Indeed, Franz explained, Haeckel was a socialist, but certainly not of the Marxian persuasion—implying of course that he was a National Socialist. Franz also recalled Bismarck's visit to Jena in 1892, and he invoked Haeckel's name as a symbol of the heroic in life and as a person who should serve as a model for Nazi youth.[132]

In another eulogy written for Haeckel's Centenary, the noted biologist and anthropologist, Professor Gerhard Heberer also claimed Haeckel as a prophet of National Socialism. 'It is to be recalled at this opportunity,' he wrote, 'that Haeckel was one of the first fighters for eugenic measures. His proposals were being brought into reality in the new Reich.'[135] And Heberer also noted the Germanic content of Haeckel's thought. Referring to the ultimate significance of the

Weltätsel, Heberer contended that in the 'final analysis [the *Weltätsel*] was a protest of the Germanic spirit against the [spirit] of the Mediterranean.'[134]

There were, in addition to these celebrations at Jena, frequent references to Haeckel as a precursor of National Socialism in the various journals of racial biology which were published under the Nazis. In February 1934, also to commemorate the Centenary of Haeckel's birth, *Der Biologe*, distributed by the enthusiastically pro-Nazi publishing firm of J. F. Lehmann, devoted an entire issue to Haeckel. One of the articles praised Haeckel as a pioneer in the development of National Socialism and the author remarked how Haeckel could hardly have realized during his own lifetime how faithfully the Nazi leadership would be willing and able to carry out his ideas, especially in the realm of eugenics.[135] In another issue of the same journal, in May, 1934, the well-known Nazi racial biologist, Professor Ernst Lehmann, lauded Haeckel as a 'revolutionary of the spirit' and argued that the essence of the National Socialist striving to attain a bond with nature was akin to the strivings of Haeckel.[136] And in an article inspired by the naturalistic principles of Volkism written during the previous summer, Professor Lehmann located the essence and origin of National Socialism in the Darwinian revolution and credited Haeckel's role in the growth and diffusion of Naziism.'[137]

Thus, among many Nazi scientists and intellectuals there was general acclaim for Haeckel as a forerunner of National Socialism. It is noteworthy that the official ideologist of Nazi Germany, Alfred Rosenberg, wrote of his own intellectual debt to the Haeckelian tradition. In his memoirs he described the formative influence of his studies at the *Realgymnasium* in Reval. This school, Rosenberg's editors explain, was 'completely based on the spirit of the scientific positiveness of the nineteenth century, without classical precepts,' and thoroughly shaped Rosenberg's early mind. The school's director was admiringly described by Rosenberg as a 'naturalist' who 'owned a large butterfly collection, wrote on the geological history of Estonia, and corresponded with many of the scientific institutes of the Reich.' This same director, Rosenberg added, 'sent his only son to Jena' where 'Haeckel and Eucken were making this university world famous.' And as a consequence of his *Gymnasium* background, Rosenberg's editors add,

'Rosenberg was never able to shed the influence of the Monists of Haeckel's caliber, and the foundation for his later anti-Christian philosophy was obviously laid there and then. This adulation for the supremacy of science, elevated to the realm of philosophy, is encountered time and again later on, specifically in the field of hereditary biology.'[138]

Among some of Haeckel's other eulogizers in the Third Reich, might be mentioned Hans F. K. Günther, Naziism's leading racial anthropologist, who, interestingly enough, joined the faculty of the University of Jena shortly before the Nazi revolution.[139] In addition, Haeckel was celebrated in the pages of the official ideological journal of the Nazi party, *Nationalsozialistische Monatshefte*,[140] and a biography of him was published in 1935 under the auspices of the *Institut für menschliche Erbforschung und Rassenpolitik*.[141] Haeckel's Nazi biographer, Heinz Bruecher, gave assurances not only of his importance for the development of the basic doctrines of National Socialism but also of his proper biological background—his Aryanism, his blond hair, and his blue eyes.

And even among those Nazi leaders where there is no specific mention of Haeckel, nonetheless, the influence of Haeckelian ideology is clearly in evidence. In Himmler, for example, biological analogy pervades much of his thinking. Trained early in life in agricultural genetics Himmler attempted to use his knowledge for the selection of members of the SS. He thought of himself as operating completely within the framework of science and in his famous conversations with his physical therapist, Dr. Felix Kersten, he revealed how the idea of nature dominated his thinking and gave evidence of the same mystical reverence for nature and its powers which had characterized Hitler.[142] But it was not only among the main Nazi leaders that Haeckelian ideas were to be found. The entire literature of National Socialism was suffused with veneration of nature and adherence to the dictates of science. The Nazi state, for example, 'publicized' itself as the 'biological will of the German people' and National Socialism was defined as 'political biology.'[143] In innumerable scholarly journals and books the biological basis of the new state was stressed and the rebirth of the German people was linked to the laws of biology.[144] In fact, Naziism completely assimilated the fundamental ideas of Haeckel and the Monists.

Among Haeckel's closest followers in the Monist League, National Socialism was openly and enthusiastically welcomed as the ideology which they had been espousing for years. In 1933, the Monist League was dissolved and a new cultural organization came into existence in its place, the *Ernst Haeckel Gesellschaft*. It was sponsored by the well-known Gauleiter of Thuringia, Fritz Sauckel, who was to be tried and condemned to death at the Nuremberg trials after the War.[145] The leading member of the *Ernst Haeckel Gesellschaft* was Heinrich Schmidt, Haeckel's close disciple and biographer, and editor of his collected works. In 1933, Schmidt launched a new nature-philosophical journal called *Natur und Geist*. The journal was completely dedicated to the ideas of National Socialism and continually expressed a more than usual fawning admiration for Hitler and the new regime. *Natur und Geist* was edited as a continuing memorial to Haeckel and its articles and editorial comment were dedicated to the unity of Haeckelian Monism and National Socialism.[146]

One question remains to be answered, however. Haeckel was clearly accorded recognition by some Nazi intellectuals and by his followers as a forerunner of the Third Reich. Yet at the same time, it is also apparent that Haeckel did not figure in Nazi propaganda as a major prophet of National Socialism. He never attained the status of Lagarde or of Houston Stewart Chamberlain in the annals of Nazi history. And the reason is clear. While Darwinism was part of the Nazi educational curriculum in biology, official National Socialist ideology was suspicious of the idea of human evolution and, while not outrightly denying it, tended to play down the theory of the animal origin of man. It must be remembered that the Nazis had assigned a heroic and eternally superior character and racial constitution to the Aryans. It was therefore hardly ideologically admissible at the same time to allow for the evolution of the Aryans from a group of inferior anthropoid progenitors. Any theory of this kind would have destroyed the notion that the Aryans were in possession of racial superiority from the beginning. This dilemma of the Nazis, however, in regard to the complete acceptance of the idea of evolution was in fact an Haeckelian dilemma magnified many times. Haeckel and the Monists had also tried to disseminate their belief in man's immutability in a world which by the fundamental tenets of their own theory was assumed to be constantly in motion.[147]

NOTES

1. Bronder, *Bevor Hitler kam*, p. 300.
2. A full statement on the nature of the contest is to be found in Heinrich Ziegler's introduction to *Natur und Staat. Beiträge zur naturwissenschaftlichen Gesellschaftslehre, eine Sammlung von Preisschriften*, I, pp. 1–221. For an account by a Monist of how Haeckel and the collection *Natur und Staat*, led him to the discovery of Woltmann, racial ideology, eugenics, and to the 'circle of those who honor Gobineau,' see Friedrich Siebert (no title), in Schmidt (ed.), *Was wir Ernst Haeckel verdanken*, I, 345.
3. For Schallmayer's account of the disagreement with Ludwig Woltmann over the Krupp essay contest, see his *Vererbung und Auslese*, pp. xiv–xvi.
4. For a more complete account of Woltmann's ideas, see Mosse, *The Crisis of German Ideology*, pp. 99–103.
5. For Woltmann as a member of the Social Democratic Party, see Lichtheim, *Marxism. An Historical and Critical Study*, p. 292. Lichtheim, however, does not deal with the racist side of Woltmann's thought.
6. Ludwig Woltmann, *Politische Anthropologie* (Leipzig: Dorner, 1936), *passim*.
7. For an extended study of Otto Ammon and his link with National Socialism, see Conrad-Martius, *Utopien der Menschenzüchtung*, Chapter I, Part 1. For a Monist appreciation of Ammon, see Ziegler, *Die Naturwissenschaft und die sozialdemokratische Theorie*, p. 13.
8. See Haeckel, *Die Welträtsel* ([E.] Berlin: Akademie, 1961), p. 442.
9. Otto Ammon, *Der Darwinismus gegen die Sozialdemokratie* (Hamburg: A. G., 1891), p. 14.
10. *Ibid*.
11. *Ibid*.
12. For an extended study of Tille and Ploetz and their connection with National Socialism, see Conrad-Martius, *Utopien der Menschenzüchtung*, Chapter I, Part 3, and Chapter II, Part 2.
13. Ernst Haeckel, 'Die Wissenschaft und der Umsturz,' *Gemeinverständliche Vorträge und Abhandlungen*, II, 375.
14. Haeckel also had high praise for this book. See Ernst Haeckel to Bartolomäus von Carneri, June 17, 1895, in *Carneri's Briefwechsel mit Ernst Haeckel und Friedrich Jodl*, p. 75.
15. For additional material on Ploetz, see Zmarzlik, 'Der Sozialdarwinismus in Deutschland als geschichtliches Problem,' p. 264. And for praise of Ploetz by a Monist, see Forel, *Out of My Life and Work*, p. 207.
16. In 1917, Lenz wrote a doctoral dissertation for Ploetz entitled 'An Ethic Revised',

and it was published in 1933. The thesis integrated racial and social Darwinist ideas and the author himself described it as 'containing all of the important features of the National Socialist philosophy.' For the source of this quote and for more on Lenz and his significance for the racial theories of the Nazis, see Helmut Krausnick, 'The Persecution of the Jews,' in *Anatomy of the SS State* (New York: Walker, 1969), pp. 16-17.

17. For additional comments on the significance of the *Archiv*, see Zmarzlik, 'Der Sozialdarwinismus in Deutschland als geschichtliches Problem,' p. 264.
18. On the significance of Krause for the Darwinist movement, see *ibid.*, p. 259.
19. Uschmann, *Geschichte der Zoologie und der zoologischen Anstalten in Jena*, pp. 111-112.
20. Mosse, *The Crisis of German Ideology*, p. 112.
21. *Ibid.*, pp. 113-114.
22. Walter Laqueur, *Young Germany* (London: Routledge, 1962), p. 109.
23. Peter Pulzer, *The Rise of Political Anti-Semitism in Germany and Austria* (New York: Wiley, 1964), p. 310. See also Hoess' own account of the influence of the *Artamanen* on his development in his autobiography, *Commandant of Auschwitz* (London: Weidenfeld, 1959), pp. 62-63, and 64n for Himmler as a member of the *Artamanen*.
24. See the biography of Liebenfels by Wilfred Daim, *Der Mann der Hitler die Ideen gab* (Munich: Isar, 1958). Daim tries to establish, although—it would appear—unsuccessfully, a direct link between Hitler and Liebenfels. Unfortunately no proof is available that Hitler ever read Liebenfel's publications. See Mosse, *The Crisis of German Ideology*, p. 295, on this point.
25. Fritz Bolle, 'Darwinismus und Zeitgeist,' *Zeitschrift für Religion und Geistesgeschichte*,' XIV (1962), 174-175.
26. For Rohleder as a member of the Monist League, see *Das monistische Jahrhundert*, IV (1915), 18-19.
27. *Ibid.*, p. 172.
28. *Ibid.*, p. 158.
29. See Wilhelm Boelsche, 'Friedrichshagen in der Literatur,' in *Auf dem Menschenstern; Gedanken zu Natur und Kunst* (Dresden: Reissner, 1909).
30. On Bruck's first marriage, see Stern, *The Politics of Cultural Despair*, p. 186.
    There is also a description of the Monist League in Hedda Eulenburg's autobiography, *Im Doppelglück von Kunst und Leben* (Düsseldorf: Die Faehre, n.d. [ca. 1950]).
31. Ernst Haeckel, *Gottnatur (Theophysis): Studien über monistische Religion*, in *Gemeinverständliche Werke*, Heinrich Schmidt, ed. (Leipzig und Berlin: Kroner, 1924), III, 469.
32. For a more detailed analysis of Eugen Diederichs, see Mosse, *The Crisis of German Ideology*, pp. 52-63. On the significance of the *Tat* Circle, see Laqueur, *Young Germany. A History of the German Youth Movement*, pp. 183, 184, and

Kurt Sontheimer, 'Der Tatkreis,' *Vierteljahreshefte für Zeitgeschichte*, VII (1959), 229–260.

33. This is maintained, for example, by the most sensitive recent historian of the Volkish movement, Mosse. In his *Culture of Western Europe*, p. 214, he writes: 'Young people tried to escape the prison of bourgeois convention by fleeing to the countryside and, with the *Wandervoegel* (Roamers), began the history of the modern youth movements. Though much of this repudiation of the material world was of an antibourgeois nature, middle-class society itself was not wholly materialistic and given over totally to books like Haeckel's *Riddle of the Universe* (1899).'
34. For an impassioned recounting of the influence of Haeckel on young people in Germany, see the many articles in Schmidt, *Was wir Ernst Haeckel verdanken*, I, II, especially Heinrich Michaelis, 'Ernst Haeckel und die deutsche Jugend,' I, 267–272, and Ludwig Gurlitt (no title), I, 234–240.
35. Mosse, *The Crisis of German Ideology*, p. 157.
36. Else Frobenius, *Mit uns zieht die neue Zeit. Eine Geschichte der deutschen Jugend Bewegung* (Berlin: Deutsche Buchgemeinschaft, 1927), p. 26, and Stern, *The Politics of Cultural Despair*, p. 226.
37. Mosse, *The Crisis of German Ideology*, p. 173; Stern, *The Politics of Cultural Despair*, 74n and 84n. Stern writes: 'Among those who had been most powerfully influenced by Lagarde's critique of education was Ludwig Gurlitt, who carried the banner of Lagarde into his frequent battles with officialdom.'
38. Mosse, *The Crisis of German Ideology*, p. 157.
39. See the account of the activities of *Sonne* in its periodical, *Sonne*, published as a supplement to *Das monistische Jahrhundert*, 1914–1915. For Monist praise of the German youth movement, see Lutz Hammerschlag, 'Vom Freideutschen Jugendtag auf dem Höhen Meissner,' *Das monistische Jahrhundert* II (1913–14), 843–848, and for Monist praise of the proto-Nazi youth group of Hermann Popert, the *Vortrupp*, see Max Artur Jordan, 'Die neue Jugend,' *Sonne*, May 23, 1914, 83.
40. For an account of *Jugendstil*, see Hermann Jost, *Jugendstil, Ein Forschungsbericht, 1918–1964* (Stuttgart: Metzlersche Verlagsbuchhandlung, 1965).
41. *Das monistische Jahrhundert*, I (1912–13), 749.
42. Quoted in Laqueur, *Young Germany*, p. 33. Laqueur also mentions Schwaner's correspondence with Walter Rathenau. For some brief comments on the relationship of Rathenau, the Jew, and Schwaner, the Germanic nationalist, see Count Harry Kessler, *Walter Rathenau* (New York: Harcourt, 1930), pp. 66, 222, 228.
43. Bronder, *Bevor Hitler Kam*, p. 75.
44. Means, *Things That Are Caesar's*, p. 165.
45. Fahrenkrog executed a number of illustrated books on Germanic religion for use by members of the GGG. He also painted illustrations of the pagan gods Baldur and Thor which were sold to support the Volkist, Tarnhari, the

publisher of the *Swastika Letter*, and the friend of Dietrich Eckart, Hitler's mentor. See Mosse, *The Crisis of German Ideology*, p. 77, and his article on Tarnhari, 'Mystical Origins of National Socialism,' *Journal of the History of Ideas*, XII (1961), 81–96.

46. Means, *Things That Are Caesar's*, pp. 165–166. In this connection mention should also be made of the work of Professor Arthur Drews, who worked very closely with the Monist League. Although Drews was an 'idealistic' Monist and therefore incurred the displeasure of Haeckel, he nonetheless worked together with many Monists to spread the idea that Christ was not an historical figure, but only the product of a myth.

    For an account of a major activity against the historical Christ held jointly by Drews and the Monist League, see Arthur Drews et al, *Hat Jesus gelebt? Reden gehalten auf dem Berliner Religionsgespräch des deutschen Monistenbundes am 31. Januar und 1 Februar 1910* (Berlin: Verlag des Deutschen Monistenbundes, 1910).

    For Drew's place in the Germanic Faith Movement see Means, *Things That Are Caesar's*, p. 59.

47. Haeckel, *The Riddle of the Universe*, p. 328. Even as a young student Haeckel showed strong anti-Jewish feelings. He gleefully wrote to his parents from Würzburg in 1853 that an 'insolent Jew boy' a 'disgusting insolent' person was injured in a duel. He wrote that his 'very nice' gentile friends 'slashed his Jewish face about handsomely, without receiving even a scratch in return.' See Haeckel, *The Story of the Development of a Youth*, p. 83. The popularity of Haeckel's anti-Semitism is also revealed by an incident related to me by a friend, Mr. Adolph Nussenow of New York. He recalls that when he was a student in Leipzig during the period of the Kapp *Putsch* (1920), he would frequently find anti-Semitic slogans by Haeckel on stickers which were attached to his desk.

48. Hermann Bahr, *Der Antisemitismus. Ein internationales Interview* (Berlin: Fischer, 1894).
49. *Ibid.*, p. 66.
50. *Ibid.*, p. 67.
51. *Ibid.*
52. *Ibid.*
53. *Ibid.*, p. 68.
54. But there were also active anti-Semites in the Monist League. For example, Max Mauerenbrecher, the Germanic Faith Movement leader, and Heinrich Pudor, the strong advocate of social eugenics. On Mauerenbrecher's anti-Semitism, see Werner Maser, *Die Frühgeschichte der NSDAP* (Frankfurt a.M.: Athenaum, 1965), p. 177 n.; and on Pudor's, see Mosse, *The Crisis of German Ideology*, p. 137. Monist concern with a 'Jewish question' can also be detected in an article which appeared in the journal of the youth organisation of the Monist League. The author raised the problem as to whether it was patriotic or not for merchants to sell to Jews and to foreigners and asked for comments from his readers. See Wilhelm Heydorn, 'Die englischen Stoffe,' *Sonne*, February 14,

1914, p. 29. It is also a measure of Monist concern about the Jews when during the First World War one Monist declared himself ready to accord full rights to the Jews because they had demonstrated their loyalty and patriotism in the conflict. See Heinz Potthoff, 'Erziehung durch den Krieg,' *Das monistische Jahrhundert*, III (1914–15), 923.

55. Hermann Schnell, 'Die Zukunft der Juden im Lichte des Monismus,' *Das monistische Jahrhundert*, II (1913–1914), 311.
56. Ibid.
57. Edgar Herbst, 'Bedenken gegen den Austritt aus der Religionsgemeinschaft unter den Juden,' *Das monistische Jahrhundert*, II (1913–1914), 1168.
58. Schnell, 'Die Zukunft der Juden im Lichte des Monismus,' p. 317.
59. Werner Maser *Hitler's Mein Kampf: An Analysis* (London: Faber and Faber, 1970), p. 67. Maser does not go into detail on Haeckel's influence on Hitler but lists him as a general source together with other Monists like Wilhelm Boelsche and Fridtjof Nansen.

    There is also a brief discussion by Percy Schramm of the influence of Haeckel and a few other Monists on Hitler's pantheism: see the introduction to Henry Picker (ed.), *Hitler's Tischgespräche im Führerhauptquartier, 1941–1942* (Stuttgart: Seewald, 1965).

60. For an analysis of Boelsche's influence on Haeckel, see Maser, *Hitler's Mein Kampf: An Analysis*, pp. 67–69. Maser writes that Boelsche's book, *Vom Bazillus zum Affenmenschen*, was published in 1921. The book was actually widely known and had gone through many editions since 1900 when it was first published.
61. Picker, *Hitler's Tischgespräche im Führerhauptquartier, 1941–1942*, p. 363 n.
62. For an excerpt from a letter which Nansen wrote to Haeckel expressing his deepest intellectual and personal appreciation, see Schmidt, *Denkmal eines grossen Lebens*, p. 95.
63. There is, however, one other possible direct source. In one of his conversations with Rauschning, Hitler spoke of the book, *Urwelt, Sage und Menschheit*, written probably by the nature mystic Edgar Dacqué. Dacqué was a noted zoologist and a member of the Monist dominated *Münchner Verein für Naturkunde*. In a number of books he developed the idea of the importance of evolution and biology for an understanding of human culture, although it is true that he was a bit more mystical than ordinary Monists. Apparently Hitler read Dacqué and was impressed by him. For the connection between Hitler and Dacqué, see Mosse, *The Crisis of German Ideology*, pp. 306, and 356 n. For Dacqué and the *Münchner Verein für Naturkunde*, see the collection of Monist articles in *Die Abstammungslehre* (Jena: G. Fischer, 1911). For Monist praise of Dacqué, see U[nold], *Der Monismus*, V (1910), 462.
64. On this early period in Hitler's life, see Maser, *Hitler's Mein Kampf: An Analysis*, pp. 79–92.
65. Ibid., 63–66.
66. For Hitler's reference to Haeckel, see Hermann Rauschning, *The Voice of Destruction* (New York: Putnam, 1940), p. 50; and for the importance which is attributed

to Darwin in Hitler's thought, see, for example, Maser's recent work, *Hitler's Mein Kampf: An Analysis*, p. 77, where within the established tradition Darwin—not Haeckel—is mentioned as the general source for Hitler's notions of biology, of worship of force and struggle, and his rejection of 'aesthetic'—i.e. moral causality in history. Maser concludes that Hitler had absorbed the ideas of Darwin and that he had 'clung consistently to the concepts he had formed before the First World War; he says as much in *Mein Kampf*'. But again this was precisely the period in which the *Welträtsel* attained the status of a best seller, whereas Darwin's ideas were already ancient and foreign history.

67. See Nolte, *Three Faces of Fascism*, pp. 420-425.
68. For a sensitive analysis of the meaning of science in Hitler's thought, see Solomon F. Bloom, 'The Peasant Caesar, Hitler's Union of German Imperialism and Eastern Reaction,' *Commentary*, XXIII (1957), 408
69. *Ibid.*, p. 408.
70. Adolf Hitler, *Hitler's Secret Conversations, 1941-1944* (New York: Farrar, 1953), p. 5.
71. Haeckel, *Riddle of the Universe*, p. 380.
72. Hitler, *Hitler's Secret Conversations, 1941-1944*, p. 5.
73. *Ibid.*, p. 116.
74. *Ibid.*, p. 321.
75. *Ibid.*, p. 412. How seriously and literally Hitler accepted this idea is indicated by the following: 'Take the example,' he wrote, 'of the bicycle; it suffices for me to remove in imagination the rims and the tires from the wheels, to see that the movements of the spokes are exactly those of a man walking.' It did not seem to occur to Hitler that the first wheels did not have spokes. He continued that 'in aviation, too, we see that the natural laws retain all their original value.... Nature, obviously, has rejected the "lighter-than-air" principle; she has provided no bird with any sort of balloon, as she has done in the case of the fish.' Hitler, therefore, refused to ride in a Zeppelin because he regarded it as an anti-natural vehicle. He also suggested that ships should be propelled from the side to imitate the fins of fish. See *Ibid.*, pp. 412-413.
76. *Ibid.*, p. 125.
77. Adolf Hitler, *Hitler's Secret Book* (New York: Grove Press, 1961), p. 7.
78. Hitler, *Hitler's Secret Conversations*, p. 32.
79. Hitler, *Hitler's Secret Book*, p. 5.
80. *Ibid.*
81. Haeckel, *The History of Creation*, I, 170.
82. Hitler, *Hitler's Secret Book*, p. 18.
83. Haeckel, *History of Creation*, II, 366.
84. Quoted in Heinz Bruecher, *Ernst Haeckels Bluts- und Geisteserbe* (Munich: Lehmann, 1936), p. 91.
85. Haeckel, *Riddle of the Universe*, p. 125.
86. Hitler, *Hitler's Secret Conversations*, p. 71.

87. See, for example, Arnold Dodel, *Moses oder Darwin*, in his collected works *Aus Leben und Wissenschaft*, I (Stuttgart: Dietz, 1922), pp. 114-115, and Ziegler, *Der Darwinismus gegen die Sozialdemokratie*, p. 22 n. Ziegler quoted another anthropologist who wrote that 'neither have the sharply defined racial characteristics of the Semites in Europe been weakened nor, even less, have their characteristics approached that of ours.'
88. Hitler, *Hitler's Secret Conversations*, p. 393.
89. *Ibid.*, p. 269.
90. *Ibid.*, p. 115.
91. *Ibid.*, p. 255.
92. See the analysis of the Monist, Heinrich Pudor in Mosse, *The Crisis of German Ideology*, p. 137.
93. Norman Cohn, *Warrant for Genocide* (London: Eyre, 1967), p. 184.
94. Haeckel, *Riddle of the Universe*, p. 315.
95. Hitler, *Hitler's Secret Conversations*, p. 6.
96. *Ibid.*, p.207.
97. Haeckel, *Riddle of the Universe*, pp. 314-315.
98. Hitler, *Hitler's Secret Conversations*, p. 205.
99. *Ibid.*, p. 6.
100. *Ibid.*, p. 262.
101. Haeckel, *Riddle of the Universe*, p. 353.
102. *ibid.*
103. *Ibid.*, p. 344.
104. Hitler, *Hitler's Secret Conversations*, p. 43.
105. *Ibid.*, p. 117.
106. *Ibid.*, p. 118.
107. *Ibid.*, p. 339.
108. See above p. 157.
109. Hitler, *Hitler's Secret Conversations*, p. 63.
110. Haeckel, *Riddle of the Universe*, p. 287.
111. Hitler, *Hitler's Secret Conversations*, p. 111.
112. *Ibid.*, p. 340.
113. *Ibid.*, p. 69.
114. *Ibid.*, p. 119.
115. *Ibid.*, p. 51.
116. *Ibid.*, p. 247.
117. *Ibid.*, p. 5.
118. *Ibid.*, p. 33.
119. *Ibid.*
120. *Ibid.*, p. 70.
121. It is also of considerable interest that Hitler's conception of art was the same as that of Haeckel and the Monists. For Hitler, as for Haeckel, art was a highly serious matter and was a vehicle whereby the people could capture the reality of the homeland. Hitler was, therefore, like Haeckel, opposed to modern art,

which he felt distorted reality. For a good insight into the artistic ideas of Hitler, see *The Speeches of Adolf Hitler, April 1922–August 1939* (New York: Oxford University Press, 1942), I, 584–592.
122. Hitler, *Hitler's Secret Conversations*, p. 5.
123. *Ibid.*, p. 50.
124. *Ibid.*, p. 141.
125. Haeckel, *Riddle of the Universe*, p. 242.
126. Hitler, *Hitler's Secret Conversations*, p. 205.
127. Haeckel, *Riddle of the Universe*, pp. 341–346.
128. Hitler, *Hitler's Secret Conversations*, p. 417.
129. Quoted in *The New York Times Magazine*, October 26, 1969, p. 97.
130. Victor Franz, *Das heutige geschichtliche Bild von Ernst Haeckel* (Jena: G. Fischer, 1934), p. 17.
131. *Ibid.*, p. 18.
132. *Ibid.*, p. 23.
133. Gerhard Heberer, *Ernst Haeckel und seine wissenschaftliche Bedeutung* (Tübingen: Heine, 1934), p. 14.
134. *Ibid.*, p. 27. It is also to be noted that Professor Heberer has attempted to keep the tradition of Haeckel alive even after the Second World War. A recent work which he has edited, *Der gerechtfertigte Haeckel* (Stuttgart: G. Fischer, 1968), was not available to me before this book went to press.
135. Werner Haeckel, 'Zum Geleit! Ernst Haeckel und die Gegenwart,' *Der Biologe*, III (1934), 33.
136. Ernst Lehmann (no title), *Der Biologe*, III (1934), 132.
137. Ernst Lehmann, 'Der Einfluss der Biologie auf unser Weltbild,' in *Öffentliche Vorträge der Universitat Tübingen, Sommersemester 1933* (Stuttgart: Kohlhammer, 1934), p. 129.
138. Alfred Rosenberg, *Memoirs of Alfred Rosenberg*, with Commentaries by Serge Lang and Ernst von Schenk (Chicago: Ziff-Davis, 1949), p. 5.
139. Hans F. K. Ginther, *Führeradel durch Sippenflege* (Munich: Lehmann, 1936), pp. 46, 91. 106.
140. Heinz Bruecher, 'Ernst Haeckel. Ein Wegbereiter biologischen Staatsdenkens,' *Nationalsozialistische Monatshefte*, VI (1935), 1088–1098.
141. Bruecher, *Ernst Haeckels Bluts- und Geisteserbe*.
142. See Felix Kerstein, *The Kersten Memoirs, 1940–1945* (New York: Macmillan, 1956), *passim*.
143. Helmust Krausnick, 'The Persecution of the Jews,' p. 15.
144. See, for example, a series entitled, *Politische Biologie: Schriften für naturgesetzliche Politik und Wissenschaft* (Munich: Lehmanns, 1936–1939).
145. Bronder, *Bevor Hitler Kam*, p. 284.
146. One of the main topics of the articles in *Natur und Geist* was the Nazi program of eugenics which the journal constantly lauded. And in 1934, Schmidt noted in the preface to his new biography of Haeckel, *Denkmal eines grossen Lebens*, p. V, that Haeckel's 'biological thought which is bound to nature is enjoying a

startling [and] energetic resurrection in the new Reich. The religious revolution of the present moves very much along the same lines as his simple but equally sublime religion of nature. Germany, which he loved so ardently, for whose unity, greatness, and power he continually interceded, Germany, which is now conscious of itself, is conscious also again of him, the great German.'

147. For more on National Socialism and Darwinism, see Conrad-Martius, *Utopien der Menschenzüchtung*, pp. 283-299.

Selected Bibliography

This bibliography lists only those works which are particularly important for an understanding of Haeckel and Monist social Darwinism. It therefore does not list all of Haeckel's works, nor does it fully duplicate the citations in the text or in the footnotes. For a complete bibliography of Haeckel's works the reader may consult Theodore Krumbach, 'Die Schriften Ernst Haeckel,' in *Naturwissenschaften* (Berlin), Vol. VII (1919). For a more complete listing of the contemporary newspaper and periodical literature surrounding the Darwinist movement in Germany, see *Bibliographie der deutschen zeitschriften Literatur* (Leipzig, 1861–1919).

I HAECKEL
  1. Works by Haeckel
  (a) books and articles
  Haeckel, Ernst. *Anthropogenie oder Entwicklungsgeschichte des Menschen (Keimes und Stammesgeschichte)*. Leipzig: W. Engelmann, 1874.
    'Die Antinomien von Immanuel Kant,' *Das freie Wort*, IV (1905), 793.
    'Beiträge zur Plastidentheorie,' *Jenaische Zeitschrift für Naturwissenschaft*, V (1870), 492–550.
    Biologische Studien. Vol. I: *Studien über Moneren und andere Protisten*. Leipzig: W. Engelmann, 1870.
    Biologische Studien. Vol. II: *Studien zur Gastraeatheorie*. Jena: Hermann Dufft, 1877.
    'Charles Darwin as an Anthropologist,' in *Darwin and Modern Science*. Essays in Commemoration of the Centenary of the Birth of Charles Darwin, ed. A. C. Seward. Cambridge: Cambridge University Press, 1909.
    'Ein Dankeswort vom 70. Geburtstag,' *Jugend*, IX (1904), 196b.
    'Energetik und Substanzgesetz. Beitrag zum sechsten Hauptversammlung des Deutschen Monistenbundes zur Magdeburg, Sep't. 1912,' *Das monistische Jahrhundert*, I (1912–1913), 412–416.

'Englands Blutschuld am Weltkriege,' *Das monistische Jahrhundert*, III (1914–1915), 538–548 [1914].

Ernst Haeckels Wanderbilder. Nach eigenen Aquarellen und Ölgemälden: Die Naturwunder der Tropenwelt Ceylon und Insulinde. Gera-Untermhaus: F. E. W. Koehler, n.d. [1905].*

Eternity. World War Thoughts on Life and Death, Religion, and the Theory of Evolution. New York: Truth Seeker, 1916 [1915].

The Evolution of Man: A Popular Exposition of the Principal Points of Human Ontogeny and Phylogeny. 2 vols. New York: D. Appleton, 1903 [1874].

Ewigkeit. Weltkriegsgedanken über Leben und Tod, Religion und Entwicklungslehre. Berlin: G. Reimer, 1915.

Freedom in Science and Teaching. With a Prefatory Note by T. H. Huxley. New York: D. Appleton, 1879.

'Die Fundamente des Monismus. Beitrag zum Ersten Monistenkongress in Hamburg. September 1911, '*Der Monismus*, VI (1911), 440.

Gemeinverständliche Vorträge und Abhandlungen aus dem Gebiete der Entwicklungslehre. Second ed., 2 vols. Bonn: Emil Strauss, 1902.

Generelle Morphologie der Organismen. 2 vols. Berlin: G. Reimer, 1866.

Gottnatur (Theophysis). Studien über monistische Religion. Gemeinverständliche Werke, ed. Heinrich Schmidt, Vol. III. Leipzig: A. Kroner, 1924.

Die heutige Entwicklungslehre im Verhältnisse zur Gesammtwissenschaft. Öffentlicher Vortrag in der allgemeinen Versammlung Deutscher Naturforscher und Ärzte zu München am 18. September 1877. Stuttgart: Schweizerbart, 1877.

The History of Creation: or the Development of the Earth and its Inhabitants by the Action of Natural Causes. A Popular Exposition of the Doctrine of Evolution in General, and that of Darwin, Goethe, and Lamarck in Particular. 2 vols. New York: D. Appleton, 1876 [1868].

India and Ceylon. New York: John W. Covell Co., 1883.

Der Kampf um den Entwicklungsgedanken. Drei Vorträge, gehalten an 14. 16. und 19. April 1905 in Saale der Singakademie zu Berlin. Berlin: G. Reimer, 1905.

Kristallseelen. Studien über das anorganische Leben. Leipzig: A. Kroner, 1917.

Kunstformen der Natur. 100 Illustrationstafeln mit beschreibendem Text. Leipzig: Verlag des Bibliographischen Instituts, 1899-1904.

Die Lebenswunder. Gemeinverständliche Studien über biologische Philosophie. Ergänzungsband zu dem Buche über die Welträtsel. Stuttgart: A. Kroner, 1904.

Der Monismus als Band zwischen Religion und Wissenschaft. Bonn: E. Strauss, 1892.

Monism as Connecting Religion and Science. The Confession of Faith of a Man of Science. London: A. and C. Black, 1894 [1892].

Monismus und Naturgesetz. Flugschriften des deutschen Monistenbundes. Heft 1. Berlin: Deutscher Monistenbund, 1906.

---

* Where journal articles by Haeckel have been reprinted in book form, the book citation is given, with the original date of the article's publication at the end of the entry in bracktes. The first publication dates of other translated or reprinted material are similarly indicated.

SELECTED BIBLIOGRAPHY

'Monismus und Papismus,' *Der Monismus*, II (1907), 1–5.

My Church Departure. Being Haeckel's Reasons as Stated by Himself, for his Late Withdrawal from the Free Evangelical Church. New York: Truth Seeker, 1911. [1910].

Die Natur als Künstlerin. Berlin: Vita Deutsches Verlagshaus, 1913.

Die Naturanschauung von Darwin, Goethe und Lamarck. Vortrag auf der Naturforscher Versammlung zu Eisenach am 18 September 1882. Jena: G. Fischer, 1882.

Natürliche Schopfungsgeschichte. Gemeinverständliche wissenschaftliche Vorträge über die Entwicklungslehre im Allgemeinen und diejenige von Darwin, Goethe, und Lamarck im Besonderen, über die Anwendung derselben auf den Ursprung des Menschen und andere damit zusammenhangende Grundfragen der Naturwissenschaft. Berlin: G. Reimer, 1868.

'Ostwald als monistische Naturforscher,' in *Festschrift zum 60. Geburtstag Wilhelm Ostwalds*. Vienna: Anzengruber-Verlag Brüder Suchitzky, 1913.

'Das Präsidium des deutschen Monistendundes,' *Der Monismus*, I (1906), 1–4.

'Prinzipien des reinen Monismus,' *Freie Bühne*, III (1892), 1166–69.

Die Radiolarien (Rhizopoda radiaria). Eine Monograph. 2 vols. Berlin: G. Reimer, 1862.

The Riddle of the Universe at the Close of the Nineteenth Century. New York: Harper, 1900 [1899].

Sandalion. The Answer of Ernst Haeckel to the Falsehoods of the Jesuits, Catholic and Protestant. New York: Truth Seeker, 1911 [1910].

'Ueber Arbeitstheilung in Natur- und Menschenleben. Vortrag gehalten am 17. December 1868 im Salle des Berliner Handwerder-Vereins,' in *Gemeinverständliche Vorträge und Abhandlungen aus dem Gebiete der Entwicklungslehre*, Vol. 1. Bonn: Emil Strauss, 1902 [1869].

Ueber die Biologie in Jena während des 19. Jahrhunderts. Jena: G. Fischer, 1905.

'Ueber die Entstehung des Menschengeschlechts. Vortrag, gehalten im October 1865 in einem Privatkreise zu Jena,' in *Gemeinverständliche Vorträge und Abhandlungen aus dem Gebiete der Entwicklungslehre*, Vol. I. Bonn: Emil Strauss, 1902.

'Ueber die Entwicklungs-Theorie Darwin's. Vortrag, gehalten am 19. September 1863 in der ersten allgemeinen Sitzung der 38. Versammlung Deutscher Naturforscher und Aerzte zu Stettin,' in *Gemeinverständliche Vorträge und Abhandlungen aus dem Gebiete der Entwicklungslehre*, Vol. I. Bonn: Strauss, 1902.

'Über Entwicklungsgang und Aufgabe der Zoologie. Rede, gehalten beim Eintritt in die philosophische Fakultät zu Jena am 19. Januar 1869,' *Jenaische Zeitschrift für Naturwissenschaft*, V (1869), 353 370.

Über unsere gegenwartige Kenntnis vom Ursprung des menschen. Vortrag, gehalten auf dem 5. Internationalen Zoologenkongress im Cambridge am 26. August 1898. Jena: Emil Strauss, 1898.

'Ueber die Wellenzeugung der Lebenstheilchen oder die Perigenesis der Plastidule. Vortrag, gehalten am 19. November 1875 in der medicinisch-naturwissenschaftlichen Gesellschaft zu Jena,' in *Gemeinverständliche Vorträge und Abhandlungen aus dem Gebiete der Entwicklungslehre*, Vol. II. Bonn: Emil Strauss, 1902.

'Die Weltanschauung der monistischen Wissenschaft,' *Freie Bühne*, III (1892), 1155–66.

'Die Weltanschauung des neuen Curses,' in *Gemeinverständliche Vorträge und Abhandlungen aus dem Gebiete der Entwicklungslehre*, Vol. II. Bonn: Emil Strauss, 1902. [1892].

Das Weltbild von Darwin und Lamarck. Festrede zur 100 jährigen Geburtstag-Feier von Charles Darwin am 12. Februar 1909 gehalten im Volkshause zu Jena. Leipzig: A. Kroner, 1909.

'Weltkrieg und Naturgeschichte,' *Nord und Süd*, CLI (1914), 140–147.

Die Welträtsel. Studien über monistische Philosophie. Bonn: Emil Strauss, 1899.

'Die Wissenschaft und der Umsturz,' in *Gemeinverständliche Vorträge und Abhandlungen aus dem Gebiete der Entwicklungslehre*, Vol. II. Bonn: Emil Strauss, 1902. [1895].

The Wonders of Life. New York: Harper, 1904.

'Zellseelen und Seelenzellen,' *Deutsche Rundschau*, XVI (1878), 40–60.

'Ziele und Wege der heutigen Entwicklungsgeschichte,' *Jenaische Zeitschrift für Naturwissenschaft*, X (1875), 1–100.

(b) letters

Carneri, Bartholomäus von. *Bartholomäus von Carneri's Briefwechsel mit Ernst Haeckel und Friedrich Jodl.* Leipzig: H. F. Koehler, 1922.

Franz, Victor. 'Hermann Allmers und Ernst Haeckel in noch unbekannten Briefen,' in *Ernst Haeckel. Sein Leben, Wirken und Denken*, ed. Victor Franz, Vol. II. Leipzig: W. Gronau, 1944.

'Der Meister und die Meisterschüler. Haeckel und die Hertwig's in ihrem Briefwechsel,' in *Ernst Haeckel. Sein Leben, Denken und Wirken*, ed. Victor Franz, Vol. I. Leipzig: W. Gronau, 1943.

Haeckel, Ernst. *Ernst Haeckel, Forscher, Künstler, Mensch; Briefe ausgewählt und erlautert von Georg Uschmann.* 3rd ed. Leipzig: Urania, 1961.

Himmelhoch jauchzend; Errinerungen und Briefe der Liebe. Dresden: C. Reissner, 1927.

Italienfahrt. Briefe an die Braut 1859–1860. Leipzig: Koehler, 1921.

The Love Letters of Ernst Haeckel, Written Between 1898 and 1903. New York: Harper, 1930.

The Story of the Development of a Youth; Letters to his Parents 1852–1856, New York: Harper, 1923.

Von Teneriffa bis zum Sinai; Reisseskizzen. Leipzig: A. Kroner, 1923.

Koop, Rudolf. (ed.) *Haeckel und Allmers. Die Geschichte einer Freundschaft in Briefen der Freunde.* Bremen: Arthur Geist, 1941.

2. Works on Haeckel

Adickes, Erich. *Kant contra Haeckel; erkenntnistheorie gegen naturwissenschaftlichen Dogmatismus*. Berlin: Reuther und Reichard, 1910.

Boelsche, Wilhelm. *Haeckel, His Life and Work; with Introduction and supplementary chapter by the translator, Joseph McCabe*. Philadelphia: Jacobs, 1906.

Breucher, Heinz. *Ernst Haeckels Bluts- und Geisteserbe*. Munich: J. F. Lehmann, 1936.

'Ernst Haeckel. Ein Wegbereiter biologischen Staatsdenkens,' *Nationalsozialistische Monatshefte*, VI (1935), 1088-98.

Carus, Paul. 'God-Nature: a Discussion of Haeckel's Religion,' *Open Court*, XXVIII (1914), 385-404.

Chwolson, Orest Daniilovich. *Hegel, Haeckel, und das Zwölfte Gebot; eine kritische Studie*. Braunschweig: F. Vieweg un Sohn, 1906.

Dennert, E. *At the Deathbed of Darwinism*. Burlington, Ia.: German Literary Board, 1904.

Franz, Victor. (ed.) *Ernst Haeckel. Sein Leben, Denken und Wirken. Eine Schriftenfolge für seine zahlreichen Freunde und Anhänger*. 2 vols. Leipzig: W. Gronau, 1943, 1944.

Das heutige geschichtliche Bild von Ernst Haeckel. Jena: G. Fischer, 1934.

Heberer, Gerhard. *Ernst Haeckel und seine wissenschaftliche Bedeutung*. Tübingen: Franz F. Heine, 1934.

Der gerechtfertigte Haeckel. Stuttgart: G. Fischer, 1968.

Hemleben, Johannes. *Ernst Haeckel in Selbstzeugnissen und Bilddokumenten*. Hamburg: Rowohlt, 1964.

Rudolf Steiner und Ernst Haeckel. Stuttgart: Verlag Freies Geistesleben, 1965.

Klemm, Peter. *Ernst Haeckel. Der Ketzer von Jena*. Leipzig: Urania, 1966.

Klohr, Olof. 'Introduction,' to Ernst Haeckel, *Die Welträtsel*. [East] Berlin: Akademie-Verlag, 1961.

Lodge, Sir Oliver Joseph. *Life and Matter. A Criticism of Haeckel's 'Riddle of the Universe.'* New York and London: G. P. Putnam's Sons, 1905.

Paulsen, Friedrich. 'Ernst Haeckel als Philosoph,' *Preussusche Jahrbuecher*, CI (1900) 29-72.

Schmidt, Heinrich. *Ernst Haeckel. Denkmal eines grossen Lebens*. Jena: Frommann, 1934.

Der Kampf um die 'Welträtsel.' Ernst Haeckel, die 'Welträtsel,' und die Kritik. Bonn: Emil Strauss, 1900.

(ed) *Was wir Ernst Haeckel verdanken. Ein buch der Verehrung und Dankbarkeit*. 2 vols. Leipzig: Unesma, 1914.

Steiner, Rudolf. *Haeckel, die Welträtsel und die Theosophie*. Dornach, Switzerland: Philosophisch-Anthropologischer Verlag, 1926.

Uschmann, Georg. *Geschichte der Zoologie und der zoologischen Anstalten in Jena 1779-1919*. Jena: G. Fischer, 1959.

Wasmann, Erich. *Ernst Haeckel's Kulturarbeit*. Freiburg im Breisgau: Herdsche Verlagshandlung, 1916.

II The Monist League

1. Journals of the Monist League

   Mitteilungen des deutschen Monistenbundes. Munich, 1916–1919.
   Der Monismus. Zeitschrift für einheitliche Weltanschauung und Kulturpolitik. (Blätter des deutschen Monistenbundes). Berlin, 1906–1912.
   Das monistische Jahrhundert. Zeitschrift für wissenschaftliche Weltanschauung und Weltgestaltung. Jena, 1912–1915.
   Monistische Monatshefte. Munich, 1919–1933.
   Sonne. Leipzig, 1914–1915.

2. Selected Works by Monist Authors

   Boelsche, Wilhelm. *Die Abstammung des Menschen.* Stuttgart: Kosmos, 1904.
   ‘Friedrichshagen in der Literatur,’ in *Auf dem Menschenstern; Gedanken zu Natur und Kunst.* Dresden: C. Reissner, 1909.
   Das Liebesleben in der Natur; eine entwicklungsgeschichte der Liebe. 2 vols. in 3. Jena: Diederichs, 1911–1927.
   Vom Brazillus zum Affenmenschen. Leipzig: Eugen Diederichs, 1900.
   Von Sonnen und Sonnentaubschen. Kosmische Wanderungen. Mit vier Farbigen und vier Schwarzen Tafeln nach original-Aquarellen von Professor Ernst Haeckel. Berlin: G. Bondi, 1910.
   Carneri, Bartholomäus von, *Sittlichkeit und Darwinismus.* Vienna: W. Braumüller, 1871.
   Drews, Arthur, et. al. *Hat Jesus gelebt? Reden gehalten auf dem Berliner Religionsgespräch des deutschen Monistenbundes am 31. Januar und 1. Februar 1910.* Berlin und Leipzig: Verlag des Deutschen Monistenbundes, 1910.
   Eulenberg, Hedda. *Im Doppelglück von Kunst und Leben.* Düsseldorf: Die Faehre, n. d. [ca. 1950].
   Eulenberg, Herbert. *Katinka die Fliege, ein zeitgenössicher Roman.* Leipzig: Rowohlt, 1911.
   Forel, August. *Out of My Life and Work.* New York: W. W. Norton, 1937.
   Gurlitt, Ludwig. *Der Deutsche und seine Schule: Errinerungen, Beobachtungen, und Wünsche eines Lehrers.* 2nd ed. Berlin: Wiegandt und Grieben, 1906.
   Der Deutsche und sein Vaterland; Politisch-pädagogische Betrachtungen eines Modernen. 4th ed. Berlin: Wiegandt und Grieben, 1902.
   Jager, Gustav. *Die Darwinsche Theorie und ihre Stellung zu Moral u. Religion.* Stuttgart. Hoffmann, 1869.
   Jodl, Friedrich. *Der Monismus und die Kulturprobleme der Gegenwart: Vortrag auf dem Ersten Monisten-Kongresse am 11. September 1911 zu Hamburg.* Leipzig: A. Kroner, 1911.
   Krause, Ernst. *Charles Darwin und sein verhältniss zu Deutschland.* Leipzig: E. Gunther, 1885.
   Werden und Vergehen. Eine entwicklungs-Geschichte des Naturganzen in gemeinverständlicher Fassung. 4th ed. Berlin: Gebrüder Bornträger, 1901.

Ostwald, Wilhelm. *Lebenslinien*. 3 vols. Berlin: Klasing, 1927.
Monism as the Goal of Civilization. Hamburg: The International Committee of Monism, 1913.
Monistische Sonntags-Predigten. 3 vols. Leipzig: Akademische Verlagsgesellschaft, 1913.
Vorlesungen über Naturphilosophie. Leipzig: Veit, 1902.
Schallmayer, Wilhelm. *Beiträge zu einer Nationalbiologie*. Jena: H. Costenoble, 1905.
Vererbung und Auslese im Lebenslauf der Völker. Eine staatswissenschaftliche Studie auf grund der neueren Biologie. 2nd ed. Jena: G. Fischer, 1910.
Schmidt, Heinrich. *Der Kampf ums Dasein*. Jena: Urania, 1930.
Unold, Johannes. *Aufgabe und Ziele des Menschenlebens*. 5th ed. Leipzig und Berlin: B. G. Teubner, 1920.
Das Deutschtum in Chile. Ein Zeugnis erfolgreicher deutscher Kulturarbeit. Munich: J. F. Lehmann, 1910.
Die höchsten Kulturaufgaben des modernen Staates. Munich: J. F. Lehmann, 1902.
Der Monismus und seine Ideale. Leipzig: T. Thomas, 1908.
Politik im Lichte der Entwicklungslehre. Ein beitrag zur staatsbürgerlichen Erziehung. Munich: E. Reinhardt, 1912.
Ziegler, Heinrich. *Die Naturwissenschaft und die sozialdemokratische Theorie, ihr Verhältniss dargelegt auf grund der Werke von Darwin und Bebel*. Stuttgart: Enke, 1893.
Die Vererbungslehre in der Biologie und in der Soziologie. Jena: G. Fischer, 1918.
'Das Verhältniss der Sozialdemokratie zu Darwinismus,' *Zeitschrift für Sozialwissenschaft*, II (1899), 424-432.

III. Other Selected Works

Abb, Gustav, (ed.) *Aus Fünfzig Jahren deutscher Wissenschaft*. Berlin: W. de Gruyter, 1930.
Abrams, M. H. *The Mirror and the Lamp: Romantic Theory and the Critical Tradition*. Oxford: Oxford University Press, 1953.
Ackerknecht, Erwin. *Rudolf Virchow*. Madison, Wis.: University of Wisconsin Press, 1951.
Adorno, T. W., et al. *The Authoritarian Personality*. New York: Harper, 1950.
Aliotta, Antonio. *The Idealistic Reaction Against Science*. London: Macmillan, 1914.
Aheau, René. *Hitler et les Sociétés Secrètes*. Paris: Grasset, 1969.
Ammon, Otto. *Der Darwinismus gegen die Sozialdemokratie. Anthropologische Plaudereien*. Hamburg: Verlagsanstalt und Druckerei A.-G., 1891.
Die Gesellschaftsordnung und ihre natürliche Grundlagen. Jena: G. Fischer, 1895.
Die natürliche Auslese beim Menschen. Jena: G. Fischer, 1893.
Anderson, Eugene N. *The Social and Political Conflict in Prussia, 1858-1864*. Lincoln, Neb.: University of Nebraska Press, 1954.
Apel, Max, (ed.) *Darwin. Seine bedeutung im Ringen von Weltanschauung und Lebenswert*. Berlin: Hilfe, 1909.

Archiv für Rassen- und Gesellschaftsbiologie einschliesslich Rassen- und Gesellschafts-Hygienie. Leipzig, 1904–1944.

Arendt, Hannah. *The Origins of Totalitarianism.* New York: Harcourt, Brace, 1951.

Aron, Raymond. *German Sociology.* London: Heinemann, 1957.

Das Ausland. Stuttgart, 1828–1893.

Bahr, Hermann. *Der Antisemitismus. Ein internationales Interview.* Berlin: G. Fischer, 1894.

Banton, Michael P. (ed.) *Darwinism and the Study of Society.* Chicago: Quadrangle Books, 1961.

Barbu, Zevedei. *Democracy and Dictatorship. Their Psychology and Patterns of Life.* New York: Grove Press, 1956.

Barnett, S. A. (ed.) *A Century of Darwin.* London: Heinemann, 1958.

Bartels, Adolf. *Der völkische Gedanke. Ein Wegweiser.* Weimar: Fink, 1923.

Barth, Karl. *From Rousseau to Ritschl.* London: SCM Press, 1959.

Barzun, Jacques. *Darwin, Marx, Wagner; Critique of a Heritage.* Boston: Little, Brown, 1941.

Race; a Study in Superstition. New York: Harper, 1937.

Baumer, Franklin Le Van. *Religion and the Rise of Scepticism.* New York: Harcourt, Brace, 1960.

Bebel, August. *Woman in the Past, Present, and Future. (Woman Under Socialism).* San Francisco: G. B. Benham, 1897 [1884].

Beer, Sir Gavin de. *Embryos and Ancestors.* 3rd ed. Oxford: Oxford University Press, 1958 [1940].

Bentley, Eric Russell. *A Century of Hero-Worship. A Study of the Idea of Heroism in Carlyle and Nietzsche, with notes on Wagner, Spengler, Stephan George, and D. H. Lawrence.* 2nd ed. Boston: Beacon, 1957.

Berg, Leo. *Der Übermensch in der modernen Literatur. Ein Kapitel Geistesgeschichte des neunzehnten Jahrhunderts.* Munich: Langen, 1897.

Bernal, J. D. *Science in History.* 2nd ed. London: Watts, 1957 [1954].

Bernhardi, General Friedrich von. *Germany and the Next War.* London: E. Arnold, 1912.

Bie, R. *Die deutsche Malerie der Gegenwart.* Weimar: A. Duncker, 1930.

Binkley, Robert C. *Realism and Nationalism, 1852–1871.* New York: Harper 1935.

Der Biologe. Munich, III (1934).

Bithell, Jethro. *Modern German Literature.* London: Methuen, 1939.

Bloom, Solomon F. 'The Peasant Caesar. Hitler's Union of German Imperialism and Eastern Reaction,' *Commentary,* XXIII (1957), 406–418.

Böhm, Franz. *Anti-Cartesianismus. Deutsche Philosophie im Widerstand.* Leipzig: Meiner, 1938.

Bolle, Fritz. 'Darwinismus und Zeitgeist,' *Zeitschrift für Religion und Geistesgeschichte,* XIV (1962), 143–178.

Bonhard, Otto. *Geschichte der Alldeutscher Verband.* Leipzig: Weicher, 1920.

SELECTED BIBLIOGRAPHY

Bowen, Ralph. *German Theories of the Corporative State*. New York: Whittlesey House, 1947.

Bronder, Dietrich. *Bevor Hitler kam*. Hannover: Pfeiffer, 1964.

Broszat, M. *Der Nationalsozialismus. Weltanschauung, Programm und Wirklichkeit*. Stuttgart: Deutsche Verlags-Anstalt, 1960.

'Die völkische Ideologie und der Nationalsocialismus,' *Deutsche Rundschau*, LXXXIV (1958), 53–68.

Bruck, W. F. *Social and Economic History of Germany from William II to Hitler, 1888–1938*. London: Oxford University Press, 1938.

Buchheim, Hans. *Glaubenskrise im Dritten Reich. Drei Kapitel nationalsozialistischer Religionspolitik*. Stuttgart: Deutsche Verlags-Anstalt, 1953.

Buechner, Ludwig. *Force and Matter*. London: Trübner, 1870.

Die Macht der Vererbung und ihr einfluss auf dem moralischen und geistigen Fortschritt der Menschheit. Leipzig: A. Kroner, 1882.

Butler, Rohan d'O. *The Roots of National Socialism, 1789–1933*, London: Faber, 1941.

Cameron, Thomas W. (ed.) *Evolution: Its Science and Doctrine. Symposium presented to the Royal Society of Canada* in 1959. Toronto: University of Toronto Press, 1960.

Cannon, H. Graham. *Lamarck and Modern Genetics*. Manchester: Manchester University Press, 1959.

Carter, George Stuart. *A Hundred Years of Evolution*. London: Sidgwick and Jackson, 1958.

Carus, Victor. *Geschichte der Zoologie bis auf Johannes Müller und Charles Darwin*. Munich: Oldenbourg, 1872.

Casserley, J. V. Langmead. *The Retreat from Christianity in the Modern World*. Longmans, Green, 1952.

Cassirer, Ernst. *The Problem of Knowledge. Philosophy, Science, and History since Hegel*. New Haven: Yale University Press, 1950.

Chamberlain, Houston Stewart. *Foundations of the Nineteenth Century*. London: J. Lane, 1911 [1899].

Christie, Richard and Jahoda, Marie (eds.) *Studies in Scope and Method of the Authoritarian Personality*. Glencoe, Ill.: Free Press, 1954.

Cohn, Norman. *Warrant for Genocide*. London: Eyre and Spottiswoode, 1967.

Conrad-Martius, Hedwig. *Utopien der Menschenzüchtung. Der Sozialdarwinismus und seine Folgen*. Munich: Kösel Verlag, 1955.

Cunow, Heinrich. 'Darwinismus contra Sozialismus,' *Die neue Zeit*, VIII (1890), 326–333.

Dahrendorf, Rolf. *Society and Democracy in Germany*. Garden City, New York: Doubleday, 1967 [1965].

Daim, Wilfred. *Der Mann der Hitler die Ideen gab*. Munich: Isar Verlag, 1958.

Damaschke, Adolf. *Die Bodenreform*. Berlin: J. Rade, 1902.

Dampier, Sir William Cecil. *A History of Science and its Relations with Philosophy and Religion*. Cambridge: Cambridge University Press, 1961 [1929].

Darlington, C. D. *Darwin's Place in History*. Oxford: Blackwell, 1959.

Darwin, Charles. *Autobiography*. New York: Harcourt, Brace, 1958.
The Descent of Man and Selection in Relation to Sex. New York: D. Appleton, 1930. [1871].
Life and Letters of Charles Darwin. 2 vols. New York: D. Appleton, 1898.
More Letters of Charles Darwin. 2 vols. London: J. Murray, 1903.
The Origin of Species. A Variorum text edited by Morse Peckham. Philadelphie: University of Pennsylvania Press, 1859.
The Variation of Animals and Plants under Domestication. 2 vols. London: J. Murray, 1905 [1868].

Dawes, Ben. *A Hundred Years of Biology*. London: Duckworth, 1952.

Deak, Istvan. *Weimar Germany's Left-Wing Intellectuals*. Berkeley and Los Angeles: University of California Press, 1968.

Denis, Maurice. *Théories*. 4th ed. Paris: Rouart et Watelin, 1920 [1912].

Dewey, John. *German Philosophy and Politics*. New York: H. Holt, 1915.
The Influence of Darwin on Philosophy. New York: H. Holt, 1910.

Dietzgen, Joseph. *Some of the Philosophical Essays on Socialism and Science, Religion, Ethics, Critique-of-Reason, and the World at Large*. Chicago: Kerr, 1917.

Dill, Marshall Jr. *Germany. A Modern History*. Ann Arbor: University of Michigan Press, 1961.

Dokumente des Fortschritts. Berlin, 1907-1918.

Douglass, Paul F. *God Among the Germans*. Philadelphia: University of Pennsylvania Press, 1935.

Draper, J. W. *History of the Conflict Between Religion and Science*. New York: D. Appleton, 1876.

Driesch, Hans. 'The Covert Presumption of all Theories of Descent,' in *The Science and Philosophy of the Organism*. London: A. and C. Black, 1908.
Lebenserrinerungen. Munich: E. Reinhardt, 1951.

DuBois-Reymond, Emil. *Über die grenzen der Naturerkennens. Die sieben Welträthsel*. Leipzig: Veit, 1882.

Eiseley, Loren. *Darwin's Century. Evolution and the Men who Discovered it*. Garden City, New York: Doubleday, 1958.

Ellegard, Alvar. *Darwin and the General Reader. The Reception of Darwin's Theory of Evolution in the British Periodical Press, 1859-72*. Gotenburg: Gotenburg Studies in English, 1958.
'The Darwinian Theory and Nineteenth Century Philosophies of Science,' *Journal of the History of Ideas*, XVIII (1957), 362-393.

Engels, Friedrich. *Dialectics of Nature*. New York: International, 1940.
Herr Eugen Dühring's Revolution in Science (Anti-Dühring). New York: International, 1939. [1878].
'Ludwig Feuerbach and the End of Classical German Philosophy,' *Marx and Engels: Basic Writings on Politics and Philosophy*, ed. Lewis S. Feuer. Garden City, New York: Doubleday, 1959.

SELECTED BIBLIOGRAPHY

Ferri, Enrico. *Socialism and Modern Science*. New York: International Library Publishing Co., 1905 [1895].
Fischer, Fritz. *Germany's Aims in the First World War*. New York: Norton, 1967.
Fleming, Donald H. 'The Centenary of *The Origin of Species*,' *Journal of the History of Ideas*, XX (1959), 437–446.
— 'Introduction,' to Jacques Loeb, *The Mechanistic Basis of Life*. Cambridge, Mass.: The Belknap Press, 1964.
Flenley, Ralph. *Modern German History*. London: Dent, 1953.
Fothergill, Philip G. *Historical Aspects of Organic Evolution*. London: Hollis and Carter, 1952.
Freie Bühne für Entwicklungskampf der Zeit. Berlin, 1894–1903.
Das freie Wort. Frankfurter Halbmonatschrift für Fortschritt auf allen Gebieten des Geistigen Lebens. Frankfurt, a. M., 1901–1920.
Friedell, Egon. *A Cultural History of the Modern Age; The Crisis of the European Soul from the Black Death to the World War*. Vol. III, book 5. *Imperialism and Impressionism: from the Franco-Prussian War to the World War*. New York: A. Knopf, 1953–54 [1927–31].
Fritsch, Theodor. *Handbuch der Judenfrage*. Leipzig: Hammer Verlag, 1933.
Frobenius, Else. *Mit uns zieht die neue Zeit. Eine Geschichte der deutschen Jugendbewegung*. Berlin: Deutsche Buchgemeinschaft, 1927.
Fromm, Erich. *Escape from Freedom*. New York: Rinehart, 1941.
Gerstenhauer, Max Robert. *Der völkische Gedanke in Vergangenheit und Zukunft. Aus der Geschichte der völkischen Bewegung*. Leipzig: Armanen, 1933.
Gillispie, Charles C. *Genesis and Geology*. Cambridge, Mass.: Harvard University Press, 1951.
— 'Lamarck and Darwin in the History of Science,' in *Forerunners of Darwin*, ed. Bentley Glass. Baltimore: Johns Hopkins University Press, 1959.
Ginsberg, Morris. *The Idea of Progress. A Re-evaluation*. Boston: Beacon, 1953.
Glass, Bentley, 'The Germination of the Idea of Biological Species,' in *Forerunners of Darwin*, ed. Bentley Glass. Baltimore: Johns Hopkins University Press, 1959.
Gode-von Aesch, Alexander Gottfried Friedrich. *Natural Science in German Romanticism*. New York: Columbia University Press, 1941.
Guenther, H. F. K. *Führeradel durch Sippenpflege*. Munich: J. F. Lehmann, 1936.
Gumplowicz, Ludwig. *Der Rassenkampf*. Innsbruck: Wagner, 1883.
Haecker, Walter. *Die ererbten Anlagen und die Bemessung ihres Werter für das politischen Leben*. Jena: G. Fischer, 1907.
Haldane, John S. *The Philosophical Basis of Biology*. London: Hodder and Stoughton, 1931.
Harpf, Adolf. *Darwin in der Ethik: Festschrift zum achtzigsten Geburtstage Carneri's*. Leoben Prosl.: Hans Prosl, 1901.
Hartmann, Eduard. *Wahrheit und Irrtum im Darwinismus*. Berlin: Duncker, 1875.
Hauptmann, Gerhardt. *Das Abendteuer meiner Jugend*. Berlin: S. Fischer, 1937.

Hayek, F. A. *The Counter-Revolution of Science. Studies in the Abuse of Reason*. Glencoe, Ill.: Free Press, 1952.

Hayes, Carlton. *A Generation of Materialism*. New York: Harper, 1941.

Heberer, Gerhard (ed.) *Hundert Jahre Evolutionsforschung. Das wissenschaftliche Vermächtniss Charles Darwin*. Stuttgart: G. Fischer, 1960.

Heine, Heinrich. *Religion and Philosophy on Germany*. Boston: Beacon, 1959. [1834].

Henning, Max. *Handbuch der freigeistigen Bewegung Deutschlands, Österreichs und der Schweiz*. Frankfurt a. M.: Neuer Frankfurter Verlag, 1914.

Hentschel, Cedric. *The Byronic Teuton. Aspects of German Pessimism, 1800–1937*. London: Methuen, 1940.

Hentschel, Willibald. *Mittgart: Eine Weg zur erneuerung der germanischen Rasse*. Leipzig: Fritsch, 1906.

— *Varuna. Das Gesetz des aufsteigenden und sinkenden Lebens in der Geschichte*. Leipzig: Fritsch, 1907.

— *Vom aufsteigenden Leben*. Leipzig: Matthes, 1913.

Hertwig, Oskar. *Das Werden der Organismen. Zur widerlegung von Darwin's Zufallstheorie durch das Gesetz der Entwicklung*. Jena: G. Fischer, 1916.

— *Zur Abwehr des ethischen, des politischen, des sozialen Darwinismus*. Jena: G. Fischer, 1918.

Hesse, Albert. *Natur und Gesellschaft*. Jena: G. Fischer, 1904.

Himmelfarb, Gertrude. *Darwin and the Darwinian Revolution*. Garden City, New York: Doubleday, 1959.

— 'Varieties of Social Darwinism,' in *Victorian Minds*. New York: Knopf, 1968.

Hitler, Adolf. *Hitler's Secret Book*. New York: Grove Press, 1961.

— *Hitler's Secret Conversations, 1941–1955*. New York: Farrar, Straus and Young, 1953.

— *Mein Kampf*. New York: Reynal and Hitchcock, 1940.

— *The Speeches of Adolf Hitler, April 1922–August 1939*. 2 vols. New York: Oxford University Press, 1942.

Hobhouse, Leonard T. *Social Evolution and Political Theory*. New York: Columbia University Press, 1911.

Hoess, Rudolf. *Commandant of Auschwitz*. London: Weidenfeld and Nicolson, 1959.

Hoffding, Harald. *A History of Modern Philosophy*. London: Macmillan, 1900.

Hofmann, Werner. *The Earthly Paradise. Art in the Nineteenth Century*. New York: George Braziller, 1961.

Hofstadter, Richard. *Social Darwinism in American Thought*. Philadelphia: University of Pennsylvania Press, 1945.

Holborn, Hajo. 'Der deutsche Idealismus in sozialgeschichtlicher Beleuchtung,' *Historische Zeitschrift*, LCXXIV (1952), 359–384.

Hughes, H. Stuart. *Consciousness and Society. The Reorientation of European Social Thought, 1890–1930*. New York: Knopf, 1958.

SELECTED BIBLIOGRAPHY

Huxley, Julian. *Evolution in Action*. New York: Harper, 1953.
   Evolution. The Modern Synthesis. London: Allen and Unwin, 1942.
Huxley, Thomas Henry. *Darwiniana*. New York: D. Appleton and Co., 1893.
   Evolution and Ethics. New York: Humboldt, 1894.
Irvine, William. *Apes, Angels, and Victorians; the Story of Darwin, Huxley, and Evolution*. New York: McGraw-Hill, 1955.
Jackson, Holbrook. *The Eighteen Nineties. A Review of Art and Ideas at the Close of the Nineteenth Century*. London: Cape, 1927.
Jenaische Zeitschrift für Naturwissenschaft. Jena, 1864-96.
Jenks, William A. *Vienna and the Young Hitler*. New York: Columbia University Press, 1960.
Jetzinger, Franz. *Hitler's Youth*. London: Hutchinson, 1958.
Jost, Hermann. *Jugendstil; Ein Forschungsbericht, 1918-1964*. Stuttgart: Metzlersche Verlagsbuchhandlung, 1965.
Kandinsky, Wassily. *On the Spiritual in Art*. New York: Solomon R. Guggenheim Foundation, 1946 [1912].
Kaufmann, Walter. *Nietzsche; Philosopher, Psychologist, Antichrist*. Princeton: Princeton University Press, 1950.
Kautsky, Karl. 'Darwinismus und Marxismus,' *Die neue Zeit*, XIII (1894-95), 709-716.
   'Darwinismus und Marxismus,' *Oesterreichischer Arbeiterkalender*, XI (1890), 49-54.
Klemperer, Klemens von. *Germany's New Conservatism*. Princeton: Princeton University Press, 1957.
Kohlbrügge, J. H. F. 'J. B. Lamarck und der Einfluss seiner Descendenztheorie von 1809-1859,' *Zeitschrift für Morphologie und Anthropologie*, XVIII (1914), 191-206.
   'War Darwin ein originelles Genie' *Biologisches Zentralblatt*, XXXV (1915), 93-111.
Kolnai, Aurel. *The War Against the West*. New York: Viking Press, 1938.
Kosmos. Zeitschrift für einheitliche Weltanschauung auf grund Entwicklungslehre. Leipzig, 1877-1886.
Kossmann, H. 'Darwinismus und Socialdemokratie,' *Deutsche Rundschau*, XVII (1878), 278-292.
   'Socialismus und Darwinismus,' *Nord und Süd*, CXXXVIII (1891), 326-342.
Krause, Ernst. *Die Trojaburgen Nordeuropas: ihr Zusammenhang mit der indogermanischen Trojasage von der entführten Sonnenfrau (Syrith, Ariadne, Helena), dem Trojaspielen Schwert- und Labyrinthtänzen zur Feier ihrer Lenzbefreiung*. Glogau: Flemming, 1893.
   Tuisko-Land, der arischen Stämme und Götter Urheimat. Glogau: Flemming, 1891.
Krausnick, Helmut. 'The Persecution of the Jews,' in *Anatomy of the SS State*. New York: Walker, 1968.
Krieck, Ernst. *Volk im Werden*. Oldenbourg i.O.: Stalling, 1932.

Krieger, Leonard. *The German Idea of Freedom; History of a Political Tradition*. Boston: Beacon, 1957.
Krikorian, Yervant. (ed.) *Naturalism and the Human Spirit*. New York: Columbia University Press, 1944.
Kruck, Alfred. *Geschichte des Alldeutschen Verbandes, 1890–1939*. Wiesbaden: Steiner, 1954.
Kubizek, August. *Young Hitler: The Story of our Friendship*. London: Wingate, 1954.
Künneth, Walther. *Der grosse Abfall. Eine geschichtstheologische Untersuchung der Bewegung zwischen Nationalsozialismus und Christentum*. Hamburg: Wittig, 1947.
Kupisch, Karl. *Zwischen Idealismus und Massendemokratie. Eine Geschichte der evangelischen Kirche in Deutschland von 1815–1945*. Berlin: Lettner, 1955.
Lagarde, Paul de. *Deutsche Schriften*. Göttingen: Dieterich, 1937 [1878].
Lamarck, Jean. *Zoological Philosophy*. London: Macmillan, 1914 [1809].
Lange, Friedrich A. *The History of Materialism and Criticism of its Recent Importance*. New York: Harcourt, Brace, 1925 [1865].
Langbehn, Julius. *Rembrandt als Erzieher*. Berlin: Fritsch, 1944 [1891].
Laqueur, Walter. 'Review of *The Crisis of German Ideology* by George L. Mosse,' *The New York Review of Books*, January 14, 1965.
  Young Germany; a History of the German Youth Movement. London: Routledge and Kegan Paul, 1962.
Lebovics, Herman. *Social Conservatism and the Middle Classes in Germany, 1914–1933*. Princeton: Princeton University Press, 1969.
Lichtheim, George. *Marxism; an Historical and Critical Study*. New York: Prager, 1961.
Lilge, Frederic. *The Abuse of Learning: the Failure of the German University*. New York: Macmillan, 1948.
Loeb, Jacques. *The Mechanistic Conception of Life*. Cambridge, Mass.: The Belknap Press, 1964 [1912].
Löwith, Karl. *From Hegel to Nietzsche; the Revolution in Nineteenth Century Thought*. New York: Holt, Rinehart, and Winston, 1964 [1941].
Lovejoy, Arthur. 'The Argument for Organic Evolution Before *The Origin of Species*;' 'Buffon and the Problem of Species;' 'Herder; Progressionism without Transformism;' 'Kant and Evolution;' 'Recent Criticism of the Darwinian Theory of Recapitulation; its Grounds and its Initiator,' in *Forerunners of Darwin*, ed. Bentley Glass. Baltimore: Johns Hopkins University Press, 1959.
  The Great Chain of Being; a Study in the History of an Idea. Cambridge, Mass.: Harvard University Press, 1957 [1936].
Lübbe, Hermann. *Politische Philosophie in Deutschland. Studien zu ihrer Geschichte*. Basel-Stuttgart: Schwabe, 1963.
Lütgert, Wilhelm D. *Das Ende des Idealismus im Zeitalter Bismarcks*. Gütersloh: Bertelsmann, 1930.

SELECTED BIBLIOGRAPHY

Lukacs, Georg. *Die Zerstörung der Vernunft*. East Berlin: Aufbau, 1954.
Magnus, Rudolf. *Goethe as a Scientist*. New York: Schuman, 1949.
Malia, Martin. *Alexander Herzen and the Birth of Russian Socialism, 1812-1855*. Cambridge, Mass.: Harvard University Press, 1961.
Man, Race, and Darwin; Papers Read at a Joint Conference of the Royal Anthropological Institute of Great Britain and Ireland and the Institute of Race Relations. Oxford: Oxford University Press, 1960.
Marcuse, Herbert. 'Der Kampf gegen den Liberalismus in der totalitären Staatsauffassung,' *Zeitschrift für Sozialforschung*, III (1934), 161-194.
—— *Reason and Revolution; Hegel and the Rise of Social Theory*. New York: Humanities, 1954. [1941].
Marty, Martin E. *Varieties of Unbelief*. New York: Holt, Rinehart, and Winston, 1964.
Marx, Karl. *Briefwechsel. Karl Marx-Friedrich Engels: Historisch-kritische Gesammtausgabe*. Part 3, Vol. III. Frankfurt und Berlin: Marx-Engels Verlag, 1927-1932.
—— *Correspondence*. New York: International, 1942.
—— *Selected Works*. 2 vols. New York: International, 1942.
—— 'Theses on Feuerbach,' in *Marx and Engels: Basic Writings on Politics and Philosophy*, ed. Lewis Feuer. Garden City, New York: Doubleday, 1959.
Maser, Werner. *Die Frühgeschichte der NSDAP. Hitlers Weg bis 1924*. Frankfurt a.M.: Athenaum, 1965.
—— *Hitler's Mein Kampf: An Analysis*. London: Faber and Faber, 1970 [1966].
Mason, Stephen Finney. *History of Science*. London: Routledge and Paul, 1953.
—— 'The Idea of Progress and Theories of Evolution in Science,' *Centaurus*, III (1953), 90-106.
Massing, Paul W. *Rehearsal for Destruction. A Study of Political Anti-Semitism in Imperial Germany*. New York: Harper, 1949.
Masur, Gerhard. *Prophets of Yesterday; Studies in European Culture, 1890-1914*. New York: Macmillan, 1961.
Mayer, Carl. 'On the Intellectual Origin of National Socialism,' *Social Research*, IX (1942), 225-247.
Means, Paul F. *Things That are Caesar's; Genesis of the German Church Conflict*. New York: Round Table Press, 1935.
Merz, John Theodore. *A History of European Thought in the Nineteenth Century*. 4 vols. London: Blackwood, 1903-1914.
Metnitz, Gustav Adolf von. *Die deutsche Nationalbewegung, 1871-1933*. Berlin: Junker und Dunhaupt, 1939.
Meyer, Henry Cord. *Mitteleuropa in German Thought and Action, 1815-1945*. The Hague: Nijhoff, 1955.
Michaelis, Curt. *Prinzipien der natürlichen und sozialen Entwicklungsgeschichte des Menschen*. Jena: G. Fischer, 1904.
Moeller van den Bruck, Arthur. *Germany's Third Empire*. London: Allen and Unwin, 1934 [1923].

Mohler, Armin. *Die konservative Revolution in Deutschland, 1918–1932.* Stuttgart: Vorwerk, 1950.

Mosse, George L. *The Crisis of German Ideology; Intellectual Origins of the Third Reich.* New York: Grosset and Dunlap, 1964.

―― *The Culture of Western Europe; the Nineteenth and Twentieth Centuries.* [New York]: Rand McNally, 1962.

―― 'The Genesis of Fascism,' *Journal of Contemporary History*, I (1966), 14–26.

―― 'Mystical Origins of National Socialism,' *Journal of the History of Ideas*, XII (1961), 81–96.

Nagel, Ernest. *The Structure of Science; Problems in the Logic of Scientific Explanation.* New York: Harcourt, Brace, and World, 1961.

Nasmyth, Georg. *Social Progress and the Darwinian Theory.* New York: G. P. Putnam's, 1916.

Natur und Geist. Monatshefte für Wissenschaft, Weltanschauung und Lebensgestaltung. Jena, 1933–1938.

Natur und Staat. Beiträge zur naturwissenschaftlichen Gesellschaftslehre, eine Sammlung von Preisschriften. 10 vols. Jena: G. Fischer, 1903–1918.

Neue Weltanschauung. Berlin, 1904–1921.

Neumann, Franz. *Behemoth. The Structure and Practice of National Socialism.* London: Gollancz, 1942.

Neurohr, Jean F. *Der Mythos vom Dritten Reich. Zur Geistesgeschichte des Nationalsozialismus.* Stuttgart: Cotta, 1957.

Nicolas, Marius Paul. *De Nietzsche à Hitler.* Paris: Fasquelle, 1936.

Niekisch, Ernst. *Der Reich der niederen Dämonen.* Hamburg: Rowohlt, 1953.

Nietzsche, Friedrich. *Thoughts Out of Season.* New York: Macmillan, 1911 [1872].

Nolte, Ernst. *Three Faces of Fascism.* New York: Holt, Rinehart, and Winston, 1966.

Nordenskiold, Erik. *The History of Biology: A Survey.* New York: Tudor, 1929 [1920–1924].

Oppenheimer, Jane. 'An Embryological Enigma in the Origin of Species,' in *Forerunners of Darwin*, ed. Bentley Glass. Baltimore: Johns Hopkins University Press, 1959.

Pauwels, Louis and Jacques Bergier. *The Morning of the Magicians.* New York: Avon, 1968 [1960].

Pearson, Karl. *The Scope and Importance to the State of the Science of National Eugenics.* London: University of London, 1911.

Phelps, Reginald. 'Before Hitler Came: Thule Society and Germanen Orden,' *Journal of Modern History*, XXV (1963), 245–261.

Pinson, Koppel. *Modern Germany; its History and Civilization.* New York: Macmillan, 1954.

Plaine, Henry L. (ed.) *Darwin, Marx, Wagner; a Symposium.* Columbus, Ohio: Ohio State University Press, 1962.

Plessner, Helmuth. *Die verspätete Nation. Über die politische Verführbarkeit bürgerlichen Geistes.* Stuttgart: Kohlhammer, 1959.

Ploetz, Alfred. *Die Tüchtigkeit unserer Rasse und der Schutz der Schwachen — Ein Versuch über Rassenhygienie und ihr Verhältniss zu den humanen Idealen, besonders zum Sozialismus.* Berlin: S. Fischer, 1895.

Polanyi, Karl. 'The Essence of Fascism,' in *Christianity and Social Revolution*, ed. John Lewis. New York: Scribner's, 1936.

Politisch-anthropologische Revue. Leipzig: 1902–1922.

Potonie, H. 'Aufzählung von Gelehrten, die in der zeit von Lamarck bis Darwin sich im Sinne der Descendenz-Theorie geäussert haben,' *Naturwissenschaftliche Wochenschrift*, V (1890). 441–445.

Prenant, Marcel. *Biology and Marxism.* New York: International, 1938.

Pelzer, Peter G. J. *The Rise of Political Anti-Semitism in Germany and Austria.* New York: Wiley, 1864.

Radl, Emmanuel. *Geschichte der biologischen Theorien.* Vol. II: *Geschichte der Entwicklungstheorien in der Biologie des XIX Jahrhunderts.* Leipzig: Engelmann, 1909.

Randall, John Herman Jr. *The Making of the Modern Mind.* Boston: Houghton-Mifflin, 1954 [1926].

Rauschning, Hermann. *The Conservative Revolution.* New York: G. P. Putnam's, 1941.

The Revolution of Nihilism; Warning to the West. New York: Longmans, Green, 1939.

The Voice of Destruction. New York: G. P. Putnam's, 1940.

Reichmann, Eva. *Hostages of Civilization; the Social Sources of National Socialist Anti-Semitism.* Boston: Beacon, 1951.

Ritchie, David G. *Darwinism and Politics.* London: Swan Sonnenschein, 1891.

Rosenberg, Alfred. *Memoirs of Alfred Rosenberg, with Commentaries by Serge Lang and Ernst von Schenk.* Chicago: Ziff-Davis, 1949.

Rosenberg, Arthur. *The Birth of the German Republic, 1871–1918.* London: Oxford Press, 1931.

Rosteutscher, J. H. W. *Die Widerkunft der Dionysos. Der naturmystische Irrationalismus in Deutschland.* Bern: Francke, 1947.

Royce, Josiah. *Lectures on Modern Idealism.* New Haven: Yale University Press, 1919.

Rudolf, Otto. *The Idea of the Holy; an Inquiry into the Non-Rational Factor in the Idea of the Divine and its Relation to the Rational.* London: Oxford University Press, 1950.

Ruggiero, Guido de. *The History of European Liberalism.* Boston: Beacon, 1959. [1927].

Russell, Edward Stuart. *Form and Function.* Oxford: J. Murray, 1916.

Sampson, R. V. *Progress in the Age of Reason; the Seventeenth Century to the Present Day.* Canbridge, Mass.: Harvard University Press, 1956.

Sandow, Alexander. 'Social Factors in the Origin of Darwinism,' *Quarterly Review of Biology*, XIX (1938), 315-326.
Santayana, George. *Egotism and German Philosophy*. London: Dent, 1916.
Schalk, Emil. *Der Wettkampf der Völker*. Jena: G. Fischer, 1905.
Schemann, Ludwig. *Gobineau und die deutsche Kultur*. Leipzig: Eckhardt, 1910.
  Die Rasse in den Geisteswissenschaften. Studien zur Geschichte des Rassengedankens. 3 vols. Munich: Lehmann, 1928-1931.
Schmidt, Oscar. *Darwinismus und Sozialdemokratie*. Bonn: Emil Strauss, 1878.
Schramm, Percy. 'Vorwort und Erlauterungen,' in *Hitler's Tischgespräche im Führerhauptquartier, 1941-1942*, ed. Henry Picker. 2nd ed. Stuttgart: Seewald, 1965.
Schuecking, Walter. *Neue Ziele der staatliche Entwicklung*. Marburg: Elwert, 1913.
Schultze, Gustav. 'Dr. Willibald Hentschel zu seinem 75. Geburtstag am 7. Nebelungs 1933,' *Die Sonne*, X (1933), 574-577.
Seillière, E. *Sur la Psychologie du Romantisme Allemande*. Paris: Editions de la Nouvelle Revue Critique, 1933.
Sell, Friedrich. *Die Tragödie des deutschen Liberalismus*. Stuttgart: Deutsche Verlags-Anstalt, 1953.
Selz, Peter. *German Expressionist Painting*. Berkeley and Los Angeles: University of California Press, 1957.
Semmel, Bernard. *Imperialism and Social Reform: English Social-Imperial Thought, 1895-1914*. Cambridge, Mass.: Harvard University Press, 1960.
Shanahan, William C. *German Protestants Face the Social Question*. Vol. I: *The Conservative Phase 1815-1871*. Notre Dame, Ind.: University of Notre Dame Press, 1954.
Shils, Edward A. 'Authoritarianism: Right and Left,' in *Studies in Scope and Method of the Authoritarian Personality*, ed. Richard Christie. Glencoe, Ill.: Free Press, 1954.
Siegel, Carl. *Geschichte der deutschen Naturphilosophie*. Leipzig: Akademische Verlagsgesellschaft, 1913.
Singer, Charles. *A History of Biology to about the Year 1900*. London and New York: Schuman, 1959 [1931].
Sokel, Walter H. *The Writer in Extremis: Expressionism in Twentieth Century German Literature*. Stanford: Stanford University Press, 1959.
Sontheimer, Kurt. *Antidemokratisches Denken in der Weimarer Republik. Die politischen Ideen des deutschen Nationalismus zwischen 1918 und 1933*. Munich: Nymphenburger, 1962.
  'Der Tatkreis,' *Vierteljahreshefte für Zeitgeschichte*, VII (1959), 229-260.
Steiner, Rudolf. *Briefe*. Vol. II: Dornach, Switzerland: Der Rudolf Steiner Nachlassverwaltung, 1953.
Stern, Fritz. 'The Political Consequences of the Unpolitical German,' *History; a Meridian Periodical*. III (1960), 104-134.
  The Politics of Cultural Despair. A Study in the Rise of the Germanic Ideology. Berkeley: University of California Press, 1961.

SELECTED BIBLIOGRAPHY

Stirk, S. D. *The Prussian Spirit. A Survey of German Literature and Politics 1914–1940*. London: Faber, 1941.

Stocking, George W. 'Lamarckianism in American Social Science, 1890–1915,' *Journal of the History of Ideas*, XXIII (1962), 239–256.

Strauss, David. *The Old Faith and the New*. New York: Holt, 1873.

Die Tat. Leipzig, 1909–1939.

Temkin, Oswei. 'The Idea of Descent in Post-Romantic German Biology: 1848–1858,' in *Forerunners of Darwin*, ed. Bentley Glass. Baltimore: Johns Hopkins University Press, 1959.

'Materialism in French and German Physiology of the early Nineteenth Century,' *Bulletin of the History of Medicine*, XX (1946), 322–327.

Tille, Alexander. *Volksdienst. Von einem Sozialaristokraten*. Berlin: Wiener, 1893.

Von Darwin bis Nietzsche, ein Buch Entwicklungsethik. Leipzig: Nauman, 1895.

Ullmann, Hermann. *Das neunzehnte Jahrhundert. Volk gegen Masse im Kampf um die Gestalt Europas*. Jena: Diederichs, 1936.

Uschmann, Georg. *Geschichte der Zoologie und der zoologischen Anstalten in Jena 1779–1919*. Jena: G. Fischer, 1959.

Vermeil, Edmond. 'L'Allemagne Hitlérienne et L'Idée International,' *L'Esprit International*, X (1936), 187–206.

Germany's Three Reichs; Their History and Culture. London: A. Dakers, 1944.

Victorian Studies. III, No. 1 (1959). ('Darwin Anniversary Issue.')

Viereck, Peter. *Metapolitics; from the Romantics to Hitler*. New York: Knopf, 1941.

Virchow, Rudolf. *The Freedom of Science in the Modern State*. London: J. Murray, 1878.

Wehberg, Heinrich. *Die Bodenreform im Lichte der humanistischen Sozialismus*. Munich: Duncker, 1913.

Weinel, Heinrich. *Jesus in the Nineteenth Century*. Edinburgh: Clark, 1914.

Weinreich, Max. *Hitler's Professors; the Part of Scholarship in Germany's Crimes Against the Jewish People*. New York: Yiddish Scientific Institute, 1946.

Wertheimer, Mildred S. *The Pan-German League 1890–1915*. New York: Columbia University Press], 1924.

White, Andrew D. *A History of the Warfare of Science with Theology*. New York: D. Appleton and Co., 1896.

Whitehead, Alfred North. *Science and the Modern World*. New York: Macmillan, 1925.

Weiner, Philip. *Evolution and the Founders of Pragmatism*. Cambridge, Mass.: Harvard University Press, 1949.

Wigand, Albert. *Der Darwinismus und die Naturforschung Newtons und Cuviers. Beiträge zur Methodik der Naturforschung und zur Speciesfrage*. 3 vols. Braunschweig: Vieweg, 1874–1877.

Willey, Basil. *Darwin and Butler. Two Versions of Evolution*. New York: Harcourt, Brace, 1960.

Nineteenth Century Studies; Coleridge to Matthew Arnold. New York: Columbia University Press, 1958.

Williams, C. M. *A Review of the System of Ethics Founded on the Theory of Evolution.* New York: Macmillan, 1893.

Williams, Raymond. *Culture and Society, 1780–1950.* New York: Columbia University Press, 1958.

Woltmann, Ludwig. *Politische Anthropologie. Woltmanns Werke.* Vol. I: Leipzig: Dorner, 1936 [1903].

Zeitschrift für den Aufbau der Entwicklungslehre. Leipzig: 1907–1909.

Ziegler, Theobold. *Die geistigen und sozialen Strömungen Deutschlands im neunzehnten Jahrhundert.* Berlin: Bondi, 1911.

Zirkle, Conway. 'Early History of the Idea of the Inheritance of Acquired Characters and Pangenesis,' *Transactions of the American Philosophical Society,* CCCXXXV (1941), 91–111.

Evolution, Marxian Biology, and the Social Scene. Philadelphia: University of Pennsylvania Press, 1959.

'Gregor Mendel and his Precursors,' *Isis,* XLII (1951), 97–104.

'Natural Selection before *The Origin of Species,*' *Proceedings of the American Philosophical Society,* LXXXIV (1941), 71–123.

Zmarzlik, Hans-Günter. 'Der Sozialdarwinismus in Deutschland als geschichtliches Problem,' *Vierteljahreshefte für Zeitgeschichte,* XI (1963), 246–273.

Index

Alienation, nature religion and rural cooperatives as a solution to, 63–68, 121–122
Allmers, Hermann, 3, 5, 7
Ammon, Otto, 148, 149
  Der Darwinismus gegen die Sozialdemokratie, 149
  Die Gesellschaftsordnung und ihre natürlichen Grundlagen, 149
  Die natürliche Auslese beim Menschen, 149
Anti-Semitism,
  in Haeckel, 157–159
  in Hitler, 164–165
  in the Monist League, 159, 164
Archiv für Rassen- und Gesellschaftsbiologie, 150
Arrhenius, Svante, xxiv
Art, Monist conception of, 71–77
Ausland, Das, 20

Bahr, Hermann, 157, 158, 159
Bartels, Adolf, 56
Bauer, Bruno, xviii
Bebel, August, 92, 110, 111, 113, 114, 124
  Die Frau und der Sozialismus, 110, 113
Biogenetic Law, 10, 78
Biologe, Der, 171
Bismarck, Otto von, xiv, xv, xvi, 18, 19, 170
Boelsche, Wilhelm, 21, 154, 160, 177
  Vom Bazillus zum Affenmenschen, 160, 178
Bolle, Fritz, 153

Borngräber, Otto, 145
Bruecher, Heinz, 172
Büchner, Ludwig, 20
Bund für Mutterschutz, xxxi
Burckhardt, Jakob, 38
Burgfrieden, 141, 142

Capitalism, criticized by Monists, 118–121
Catholic Center Party, 20, 57, 62, 63
Catholicism, 57, 59, 61–63
Cezanne, Paul, 75
Chamberlain, Houston Stewart, 40, 56, 157, 168
Christ,
  as Aryan, 157, 167
  attacked by Haeckel, 60–61
Christianity, Monist opposition to, 55–68
Cities, anti-urbanism in Haeckel and the Monist League, 17–18, 121–122
Cohn, Norman, 165–166
Communism, opposed by Haeckel and the Monists, 112–122
Condorcet, Marquis de, ix
Conrad, J., 148
Corporative state, defended by Monists, 86–90
Courbet, Gustave, 76
Cremation, advocated by Monists, 104

Dacqué, Edgar, 178
  Urwelt, Sage und Menschheit, 178
Damaschke, Adolf, 119, 120
Democracy, opposed by Monists, 83–86

INDEX

Darwin, Charles, ix–xii, xviii, xix, xxi, xxii, xxviii, 6, 7, 9–11, 28, 107–110
Darwinism, xviii–xxi, 6–8, 13, 20, 107–113
Denis, Maurice, 75
Diederichs, Eugen, 154–155
Dodel, Arnold, 21
Dokumente des Fortschritts, 22
Drews, Arthur, 177
Drexler, Anton, 30
Driesch, Hans, 12
DuBois-Reymond, Emil, xviii, 41
Duncan, Isadora, 78

Eckart, Dietrich, 30, 177
Eden, rural cooperative, 122
Education, Monist view of, 37–39
Einfuhlung, concept of, 71
Eisner, Kurt, 25, 129
Engels, Friedrich, 106–110
  Dialectics of Nature, 108
Entartete Kunst, 76
Ernst Haeckel Gesellschaft, 173
Erzberger, Matthias, 24
Ethics, opposition to traditional, 48–49, 68
Eugenics, Monist support for, 90–98
Eulenberg, Hedda, 154
Eulenberg, Herbert, 21
Evolution, xvi–xvii, xix, 11–12, 78

Fahrenkrog, Ludwig, 156, 176
Feder, Gottfried, 30, 170
  Was Will Adolf Hitler? Das Program der N.S.D.A.P., 170
Felden, Emil, 125
Feuerback, Ludwig, xviii
  Essence of Christianity, xviii
Fichte, Johann Gottlieb, xvi–xvii, 17, 87
Fidus (Karl Höppner), 154
Fincke, Ewalt, 43, 53
Fischer, Karl, 155
Forel, August, 21, 103, 104, 145, 147
Fortschrittspartei, xx

Francé, R. H., 21
Franz, Victor, 170
Free-Thought Movement, 20, 22
Freie Wort, Das, 22
Freud, Sigmund, 35, 50–51
Freytag, Gustav, 26
Fried, Alfred, xxv, xxx
Friedrichshagen, literary circle of, 154
Fritsch, Theodor, 152

Gastraea Theory, 10
Gauguin, Paul, 75
Gegenbaur, Carl, xiii, 14
George, Henry, 119
German Land Reform League, 119
Germanische Glaubens Gemeinschaft, 156
Gneisenau, Count, 2
Gobineau, Count Arthur de, xii–xxiii, 174
  The Inequality of the Human Races, xxiii
Goethe, Johann Wolfgang von, xiii–xvi, xxvii, 11, 14, 17, 78
Gogh, Vincent van, 75
Grey, Sir Edward, 133
Günther, Hans F. K., 172
Gurlitt, Ludwig, 21, 155, 176

Haeckel, Ernst
  Anthropogenie, 8, 9, 14
  'Englands Blutschuld am Weltkriege,' 24
  Ewigkeit, 24
  Generelle Morphologie, xviii, 8–9
  Gottnatur . . ., 24
  Kalkschwämme, 9
  Kristallseelen . . ., 24
  Kunstformen der Natur, 73–75
  Lebenswunder, 13
  Monismus als Band . . ., 13, 168
  Natürliche Schöpfungsgeschichte, 8, 9, 14, 41, 166
  Radiolarien, 8–9
  System der Medusen, 9
  Systematische Phylogenie, 10

INDEX

'*Ueber die Entwicklungstheorie Darwins*', 7
Welträtsel, 13–16, 20, 22, 38, 47, 60, 149, 157, 160, 161, 165–167, 170
on Art, 71–76
biological theories, 8–12
and Christianity, 55–63
on the corporative state, 82, 83, 100–102
and Darwin, xviii, xix, 6–12, 28, 161, 179
education, career, death of, xiii, 1–10, 12–26
and eugenics, 90–94, 103, 104
on free will, 47
and German nationalism, 2–5, 16, 17, 24, 25
and Hitler, 159–169
and imperialism, 126–137
and liberalism, xiv, xv
and Marxism, 108–113, 124
and materialism, 64–65
and Monist League, 20–23
and National Socialism, xii, xx, 115, 147–156, 169–174
on nature religion, 63–65
and racism, 39–40
on the state, 44
and Rudolf Steiner, 79
on sun worship, 69
and his travels, 19
and Volkish ideology, xxi–xxiv
as opposed to Western civilization, 31–39
Hammer Verlag, 152
Harnack, Adolf, 62
Hauptmann, Carl, 154
Hauptmann, Gerhardt, 154
Heberer, Gerhard, 170, 180
Hegel, G. W. F., xviii, 17
Hellwald, Friedrich, 20
Helmholtz, Hermann, xviii
Hengstenberg, Ernst, 62
Hentschel, Willibald, 152–153
Varuna, 152

Hertwig, Oscar, 12
Hertwig, Richard, 13
Himmler, Heinrich, 153, 172
Hirschfeld, Magnus xxv, xxix
Hirth, Georg, 155
Hitler, Adolf
 Tischgespräche, 159, 162, 164,
 analyzed by Norman Cohn, 165–166
 on Christ as Aryan, 167
 on Christianity, 166, 167
 on eugenics, 163–164
 on evolution, 167
 and Haeckel, 159–169
 on the Jews, 164–165
 and the Monists, 160
 on nature religion, 168, 169
 on racism, 163–164
Hess, Rudolf, 30
Hobbes, Thomas, 110
Hoess, Rudolf, 153
Hohe Meissner (youth movement convention), 156
Humboldt, Alexander von, xiii
Huschke, Agnes, 9
Huxley, Thomas Henry, xii, 13, 55–56
Huysmans, J. K., 104

Institut fur menschliche Erbforschung und Rassenpolitik, 172

Jena, 17, 18
 University of Jena, 17, 18
Jugend, 155
Jugendstil, 155

Kalthoff, Albert, 21
Kammerer, Paul, 12, 53
Kandinsky, Wassily, 75
Kant, Immanuel, 14
Kapp, Wolfgang, 24
Kautsky, Karl, 123–124
Kersten, Felix, 172
Kosmos, 20, 151
Kotzde, Wilhelm, 151

INDEX

Kowalewski, Alexander, 12
Krause, Ernst, (pseud. Carus Sterne), 151
   Die Trojaburgen Nordeuropas . . ., 151
   Tuisko-Land. . ., 151
Krupp essay contest, 148
Kulturkampf, xv, 62–63

Lagarde, Paul de, xviii, xxvi, 56, 60, 155, 157, 176
Lamarck, Jean Baptiste, 78
Land reform, 118–121
Lang, Arnold, 110
Langbehn, Julius, xviii, xxvi, 71, 155
   Rembrandt als Erzieher, 71
Lassalle, Ferdinand, 87, 107
Lehmann, Ernst, 171
Lehmann, J. F., (publishers), 171
Lehmann-Rüssbildt, Otto, xxv, xxix
Lenin, Vladimir, x
Lenz, Fritz, 150, 174–175
Liberalism,
   in Germany, xiv–xv
   and Haeckel, xiv, 82, 83
   and Monism, 83–86, 89
Lichtheim, George, 123
Liebenfels, Georg Lanz von, 153, 175
   Anthropozoikon. . .,153
   Theozoologie. . .,153
Liebermann, Max, 76
Lipps, Theodor, 71
List, Friedrich, 87
Loeb, Jacques, xxiv

Mach, Ernst, xxiv
Marx, Karl, ix, x, xi, xviii, 60, 106–110, 123, 148
   Critique of Political Economy, ix
Marxism and fascism, 123
Maser, Werner, 178, 179
Materialism, xviii, 64–65
Maurenbrecher, Max, 142, 177
Mensheviks, x
Menzel, Adolph von, 76
Metchnikoff, Eli, 9

Mitteleuropa, defined by Haeckel and Ostwald, 136, 141
Moeller van den Bruck, Arthur, xxvi, 154
   The Third Reich, 154
Monet, Claude, 76
Monism, defined, 7
Monismus, Der, 21
Monist League, xii, xx, xxiv–xxvi, 20–23
Monistische Jahrhundert, Das, 21
Mosse, George, 176
Müller, Johannes, xviii
Müller-Lyer, Franz, 21
Münchner Verein für Naturkunde, 178

Nansen, Fridtjof, 160, 178
Narodniks, x
National Socialism, xii–xiii, xx, 49–50, 147, 170–174
Nationalism, Germanic, 41–44
Nationalsozialistische Monatshefte, 172
Natur und Geist, xxx, 173
Naturphilosophie, xvi, xxvii, 6
Naumann, Friedrich, 136
Neue Weltanschauung, 22
Neue Zeit Die, 110
Nietzsche, Friedrich, 38, 45
Nolte, Ernst, 123, 162
Nord und Süd, 24
Novalis, Friedrich von, xvi
Nussenow, Adolph, 177

Obrist, Hermann, 74
Oken Lorenz, 17
Origin of Species, ix, xi, xviii, 6, 107
Ossietsky, Carl von, xxv
Ostara, Zeitschrift für Blonde, 153
Ostwald, Wilhelm,
   on imperialism, 137, 140–142
   President of Monist League, xxv, 21
   on rural cooperatives, 121, 122
   on Social Democracy, 118, 142
   on sun worship, 69

INDEX

Pan-German League, 128, 129
Pan-psychism, 10, 11, 64, 65
Parliamentarianism, rejected by Monists, 88–90
Paulsen, Friedrich, 14
Pearson, Karl, 100, 101
Peasantry, Monist support for, 120–121
Pestalozzi, Jean-Henri, 38
Plate, Ludwig, 21
Ploetz, Alexander, 149, 150
Politisch-anthropologische Revue, 148
Popert, Hermann, 176
Protestantism, 57–62
Pudor, Heinrich, 165, 177, 180

Racism, in Monist League, 39–44
Rathenau, Walter, 176
Rauschning, Hermann, 161
Redon, Odilon, 74
Religion,
  opposition to Christianity, 56–63
  nature worship, 63–71
  sun worship, 69, 70
Renan, Ernst, 56
Ritschl, Albrecht, 62
Rohleder, Hermann, 153
  Künstliche Zeugung und Anthropogenie 153
Romanticism, x–xii, xv–xix
Rosenberg, Alfred, 171, 172
Roux, Wilhelm, 12
Russian Revolution and Monist League, xxv
Russian Social Democratic Party x

Sauckel, Fritz, 173
Schallmayer, Wilhelm, 90–92, 98, 99, 102–103, 147, 148
  'Vererbung und Auslese,' 148
Scheidemann, Philipp, 24
Schelling, Friedrich von, 17
Schemann, Ludwig, 40
Schiller, Friedrich von, xiii, 117

Schlegel brothers; (August and Friedrich), xvi
Schleiermacher, Friedrich, xiii, xvi, 58
Schmidt, Heinrich, xxx, 173
Schopenhauer, Arthur, 14
Schücking, Walter, 101
Schwaner, Wilhelm, 156, 176
  Germanenbibel, 156
  Unterm Hakenkreuz, 156
Science, challenge to German nationalism, xviii conception of, in Haeckel and Hitler, 162–163
Semon, Richard, 12
Sera group, 154
Sethe, Anna, 3, 6
Seurat, Georges, 75
Sonne youth journal of Monist League, 21
Sonne, youth section of Monist League, 155
Spann, Othmar, 87
Speer, Albert, 169
Spencer, Herbert, xii
Spengler, Oswald, 87
Spontaneous Generation, 10, 11
State, Monist conception of, 44–49
Steiner, Rudolf xxviii, 79
Stern Fritz, xxvi
Stirner, Max, 45
Stöcker, Helene, xxv, xxix
Strauss, David, xviii, 56
  Life of Jesus, xviii

Tanzmann, Bruno, 152
Tarnhari, 176
Tat circle, 154, 155
Thule Gesellschaft
Tille, Alexander, xxix, 149–150
  Volksdienst..., 149
  Von Darwin bis Nietzsche, 150
Tirpitz, Admiral Alfred von, 24
Toennies, Ferdinand, xxv
Troeltsch, Ernst, 62

207

INDEX

Unold, Johannes,
  on corporative state, 87, 89
  on eugenics, 92-93
  on imperialism, 129, 130
  on liberalism, 84, 86
  on Marxism, 115-118
  on Oriental population growth, 104
  on the state, 45-46
  on the struggle for existence, 34
  Vice-President of Monist League, 21
Uslar-Gleichen, Frida von, 51

Vaterlandspartei, 24
Velde, Henry van de, xxv, 75
Verworn, Max, 12
Virchow, Rudolf, xviii, xx, 5, 11, 12, 111
Volkish ideology, xxi-xxiii
Volkserzieher, 156
Vortrupp, 176

Wakeman, Thaddeus Burr, 53
Wandervogel, 155, 176
War, as outcome of evolution, 131
Water color painting, 73
Wehberg, Heinrich, 119-120
Weimar Kartel, 22
Weltbühne, Die, xxv
Wille, Bruno, 21, 154
William I, 2
William II, xv, 24
Woltmann, Ludwig, 147-148
Woman question, Monist position on, 98-100

Zeiss, Carl, 26
Zeitschrift für den Aufbau der Entwicklungslehre, 22
Ziegler, Heinrich, 84, 86, 90, 93, 94, 96-99, 113-114, 147
  Die Naturwissenschaft und die sozialdemokratische Theorie, 113